COLLECTIVE BARGAINING

Contemporary Litigation Series

Consulting Editors for the
CONTEMPORARY LITIGATION SERIES

Professor Stephen A. Saltzburg
University of Virginia Law School

Professor Kenneth R. Redden
University of Virginia Law School

COLLECTIVE BARGAINING

GERALD E. BERENDT

THE MICHIE COMPANY
Law Publishers
CHARLOTTESVILLE, VIRGINIA

This book is dedicated to
Anna, Ben, Al, and Michael

TABLE OF CONTENTS

ACKNOWLEDGEMENTS

Many individuals have assisted this author in the preparation and completion of this book. The following students and graduates of The John Marshall Law School served as research and writing assistants and helped edit segments of the original manuscript: Sarane Siewerth, Paul Lieggi, Thomas Coens, Lynn Egan and Susan Bauer. Other students who did special research were Joseph Lorintz, Sandra Ryder, Leslie Sammarco, John Aniol, Dean Regenovich, Anthony Erbacci, Elizabeth Copley, Jonathan Karmel, David Whitacre, Robert Kleinschmidt, and Bruce Wolff.

A special note of appreciation goes to the typist, Linda Johnson, for her excellent work on a seemingly endless manuscript. Secretaries Diane Gordon and Gwen Konigsfeld also provided invaluable service.

Finally, an undertaking this large would not have been possible without the generous cooperation of Dean Fred F. Herzog and Associate Dean Helen M. Thatcher of The John Marshall Law School, as well as the editors and staff of The Michie Company.

Gerald E. Berendt

PREFACE

The practice of labor law has long been regarded as the peculiar province of a small, highly specialized segment of the bar. Those attorneys who engage in "general practice" tend to look upon the law governing labor-management relations as a mysterious web of vague statutory rights, complex administrative procedures and contradictory agency and court decisions. The uninitiated general practitioner, faced with a client's inquiry raising a basic labor law question, frequently confesses ignorance, proclaims that this is a highly technical area much like tax law, and directs the client to a colleague who specializes in the field. In most cases, the client's question has a relatively simple answer which can be easily found. Yet the self-doubting lawyer needlessly cedes the opportunity to another attorney.

Indeed, there will be instances where the general practitioner will encounter labor relations and collective bargaining problems which he or she is not equipped to handle. However, many of the questions and problems passed on to the so-called specialists could be answered and managed by an attorney properly trained in the area of general practice without extensive experience in the labor field. It is the primary purpose of this book to provide a foundation of information to aid the general practitioner in identifying those cases he or she can handle, as opposed to those which truly transcend the scope of the average attorney's expertise and experience. In addition, the book focuses on frequently encountered problems in an effort to provide suggested courses of action and advice.

The book emphasizes three areas. The first area focuses on the early stages of the labor-management relationship, the union organizational campaign, the statutory framework, the role of the National Labor Relations Board, and the impact of regulation on the union and the employer during the selection process. The second area of the book discusses the administration of the collective bargaining agreement. The third area deals with the frequently neglected problems of the individual employee, the all-too-often forgotten participant, beneficiary, and sometimes victim in the collective bargaining system.

CHAPTER 1

THE NATIONAL LABOR RELATIONS ACT AND THE NATIONAL LABOR RELATIONS BOARD

The practicing attorney may be called upon to represent management, labor, or individual employees at any one of many points in the broad continuim of the collective bargaining relationship. In logical sequence, however, the first opportunity counsel may have to advise and represent such clients arises when a labor organization commences its organizational drive among an employer's employees with the object of obtaining the right to represent those employees in collective bargaining. In the private sector, union organizational campaigns, employer response to campaigns, the selection process, and methods of obtaining representative status are primarily governed by the body of law which has developed under the National Labor Relations Act.

§ 1-1. The National Labor Relations Act.

§ 1-1(A). Generally.

Congress passed the National Labor Relations Act, familiarly known as the Wagner Act, in 1935, and shortly thereafter, the United States Supreme Court declared that the statute was constitutional. (*NLRB v. Jones E. Laughlin Steel Corp.,* 301 U.S. 1 (1937).) In subsequent years, the statute has been periodically amended, the amendments of greatest consequence coming in 1947, 1959 and, most recently, 1974. Congress' intent in passing the statute is expressed in the *Short Title and Declaration of Policy* added in 1947, which states that the Act is designed "to promote the full flow of commerce." (29 U.S.C. § 141 (1974).) In the first section of the 1935 Act, Congress declares "the policy of the United States to eliminate the causes of certain substantial obstructions to the free flow of commerce and to mitigate and eliminate these obstructions when they have occurred by encouraging the practice and procedure of collective bargaining and by protecting the exercise by workers of full freedom of association, self-organization, and designation of representative of their own choosing, for the purpose of negotiating the terms and conditions of their employment or other mutual aid or protection." (29 U.S.C. § 151 (1974).) The provisions of the statute are designed to effectuate this policy.

§ 1-1(B). Jurisdiction of the National Labor Relations Board.

Congress has delegated the responsibility of administering the National Labor Relations Act to the National Labor Relations Board. (29 U.S.C. § 153 *et seq.* (1974).) However, the Board's jurisdiction is effectively limited to workers and employers in the private sector, and then not all of these fall within the Act's coverage. (29 U.S.C. § 152(2), (3) and (11) (1974).)

§ 1-1(B)(1). Statutory Jurisdiction.

The National Labor Relations Act authorizes the Labor Board "to prevent any person from engaging in any unfair labor practice affecting commerce." (29 U.S.C. § 160(a) (1974).) In effect, Congress has given the Board jurisdiction which is coexistensive with Congress' power to legislate under the commerce clause of the Constitution. This broad delegation of authority has led the United States Supreme Court to declare "we can perceive no basis for inferring any intention of Congress to make the operation of the Act depend upon any particular volume of commerce affected more than that to which courts would apply the maxim *de minimis.*" *(NLRB v. Fainblatt,* 306 U.S. 601, 607 (1939).) The Supreme Court's pronouncements in the area have led one group of experts to assert "that the full exercise of [its] power brings within the NLRB's reach every enterprise of consequence in the country." Oberer, Hanslowe, & Anderson, *Labor Law: Collective Bargaining in a Free Society,* 116 (1979).

This assessment remains valid, notwithstanding the recent aberration in *NLRB v. Catholic Bishop of Chicago,* 440 U.S. 490 (1979). In that case, a sharply divided United States Supreme Court held that the National Labor Relations Act does not afford the Labor Board jurisdiction over teachers employed in church-operated schools. Since Labor Board jurisdiction over such schools would raise serious first amendment issues, the Court reasoned that Congress did not intend such coverage absent a clear expression to the contrary. This reasoning is clearly out of step with the expansive interpretation of the Labor Board's authority expressed by the Court in earlier cases. (*See, e.g., NLRB v. Fainblatt, supra.*) Moreover, as noted by the dissenters in *Catholic Bishop of Chicago,* the Act purports to cover all employers unless they fall within any one or more of eight express exceptions, and accordingly the Court majority had no reason either to question Congress' intent or to announce a judicially created exception to the Labor Board's jurisdiction. (*NLRB v. Catholic Bishop of Chicago,* 440 U.S. 490, 511 (1979).)

§ 1-1(B)(2). Nonstatutory Exclusions.

§ 1-1(B)(2)(a). Managerial Personnel.

The National Labor Relations Act does not expressly mention the term "managerial employee." However, managerial employees have been traditionally excluded from the operation of the National Labor Relations Act. This Board practice was summarized in *Ford Motor Co. (Chicago Branch),* 66 N.L.R.B. 1317 (1946) as follows:

> We have customarily excluded from bargaining units of rank and file workers executive employees who are in a position to formulate, determine, and effectuate management policies. These employees we have considered and still deem to be "managerial," in that they express and make operative the decisions of management. (*Id.* at 1322.)

Unlike supervisory employees who were expressly excluded under the Taft-Hartley Act of 1947, managerial employees were not expressly excluded. However, in accordance with principles of statutory construction, great weight is accorded an administrative agency's consistent interpretation of its statute when Congress has not taken steps to correct or change it. Thus, the courts have upheld the Board's exclusion of managerial employees from the coverage of the Act.

In *Retail Clerks International Ass'n v. NLRB,* 366 F.2d 642 (D.C. Cir. 1966), Circuit Judge Burger explained the Board's policy on managerial employees:

> The rationale for this Board policy, though unarticulated, seems to be the reasonable belief that Congress intended to exclude from the protection of the Act those who comprised a part of "management" or were allied with it on the theory that they were the one(s) from whom the workers need protection. (366 F.2d at 645.)

The Board considered the interests of the workers to be separate from the interests of management. There was also concern that managerial employers would have a conflict of interest between their duties or responsibilities and loyalty to a labor organization.

5

In *Eastern Camera & Photo Corp.*, 140 N.L.R.B. 569, 571 (1962), the Board defined managerial employees as

> those who formulate, determine, and effectuate an employer's policies . . . . Moreover, managerial status is not necessarily conferred upon employees because they possess some authority to determine, within established limits, prices and customer discounts. In fact, the determination of an employee's "managerial" status depends upon the extent of his discretion, although even the authority to exercise considerable discretion does not render an employee managerial where his decision must conform to the employer's established policy. The Board has consistently found employees with broad authority to pledge their employer's credit to be managerial. (*Id.* at 571-72.)

This definition was consistently followed by the Board until 1971 when it decided that Congress intended to exclude from the Act only those managerial employees involved in the "formulation or implementation of labor relations policies." (*Bell Aerospace Co.*, 196 N.L.R.B. 827, 828 (1972).) Additionally, the Board held at approximately the same time that even if persons were considered managerial employees, they were still covered by the Act and entitled to its protection. (*North Arkansas Electric Cooperative, Inc.*, 185 N.L.R.B. 550 (1970).) When the courts of appeals denied enforcement to these two decisions based on their departure from past practice, the Supreme Court granted certiorari.

In *NLRB v. Bell Aerospace Co., Division of Textron, Inc.*, 416 U.S. 267 (1974), the United States Supreme Court held that

> the Board's early decisions, the purpose and legislative history of the Taft-Hartley Act of 1947, the Board's subsequent and consistent construction of the Act for more than two decades, and the decisions of the courts of appeals all point unmistakably to the conclusion that

"managerial employees" are not covered by the Act. (*Id.* at 289.)

The Court referred the Board to *Eastern Camera* for what it considered the appropriate definition of "managerial employee." The Court emphasized that the question of whether or not a person was managerial was determined in "terms of the employee's actual job responsibilities, authority, and relationship to management." (*See Id.* at 290, n. 19.)

In applying this standard to the buyers in *Bell Aerospace,* 219 N.L.R.B. 384 (1975), on remand, the Board determined they were not managerial employees. This was because they did not "exercise sufficient independent discretion in their jobs to truly align them with management. . . ." (*Id.* at 386.) In reaching this conclusion the Board deemed pertinent several factors. The buyers were governed by "numerous comprehensive manuals and instructions which show the restrictions on the buyers' discretion." There was a supervisory ratio of one supervisor to three buyers. The buyers were not authorized to "commit the company credit in amounts in excess of $5,000 without the concurrence of higher authority." Finally, buyers testified that the job was spelled out for them. (*Id.* at 386.) The Board also noted that the buyers' salary range was comparable to other employees, they had the same fringe benefits, and used the same cafeteria and parking lot.

The Board emphasized in *Washington Post Co.,* 254 N.L.R.B. 168 (1981), that the important consideration in a determination of managerial status is the actual facts relating to job performance and not the titles or job descriptions. While wage data may be somewhat probative of status, it is never conclusive or determinative. (*See also Fred Rogers Co.,* 226 N.L.R.B. 1160 (1976).) In applying the standard to numerous situations in *Washington Post Co.,* the Board gave some indications of pertinent factors for determining managerial status. It held that employees who helped plan and effectuate incentive programs, along with developing strategies and promotions concerning the programs, created a conflict of interest serious enough to take such activities into consideration when determining whether an employee was managerial. (254 N.L.R.B. at 177.) Furthermore, if an employee exercised "sole discretion" over a program which primarily involved management employees, managerial status could be attributed to him. (*Id.* at 192.) The Board went on to say that participation in a department involved with special projects could have the same result. This is especially true if the projects or planning affect jobs, personnel or equipment. (*Id.* at 199.) In *General Dynamics Corp.,* 213 N.L.R.B. 857 (1974), the Board indicated that responsibility over budgetary concerns would also raise an employee to managerial status. Specific examples of such responsibility included "signature authority to purchase equipment" and negotiating with customers regarding lower costs, manpower, and modifications. (*Id.* at 861-62.)

In *Washington Post Co.,* 254 N.L.R.B. 168 (1981), the Board also identified some of the duties which *do not* constitute a basis for exclusion from the unit based on managerial status. In doing so the Board refined its holding from *General Dynamics Corp.* that influence over the budget would raise employee status to managerial status. In *Washington Post* the Board stated that such influence does nothing to change status if it must be exercised within established guidelines and is subject to review by management. (254 N.L.R.B. at 183.)

The Board also stated that the ordering of supplies or repairs is not the sort of control over the employer's credit which is required for a finding of managerial status. (*Id.* at 188.) Training other employees also does nothing to change status because it does not involve "independent discretion or actions outside the employer's guidelines." (*Id.*) Likewise, purchasing freelance material or contracting with writers does not constitute "use of discretionary judgment in implementing or determining employer policy." (*Id.* at 209.) Along those same lines the Board denied managerial status to the acquisitions librarian who purchased books because "that is simply part of the librarian's job, and is limited in any event by budget restraints." (*Id.* at 216.)

Persons having significant budgetary responsibilities may be excluded as managerial, even though the final decision to make a capital expenditure will be determined by higher authority. (*Washington Post Co.*, 254 N.L.R.B. 168 (1981); *General Dynamics Corp., Convair Aerospace Division, San Diego Operations*, 213 N.L.R.B. 857, 860 (1974).) On the other hand, in differentiating between managerial and professional employees, the Board has concluded that professionals do not formulate or effectuate management policies since their recommendations must be approved by management officials. Basically, the Board has determined that such professionals make recommendations based on their technical expertise to management officials. Also, they do not have discretion in their job independent of their employer's established policy. (*Flintkote Co.*, 217 N.L.R.B. 497 (1975); *General Dynamics Corp., Convair Aerospace Division, San Diego Operations*, 213 N.L.R.B. 857 (1974).)

In addition to managerial employees *per se*, management trainees have also been impliedly excluded from the Act. In *Curtis Industries, Division of Curtis Noll Corp.*, 218 N.L.R.B. 1447 (1975), the Board summarized the factors which lead to exclusion of managerial trainees from a bargaining unit. These factors include:

> (1) selectivity in hiring based on "trainee's possession of relevant education or experience";
> (2) trainees "must be shown to have no alternatives other than to go into management ultimately or to leave the employ of the employer";

9

(3) "there must be a planned management trainee program"; and

(4) there must be a distinction in "wages and working conditions between the management trainees and the employee beside whom they worked." (*Id.* at 1452.)

The Supreme Court summarized the situation regarding managerial employees in *NLRB v. Yeshiva University,* 444 U.S. 672 (1980), when it stated, "Although the Board has established no firm criteria for determining when an employee is so aligned, normally an employee may be excluded as managerial only if he represents management interests by taking or recommending discretionary actions that effectively control or implement employer policy." (*Id.* at 683.) The Court compared the rationale for the exclusion of supervisory employees and indicated that the managerial exclusion was analogous. (*Id.* at 683, n. 17.) However, a finding that employees of an agreed upon bargaining unit are managerial does not allow a unilateral change. Mutual agreement of the parties or Board action is required to exclude employees as managerial during the term of the agreement regarding an agreed upon bargaining unit. (*Arizona Electric Power Cooperative, Inc.,* 250 N.L.R.B. 1132 (1980).)

In *NLRB v. Yeshiva Univeristy,* 444 U.S. 672 (1980), the Supreme Court confronted the problem of applying the exclusions of the Act to a private university. When the Act was initially passed it was not intended to cover such an institution. Thus, there was some difficulty in translating a statutory scheme designed for industry into terms applicable to the "academic arena." (444 U.S. at 692.) While the Court recognized the two types of exclusions as being analogous, it stated that the interpretation given each would be substantially different.

The exclusion for "supervisors" who use "independent judgment in overseeing other employees" would require a statutory interpretation. (*Id.* at 682.) The exclusion of managerial employees, which *Yeshiva* involved, does not require such an interpretation since it is a judicially implied exception to Labor Board jurisdiction. This exclusion covers " 'managerial employees' who are involved in developing and enforcing employer policy." (*Id.*) The Court stated in general language which employees would be covered by this exclusion. "An employee may be excluded as managerial only if he represents management interests by taking or recommending discretionary actions that effectively control or implement employer policy." (444 U.S. at 683.)

While the University agreed that its faculty were professionals under the Act, it claimed that all faculty members were managerial, and as such, were excluded from protection of the Act. The bargaining unit included assistant deans, senior professors, assistant professors, and instructors. The Court considered the decisions made by these members of the bargaining unit and concluded that "when one considers the functions of a university, it is difficult to imagine decisions more managerial than [those made by the faculty]." (444 U.S. at 686.)

The Court based this conclusion on the finding that the authority of the faculty was "absolute." (*Id.*) Faculty committees were found to have negotiated with administrators concerning employment and salary. Furthermore, through the committees, the faculty determined the university's curriculum, grading system, size of the student body, tuition, and in one instance, the very location of the school. These facts, along with the testimony of a number of Deans who stated they "could not recall an instance when a faculty recommendation had been overruled," supported the Court's conclusion that faculty authority was absolute. (444 U.S. at 677, n. 5.)

The Court rejected the Board's holding that professionals such as Yeshiva's faculty do not formulate or effectuate management policies. The Board's holding that the managerial exclusion did not apply was based on the "independent professional judgment" test. While the Court acknowledged that the faculty recommendations were based on their technical expertise, which is part and parcel of their teaching positions, it stated that such "professional expertise is indispensable to the formulation and implementation of academic policy." (444 U.S. at 689.)

In rejecting the Board's professional judgment test, the Court decided that universities such as Yeshiva "*must* rely on their faculties to participate in the making and implementation of their policies." (*Id.* (emphasis added).) What the Court did find helpful was the "aligned with management" test, under which the Board should seek to determine whose interests the employee is thought to represent. The Court held that only if an employee's activities were other than those normally performed by similarly situated professionals would he be found aligned with management.

Even though this test can be helpful the Court was quick to point out that it was only a "starting point for analysis." (444 U.S. at 690.) The Court stated quite clearly that factors not present in *Yeshiva* may become important in other contexts. But whatever the context, "the touchstone of managerial status is thus an alliance with management, and the pivotal inquiry is whether the employee in performing his duties represents his own interests or those of his employer." (444 U.S. at 696.)

§ 1-1(B)(2)(b) Confidential Personnel.

The Wagner Act became law in 1935. (49 Stat. 449.) Its express exclusions did not include confidential employees. However, the Board in interpreting the statute excluded from bargaining units of rank and file employees the group of employees with access to confidential, labor relations information of the employer. Then in *Ford Motor Co. (Chicago Branch)*, 66 N.L.R.B. 1317 (1946), the Board decided that this encompassed too broad a category of employees who were thus denied from bargaining collectively. Therefore, the exclusion was narrowed to "only those employees who assist and act in a confidential capacity to persons who exercise 'managerial' functions in the field of labor relations." ((*Id.* at 1322.)

The Taft-Hartley Act was enacted in 1947. Its express exclusions included supervisory employees, but again, no reference was made to confidential employees. Nevertheless, the Board continued to exclude such employees from rank and file bargaining units. However, the Board had from time to time expanded the definition and encompassed persons who were secretaries to persons handling grievances, and cashiers having access to labor relations. (*International Smelting & Refining Co.*, 42 N.L.R.B. 1364 (1942); *Bond Stores, Inc.*, 99 N.L.R.B. 1029 (1952).) Then in *B.F. Goodrich Co.*, 115 N.L.R.B. 722 (1956), the Board indicated its intention to adhere strictly to its *Ford* standard. Thus "confidential" was to embrace *only* those employees who "assist and act in a confidential capacity to persons who formulate, determine, and effectuate management policies in the field of labor relations." (*Id.* at 724.) Subsequently, the Board made clear that the "and" between determine and effectuate means just that and not or. (*Weyerhaeuser Co.*, 173 N.L.R.B. 1170 (1968).)

Thus there are two essential elements to the labor-nexus standard. The first is that the employee "assist in a confidential capacity," and the second is that the person assisted fulfill all three roles regarding labor relations policies (*i.e.*, formulate, determine, and effectuate). Because most employees have an arguably confidential relationship with management, and because an expansive application of the

13

exclusionary rule would deprive many employees of the right to bargain collectively, the Board has narrowly construed the definition of confidential employee.

Board decisions have established that mere access to confidential material or typing of confidential labor relations memoranda does not, without more, establish a confidential relationship. (*United States Postal Service,* 232 N.L.R.B. 556 (1978); *Ernst & Ernst National Warehouse,* 228 N.L.R.B. 590 (1977); *Los Angeles New Hospital,* 244 N.L.R.B. 960 (1979).) Neither does mere access to personnel records qualify an employee as a confidential employee. (*Hotel Employers Association of San Francisco,* 159 N.L.R.B. 143 (1966).) The board has also held that it will not exclude as "confidential," employees who "merely have access to personnel or statistical information upon which an employer's labor relations policy is based; nor will it exclude employees with access to labor relations information after it has become known to the union or the employees concerned." (*Pullman Standard Division of Pullman, Inc.,* 214 N.L.R.B. 762, 763 (1974).) An employee who had access to the project managers files, including those relating to personnel matters and such grievances as might arise, did not thereby act in a confidential capacity to him. (*Service Technology Corp., a Subsidiary of LTV Aerospace Corp.,* 196 N.L.R.B. 1036 (1972).) Neither has occasional typing of material relating to personnel problems rendered an employee confidential. (*ITT Grinnell Corp.,* 212 N.L.R.B. 734 (1974).)

The second part of the standard involves a decision regarding whether the person assisted "formulates, determines and effectuates labor relations policies." In applying this aspect of the labor-nexus test the Board has held that involvement in the grievance procedure at initial steps and compiling information for use by others in collective bargaining are insufficient. (*Holly Sugar Corp.,* 193 N.L.R.B.

1024 (1971).) A close relationship whereby one makes recommendations regarding major union problems and serious disciplinary action to the person who formulates, determines and effectuates was not considered sufficient by the Board either. (*Carolina Telephone & Telegraph Co. & Communications Workers of America, AFL-CIO,* 258 N.L.R.B. 1387 (1981).) The Board has also made clear that this relationship must exist between the employer and the employee, not some other employer whom the employer services. (*Dun & Bradstreet, Inc.,* 240 N.L.R.B. 162 (1979); *Kleinberg, Kaplan, Wolff, Cohen & Burrows, P.C.,* 253 N.L.R.B. 450 (1980); *Stroock & Stroock & Lavan,* 253 N.L.R.B. 447 (1980).)

Some dicta in *NLRB v. Bell Aerospace Co., Division of Textron, Inc.,* 416 U.S. 267 (1974), led some Circuits to dispute the interpretation the Board had given to the Statute regarding the applicable standard for determining when employees were confidential and thus excluded from rank and file bargaining units. In *Hendricks County Rural Electric Membership Corp. v. NLRB,* 603 F.2d 25 (7th Cir. 1979), the court held that the proper standard to apply was whether the employee was given information " 'that is of a confidential nature, and that is not available to the public, to competitors, or to employees generally, for use in the interest of the employer.' " (*Id.* at 30.) However the United States Supreme Court in *Hendricks,* 102 S. Ct. 216 (1981), rejected this much broader standard and reaffirmed the Board's standard for the determination of a confidential employee. It stated, "We hold that there is a reasonable basis in law for the Board's use of the 'labor nexus' test." *Id.* at 221.) They also reiterated the policy and practice of according considerable deference to an administrative agency's interpretation of its statute when Congress has not seen fit to correct that interpretation. Thus the Board's standard and its interpretation in various situations would

seem to have received the imprimatur of the Supreme
Court. Although the employee in this particular case was a
personal secretary to the chief executive officer, her duties
were very restricted and precluded access to confidential
labor relations matters. The Court did not decide that such
secretaries in general would not be excluded. In fact, they
stated, "We do not suggest that personal secretaries to the
chief executive officers of corporations will ordinarily not
constitute confidential employees." (*Id.* at 229, n. 23.) Also,
the Court did not specifically address whether employees
who were thus excluded from rank and file bargaining units
were also excluded from other aspects of the Act (*i.e.*, unfair
labor practice protections).

Thus the Board's two-part labor nexus test standard must
be met for a confidential exclusion from the Act. Whether
these employees are also excluded from the protections of
the Act is still to be determined.

§ 1-2. Administrative Structure — The National Labor Relations Board.

§ 1-2(A). NLRB Functions and Procedures.

The National Labor Relations Board performs two major
functions under the National Labor Relations Act. First, it
is responsible for the administration of the election process
through which statutory employees may exercise their
right to select a labor organization to represent them in
collective bargaining. Second, the agency administers the
Act's unfair labor practice provisions which declare
unlawful certain employer and union acts.

§ 1-2(A)(1). The General Counsel.

The General Counsel of the National Labor Relations
Board and his agents investigate unfair labor practice

charges and prosecute complaints which issue when charges are deemed meritorious. The General Counsel, who is appointed by the President with the advice and consent of the Senate, also supervises most of the attorneys and other personnel employed by the agency in the approximately 51 regional, subregional, and resident offices. The General Counsel's Division of Operations Management oversees these field operations as well as the processing of cases in the General Counsel's Washington offices. The Division of Administration manages the General Counsel's and the Labor Board's fiscal and personnel matters. The General Counsel's Office of Advice provides legal advice to the regional offices, stating the General Counsel's official policy with regard to legal issues, providing legal research services to the field offices, and cooperating with the Special Counsel to the General Counsel for Priority Injunction Litigation. The General Counsel's Division of Enforcement Litigation represents the Board in federal court enforcement and/or review proceedings, and the Office of Appeals within this Division reviews charging parties' appeals from regional director's dismissals of charges.

§ 1-2(A)(2). The Board.

The five-member Board is also appointed by the President with the advice and consent of the Senate, and the Act authorizes the President to designate one member as Chairman. The Board acts as an adjudicator in unfair labor practice cases. The unfair labor practice hearings are actually conducted by the Board's administrative law judges whose recommended orders may be adopted, modified or rejected by the Board. The Board is also charged with the responsibility of conducting representation elections in which employees choose whether they wish to be

17

represented by a labor organization for the purpose of collective bargaining. The Board has delegated this later responsibility to the Regional Directors. In addition, the Board may be called upon to determine jurisdictional disputes between unions and to conduct employee polls in national emergency disputes. (29 U.S.C. § 179.)

Each of the five members of the Board has a staff of attorneys who provide legal advice and draft Board decisions. The Board's Executive Secretary is responsible for administering the Board's case decision and handling processes, and the Solicitor advises the Board on matters of law and policy. The Board also oversees the Administrative Law Judges' Division and the Division of Information which publicizes the Board's activities and makes other information available to the public.

§ 1-2(A)(3). Representation Case Procedure.

§ 1-2(A)(3)(a). Generally.

There are several methods by which a labor organization may achieve representative status. An employer may voluntarily recognize a union which evinces majority support among the employees in question. And in cases where outrageous and pervasive employer unfair labor practices have made a fair election impossible or improbable, the National Labor Relations Board may issue a remedial order requiring the offending employer to bargain with the union. But the preferred and most commonly utilized method for a union to obtain recognition as exclusive bargaining representative of previously unorganized employees is through the Board's election and certification machinery outlined in Section 9(c) of the National Labor Relations Act. That section instructs the Board to investigate petitions filed by an employee, employees, individuals, labor groups or by an employer, and if the Board determines that a question of representation affecting commerce exists, the statute further instructs the Board to direct an election by secret ballot and to certify the results of that election. Section 9(c) also authorizes the Board to prescribe regulations governing its petition, election, and certification procedures, however, Section 9 also places several restrictions on the exercise of the Board's authority. These limitations on the Board's discretion in representation cases will be discussed below.

§ 1-2(A)(3)(b). Petitions.

Petitions should be filed in the N.L.R.B. regional office which administers the area in which the requested bargaining unit is found. If the representation unit is located in more than one region, the petition may be filed in any of the available regional offices. Filing is effective upon receipt and time-stamping in an appropriate regional office. The regional offices will provide assistance in the preparation of petitions when requested.

Representation Petitions (RC) — Section 9(c)(1)(A)(i) of the National Labor Relations Act provides that a petition for certification as bargaining agent may be filed by an employee or group of employees or any individual or labor organization acting on their behalf, alleging that a substantial number of employees wish to be represented for collective-bargaining purposes and that their employer declined to recognize their representative. The Board has designated these as RC petitions, and they are usually filed by unions. RC petitions allege that a substantial number of employees seek to be represented, and the Board has determined administratively that a 30 percent showing of interest must be submitted to support the petition.

Employer Petitions (RM) — Section 9(c)(1)(B) of the Act provides that an employer may file a petition for an election if one or more individuals or labor organizations have demanded recognition as representative of a unit of that employer's employees. An employer who files an RM petition must submit proof of a demand for recognition.

Decertification Petitions (RD) — Section (9)(c)(1)(A)(ii) provides that an employee, group of employees, individual, or labor organization may file a decertification petition asserting that the currently certified or recognized bargaining representative no longer represents the employees in the bargaining unit. A decertification petition, designated RD petition by the Board, may not be filed by an employer, a supervisor, or a confidential employee. If the Board concludes that an RD petition is supported by the requisite 30 percent showing of interest and that a question concerning representation exists, it will conduct the decertification election in a unit of employees coextensive with the previously certified or recognized unit.

Union-Security Deauthorization Petitions (UD) — Section 9(e) of the Act authorizes the Board to take a secret ballot of employees in a bargaining unit covered by a union-security agreement between their employer and a labor organization to determine whether the employees wish to rescind the authority for such a provision. Such a petition, which the Board designates as a UD petition, must be supported by a 30 percent showing of interest in rescission. Following the UD election, the Board will certify the result to the employer and the labor organization.

Clarification of Certification Petitions (UC) — Consistent with its authority to issue certifications under Section 9(c)(1) of the Act, the Board monitors and clarifies such certifications by entertaining and processing petitions to clarify certifications. Under Section 102.60(b) of the Board's rules and regulations, a UC petition, as the Board designates it, may be filed by a labor organization or an employer to clarify an existing bargaining unit in the absence of a question concerning representation. Such a petition for clarification may be filed where there is a certified bargaining representative or a recognized representative which has not been certified.

Amendment of Certification Petition (AC) — Consistent with its authority to issue certifications under Section 9(c) (1) of the Act, the Board provides in its Rules and Regulations Section 102.60(b) that an employer or labor organization may file a petition to amend a certification where there are changed circumstances, such as a change in the name of the labor organization or location of the employer. Such AC petitions, as they are designated by the Board, may be filed when there is no question concerning representation and the unit is already covered by a certification. Unlike the clarification petition, this petition may not be filed where the representative has been recognized but not certified.

§ 1-2(A)(3)(c). Question Concerning Representation.

Under Section 9(c)(1) of the Act, the Board is authorized to direct an election and certify the results if a "question of representation" exists. The Board frequently refers to this requirement as the "question concerning representation." Usually, a question concerning representation is manifested by a union's demand for recognition which the employer has rejected. However, such a demand and rejection prior to filing a petition are not necessary to raise a question concerning representation (*Advance Pattern Co.,* 80 N.L.R.B. 29 (1948)). A question concerning representation may also arise when two or more unions seek to represent a group of employees or when a union, which has been voluntarily recognized, petitions for an election in order to obtain a certification with its accompanying benefits.

§ 1-2(A)(3)(d). Showing of Interest.

Section 9(c)(1)(A) of the Act states that the employee, group of employees, individual or labor organization filing a petition must allege that "a substantial number of employees" wish to be represented for collective bargaining purposes. The Board has defined "a substantial number" as 30 percent of the employees in an appropriate bargaining unit designated in any RC or RD petition. No showing of interest is required when an employer files an RM petition pursuant to Section 9(c)(1)(B) of the Act, nor is a showing of interest needed when a clarification of certification (UC) or amendment of certification (AC) is sought. If an RC petition is filed when there is a charge alleging that the labor organization is violating Section 8(b)(7)(C)'s proscription against recognitional picketing, no showing of substantial interest is needed before the Board may direct an election. However, Section 9(e)(1) of the Act specifically, requires a 30 percent showing to support a petition to rescind a labor organization's authority to enter into contracts with union security provisions.

Ordinarily, petitioning labor organizations submit union membership or authorization cards to establish the requisite 30 percent showing of interest. Other methods for establishing the showing of interest include lists of signatures and a current or recently expired labor contract between the employer and an intervening labor organization.

If authorization cards are used, they should be dated at the time signed. Cards which are undated or not current will be rejected (*A. Werman & Sons, Inc.*, 114 N.L.R.B. 629 (1955)). A card will be counted if it authorizes the petitioning labor organization, or an organizing committee acting on petitioner's behalf, to represent the signatory for collective bargaining purposes. Similarly, union membership cards will be counted, as will cards seeking an election and certification of the petitioning union (*Levi Strauss & Co.,* 172 N.L.R.B. 732 (1968), *enf'd,* 441 F.2d 1027 (D.C. Cir. 1970)).

The Board determines the validity of a submitted showing of interest through its internal investigative procedures, and a petitioner's evidence as to the showing of interest is generally not litigable (*S.H. Kress & Co.,* 137 N.L.R.B. 1244 (1962)). A party wishing to attack the validity of a purported showing of interest should submit any evidence of fraud, duress, or coercion to the Regional Director.

§ 1-2(A)(3)(e). Employer Petitions — The Demand.

An RM petition filed by an Employer pursuant to Section 9(c)(1)(B) may be filed if one or more labor organizations has made a demand for recognition. There is no requirement that a showing of interest be provided, however, the petitioning employer must submit proof of the demand. Such proof may be the union's letter or telegram claiming majority status and demanding recognition, or absent such a document, an affidavit from the employer attesting to an oral demand by the union.

§ 1-2(A)(3)(f). The 48-Hour Rule.

The showing of interest needed to support an RC petition must be submitted at the time the petition is filed or within 48 hours thereafter, but not later than the last day on which a petition may be filed under the Board's other rules governing the timely filing of petitions (*NLRB Statements of Procedure* Section 101.17). Similarly, an employer's proof of a demand for recognition must be submitted to the Board at the time the RM petition is filed or within 48 hours thereafter. In either case, failure to comply with the 48-hour rule could result in dismissal of the petition. The Regional

Director may grant an extension of time upon a showing of good cause.

§ 1-2(A)(3)(g). Blocking Charges.

It is the general policy of the Board to consider the election process blocked if there are unresolved unfair labor practice charges affecting employees within a requested bargaining unit. Ordinarily such pending unfair labor practice charges will block the representation proceeding if the charging party is also a party to the representation case. However, representation elections may be blocked by those who are not parties to the representation proceedings and who file charges alleging violation of Sections 8(a)(2), 8(a)(5), 8(b)(3), or 8(b)(7).

If the General Counsel and his agents determine that a blocking charge lacks merit, the charge will be dismissed and the representation case will proceed to election. Otherwise, the Board will not proceed to election in the face of blocking charges unless a charging party executes a "Request to Proceed." A charging party executing a "Request to Proceed" does not waive its right to contest the validity of the subsequent election, nor are the unfair labor practices withdrawn. However, a "Request to Proceed" is ordinarily not accepted if the blocking charges allege violation of Sections 8(a)(2), 8(a)(5), or 8(b)(3), in which case the charging party must withdraw the charges in order to unblock the election proceedings.

§ 1-2(A)(3)(h). The Contract Bar.

Generally an unexpired collective bargaining agreement between an incumbent union and an employer will bar a representation election or a decertification election for a reasonable period of time. Absent unusual circumstances outlined below, the National Labor Relations Board will dismiss a representation (RC) petition or decertification (RD) petition filed during the contract bar period.

The contract bar rules are designed to promote stable labor relations, in the interest of avoiding needless disputes and disruptions of commerce. If a productive, satisfactory bargaining relationship exists, as evinced by a labor contract, it is desirable to avoid a change in bargaining agent during the term of the agreement. The contract bar rules also promote consistent and conscientious administration of the collective bargaining agreement during its terms since outside distractions to the incumbent are minimized.

Prerequisites for Contracts Operating as Bars

In order to operate as a bar, a contract must meet certain prerequisites. It must be in writing and signed by all parties prior to the filing of the rival's petition. It must contain terms and conditions of employment which are substantial and which the Board deems sufficient to stabilize the bargaining relationship. Thus, an agreement as to wages alone is not deemed sufficient and cannot serve as a bar. However, a written extension of an old contract in which the parties agreed to submit the issue of economic terms to interest arbitration was found to provide the degree of stability necessary to operate as a bar to a rival's petition. (*Stur-Dee Health Products, Inc. & Biorganic Brands, Inc.,* 248 N.L.R.B. 1100 (1980).)

In addition to the foregoing characteristics, the contract must clearly encompass what the employees sought in the petition and must embrace an appropriate unit. A contract that expressly requires ratification as a condition precedent to validity will not block an election until ratified. However, an agreement whose terms do not require ratification will operate as a bar as soon as it is signed regardless of whether the union's constitution or by-laws calls for such ratification. A contract for members only cannot serve as a bar, and a contract with an illegal union security clause (*Paragon Products Corp.,* 134 N.L.R.B. 662 (1961)) or an illegal checkoff provision (*Gary Steel Supply Co.,* 144 N.L.R.B. 470 (1963)) will be disqualified from bar status as well. On the other hand, a contract containing a hot-cargo clause which is unlawful under Section 8(e) of the act may still operate as a bar to an election (*Food Haulers, Inc.,* 136 N.L.R.B. 394 (1962)). Ordinarily, lawful "pre-hire" contracts, negotiated between parties in the construction industry pursuant to Section 8(f) of the Act, may not serve as bars to elections.

A contract meeting the foregoing prerequisites may serve as a bar for its full term not exceeding three years. Accordingly, a contract for two years will operate as a bar for two years; a contract for three years will operate as a bar for the three-year term. However, a contract for a term exceeding three years, *e.g.,* for four years, will bar an election sought by a challenger for the first three years only. A contract for a term exceeding three years will bar an election *sought by the employer or incumbent labor organization* for the full term of the agreement. (*General Cable Corp.,* 139 N.L.R.B. 1123 (1962).) Contracts of indefinite duration do not operate as bars (*Pacific Coast Association of Pulp & Paper Mfrs.,* 121 N.L.R.B. 990 (1958)).

In order to permit employees to exercise their right to choose another labor union or simply to decertify their current representative, the Board provides that a petition may be filed during the 30-day "open period" which begins 90 days before the expiration of the existing labor contract and ends 60 days prior to termination of the agreement. If no petition is filed during this open period, a petition filed during the remaining 60 days of the contract, known as the "insulated period," will be dismissed. Thus, where no dissatisfaction with the incumbent is manifested by the filing of a petition during the "open period," the incumbent union and the employer enjoy a 60-day period, insulated from petitions, during which they may continue their apparently stable bargaining relationship and execute a new agreement to replace the old one at its expiration. Execution of a new contract during the insulated period results in extension of the contract bar for the term of the new agreement, consistent with the rules and limitations surveyed above. Should no petition be filed during the open period and the parties to the expiring contract fail to reach agreement prior to expiration, a petition filed after the termination date will be entertained if filed prior to execution of a new agreement. However, if the incumbent union and the employer execute a new agreement prior to the filing of a petition during the post-termination period known as "open season," the new contract will bar the petition.

Ordinarily, the contract bar operates as described above. However, the Board recognizes certain instances of unusual circumstances which lift the contract bar.

The Board will lift the contract bar where there is a "schism," that is, an intraunion conflict at the highest level, and the unit employees covered by the contract have had an opportunity to express their judgment concerning disaffiliation within a reasonable time after the conflict began. (*Hershey Chocolate Corp.,* 121 N.L.R.B. 901 (1958).)

A labor contract with a union which is defunct will not operate as a bar. A labor organization which is unable or unwilling to represent the employees in the unit in question is said to be defunct. But one which is only temporarily unable to function or has lost all its members is not defunct, and a contract with such a labor organization may be raised as a bar to an election in the subject bargaining unit.

The National Labor Relations Board will not accord bar status to a contract executed before employees were hired or before a substantial increase in personnel. As a general rule the Labor Board will find no bar if the contract was executed when less than 30 percent of the workers employed at the time of the hearing were hired or less than 50 percent of the job classifications existing at the time of the hearing were then in existence. (*General Extrusion Co.,* 121 N.L.R.B. 1165 (1958).) This rule prevents a smaller group of employees from selecting a bargaining representative, and depriving a considerably larger group from changing representatives due to a contract bar.

§ 1-2(A)(3)(i). The Certification Bar.

Absent unusual circumstances, the National Labor Relations Board will not conduct an election in a unit in which a labor organization has been certified as the exclusive bargaining representative during the preceding year. A petition filed within one year of the certification date will be dismissed unless the certified labor organization is defunct, there is a schism in the union, or there is a radical increase in the number of employees in the bargaining unit. The certification bar applies when a union has won a Board-conducted election and has been certified, but does not apply when the employees have selected no union and the Board has certified that result. (*Centr-O-Cast & Engineering Co.,* 100 N.L.R.B. 1507 (1952).)

The certification bar was devised by the Board on a case-by-case basis and is not mandated by the statute, as is the election bar. The certification bar is designed to bind employee voters for a fixed time after the election, promoting a sense of responsibility in the electorate and coherence in administration. In addition, since the election is a solemn and costly occasion, the certification year ensures that revocation of the union's authority will be through a similarly solemn process. Finally, the certification bar permits the newly chosen union to engage in uninterrupted collective bargaining for one year, free from the distractions associated with a rival union's petition to replace that incumbent. (*Brooks v. NLRB,* 348 U.S. 96 (1954).)

Once certified, the union is entitled to one year's good faith bargaining with the employer. Thus, if an employer refuses to bargain during the certification year in violation of the Act, the Board may extend the certification period to afford the union at least one year of actual bargaining.

§ 1-2(A)(3)(j). The Election Bar.

In Section 9(c)(3) of the National Labor Relations Act, Congress has provided that the Board shall not direct an election in any bargaining unit or subdivision thereof within which a valid election has been held in the preceding twelve months. Unlike the certification bar which runs from the date of certification, the election bar runs from the date of the valid election. Although all representation petitions filed during the certification year will be dismissed by the Board, a petition filed during the last sixty days of the election bar period will be processed, and the election held pursuant to such a petition will be conducted after the twelve months have elapsed. Petitions filed within the election bar period prior to the last sixty days will be dismissed. (*Vickers, Inc.,* 124 N.L.R.B. 1051 (1959).)

Unlike the certification bar, the election bar applies regardless of who won the election. As long as the election was valid, no election may be held within the unit or a subdivision for twelve months, irrespective of whether the employees selected a representative or chose to be unrepresented.

§ 1-2(A)(3)(k). The Recognition Bar.

If an employer properly extends voluntary recognition to a labor organization, the Labor Board will afford the parties a reasonable time to bargain and execute a contract. This reasonable time, known as the recognition bar period, is determined on a case-by-case basis but rarely exceeds twelve months. A petition challenging the recognized union will be dismissed if filed during this period. (*Keller Plastics Eastern, Inc.,* 157 N.L.R.B. 583 (1966); *Ruffalo's Trucking Service, Inc.,* 114 N.L.R.B. 1549 (1955).)

In order for recognition to serve as a bar for a reasonable period, the employer must extend recognition with the good faith belief that the union represents a demonstrated majority of the employees in the bargaining unit. In addition, voluntary recognition may only come at a time when no other union is actively engaged in organizing the unit employees. (*Keller Plastics Eastern, Inc.,* 157 N.L.R.B. 583 (1966).)

§ 1-2(A)(3)(l). Unit Appropriateness.

Labor Board Authority

Section 7 of the National Labor Relations Act grants employees the right to self-organization and to representation through agents of their own choosing. Section 9(a) of the Act implements this general right with specific requirements including the provision that the representative must be selected by a majority of employees in a unit appropriate for collective-bargaining purposes. Section 9(b) empowers the National Labor Relations Board to "decide in each case whether, in order to assure employees the fullest freedom in exercising the rights guaranteed by this Act, the unit appropriate for the purposes of collective bargaining shall be the employer unit, craft unit, plant unit, or subdivision thereof. . . ." Thus, the Labor Board has broad discretion to determine issues of unit appropriateness subject only to the statutory limitations found in Section 9(b) and (c).

Limitations on Labor Board Authority

Section 9(b)(1) prevents the Board from deciding that a unit combining professional with nonprofessional employees is appropriate, unless a majority of the professional employees vote for inclusion in such a mixed unit. Although this provision is apparently designed to prevent the dilution of the rights of professional employees where they are small in number and might be involuntarily combined with a larger number of nonprofessionals, the United States Supreme Court upheld a federal district court's holding that the Labor Board was without authority to combine a large number of professionals (233) with a small number of nonprofessionals (9) without first affording the professional employees their statutory right to choose whether they wished to be included in such a mixed unit. (*Leedom v. Kyne,* 358 U.S. 184 (1958).)

Section 9(b)(2) of the Act prohibits the Labor Board from deciding that a proposed unit of craft employees is inappropriate because of prior establishment by the Labor Board of a broader unit, unless a majority of the employees in the proposed craft unit vote against separate representation. The Labor Board frequently identifies bargaining units consisting of specified craft employees on the basis of their particular skills. Nevertheless, the Board has been reluctant to permit the severance of a craft unit from an existing broader unit and has read the Section 9(b)(2) prohibition narrowly, as not foreclosing its discretion to deny craft severance after considering all the relevant circumstances in order to effectuate the policies of the Act. The Board has recognized that Congress designed the statute to foster stability in labor relations and to avoid disruptions of commerce associated with labor disputes. In an effort to balance this policy against the congressional expression of self-determination for craft employees, the Board has indicated that the circumstances relevant to their consideration includes, but is not limited to, whether the group sought is a distinct craft or trade, whether the history of collective bargaining has been stable and might be disrupted by severance of the employees requested, the extent to which the alleged craft employees have retained a separate identity while included in the broader unit, the pattern of collective bargaining in the industry as a whole, the degree of integration in the employer's operations and the interdependency of the alleged craft employees and other employees in the employer's operational processes, and whether the union seeking to sever the alleged craft employees is qualified to represent them. (*Mallinckrodt Chemical Works,* 162 N.L.R.B. 387 (1966).)

Section 9(b)(3) of the Act prohibits the Labor Board from establishing units which include plant guards with other employees. That section specifically forbids the certification of a labor organization as representative of a guard unit if that organization is part of any other labor organization which admits nonguards.

§ 1-2(B). Unfair Labor Practice Case Procedures.

§ 1-2(B)(1). Filing the Charge.

The process through which the N.L.R.B. exercises its exclusive power to investigate and issue complaints alleging unfair labor practices begins with the filing of a written charge in the appropriate regional office (N.L.R.B. Rules and Regulations §§ 102.9, 102.10). The proper choice of regional office is based on the geographic location in which the alleged unfair labor practice occurred or is occurring. Because the Board is intended to be an impartial administrator, it may not issue a complaint on its own initiative but may act only after an outside party has filed a written, signed charge. Each charge must contain either a sworn oath administered by a notary public, Board agent, or other legally qualified person, or a declaration by the person signing that the charge is true and accurate to the best of his knowledge and belief.

An unfair labor practice charge may be filed not only by a party involved in an industrial dispute — employer, union, or individual — but also by any outside person, personally aggrieved or not. This authority to entertain charges filed by any person with any motive is based on the fact that "[t]he Board was created not to adjudicate private controversies but to advance the public interest in eliminating obstructions to Interstate Commerce." (*NLRB v. Jones & Laughlin Steel Corp.,* 301 U.S. 1 (1937).) Although several challenges to the validity of Board proceedings have been based on either the identity or the motivation of the person filing the charge, the Board and the courts have taken literally the language "any person" (N.L.R.B. Rules & Regulations § 102.9). "Dubious character, evil or unlawful motives, or bad faith of the informer cannot deprive the Board of its jurisdiction to conduct the inquiry." (*NLRB v. Indiana & Michigan Electric Co.,* 318 U.S. 9 (1943).) However, although no charging party is *per se* disqualified from filing a charge, the Board has discretion to consider the motivation and character of the charging party. As the Supreme Court pointed out in *Indiana & Michigan Electric,* "[t]he Board has wide discretion in the issue of complaints. . . . It is not required by the statute to move on any charge; it is merely enabled to do so."

The actual charge is filed on one of three forms, depending upon whether the subject of the charge is an employer, a labor organization, or a "hot cargo" contract under Section 8(e) of the Act. The charging party must enter his own name and address, the name and address of the party against whom the charge is being made, the sections of the Act allegedly violated, a statement of the facts (including names, dates and places) on which the charge is based, and the required oath or declaration.

Section 10(b) of the Act provides in part that "[w]henever it is charged that any person has engaged in any such unfair labor practice, the Board . . . shall have power to issue . . . a complaint. . . ." This section has traditionally been interpreted to mean that when multiple parties are involved in the commission of an unfair labor practice, the Board may not issue an order against an employer or labor organization not named in the charge. (*NLRB v. Hopwood Refining Co.*, 98 F.2d 97 (2d Cir. 1938).) A recent case, however, indicates that the courts may construe this language somewhat more liberally. *NLRB v. Houston Distribution Services, Inc.*, 573 F.2d 260 (5th Cir. 1978), involved a situation in which employees, not knowing their employer was a wholly-owned subsidiary, filed charges against their immediate corporate employer. The Board correspondingly issued a complaint against only the named subsidiary. When the name of the parent corporation was discovered at a subsequent hearing, the parent protested that it had never been named in any charge. The court of appeals responded, "[W]e do not believe that the addition of the correct corporate entity is so completely outside the original charge that the Board could be said to have initiated a proceeding of its own motion. . . . Workingmen are not required to wander the maze of corporate structure." The authority of the Board to prevent and redress unfair labor practices, based as it is on the duty imposed by Congress to protect public rights, extends to protecting an individual who files charges despite the employer's contract with the union prohibiting the contracting parties from filing charges with the Labor Board (*F.W. Judge Optical Works, Inc.*, 78 N.L.R.B. 385 (1948).)

34

§ 1-2(B)(2). The Six-Month Statute of Limitations.

The key element to the Board's accepting a charge is timeliness. Section 10(b) of the Act establishes that the Board may issue a complaint only if the conduct complained of occurred within six months of both the filing and the service of the charge. Although the Regional Director routinely serves a copy of the charge on each alleged offender, the charging party bears the statutory responsibility of compliance with the requirement that such service he made. (N.L.R.B. Rules & Regulations § 102.14.) Either the filing in the regional office or service on the charged party may occur first, as long as both steps are completed within the statutory period. Both filing and service may be made in person or through the mails (*Olin Industries, Inc., Winchester Repeating Arms Co. Division v. NLRB*, 192 F.2d 799 (5th Cir. 1951)).

The apparent rigidity of the statute of limitations has been considerably eased by Board and judicial interpretation. First, the Board looks to the time the aggrieved party actually learned of the action constituting an unfair labor practice (*i.e.*, subjective notice). (*NLRB v. Longshoremen (ILWU), Local 30 United States Borox & Chem. Corp.*), 549 F.2d 698 (9th Cir. 1977), enf'g 223 N.L.R.B. 1257 (1976).) This tolling of the statute also occurs when the facts of an unfair labor practice are fraudulently concealed. (*NLRB v. Don Burgess Construction Corp.*, 596 F.2d 378 (9th Cir. 1979).) Second, although the Act contains no provision for the amendment of a charge, the Board and the courts have consistently recognized the power of the charging party to do so. Additional charges may be included if the actions occurred within the six-month period.

Amendment outside the statutory period will be permitted under certain circumstances. If the original charge was timely filed and served, the amended charge is allowed, even if outside the statute, as long as the additional allegations only "restate," "particularize," or "define more precisely" the charges originally filed. (*NLRB v. Gaynor News Co.,* 197 F.2d 719 (2d Cir. 1952).) Any new issue or cause of action raised in the amendment must have occurred within six months of the filing and service of the amended charge. (*Indiana Metal Products Corp. v. NLRB,* 202 F.2d 613 (7th Cir. 1953).)

Events occurring more than six months before the filing and service of the charge are not automatically barred from inclusion in the unfair labor practice charge, however, but may be used in one or two ways. First, they may be used as additional evidence to bolster an unfair labor practice charge alleging independently actionable conduct which occurred within the six-month statutory period. (*Machinists Local 1424 v. NLRB,* 362 U.S. 411 (1960). Second, they may be included in a charge of "continuing" unfair labor practices as long as the same type of objectionable conduct occurred within six months of the filing and service of the charge.

The narrow distinctions which the court is willing to draw in this area are best illustrated by two cases, *Pennwoven, Inc.,* 94 N.L.R.B. 175 (1951), *enforcement denied,* 194 F.2d 521 (3d Cir. 1952), and *Textile Machine Works, Inc.,* 105 N.L.R.B. 618 (1953). In *Textile,* the Board found a continuing violation when discriminatorily discharged employees were denied jobs after they had reapplied as new employees more than six months after their discharge. In *Pennwoven,* on the other hand, the employer's refusal to reinstate workers discharged for union activities and not called back in accordance with seniority rights was not a continuing violation. In both cases the discharges had occurred more than six months prior to the filing of the charge. The key difference was in what the employees were requesting, reinstatement to their old positions (barred) as opposed to totally new employment (permitted). No new occurrences of the objectionable conduct had occurred within the six-month period in *Pennwoven,* whereas the arbitrary refusal to hire in *Textile* served to re-activate the discharge violation.

§ 1-2(B)(3). The 72-Hour Rule, Investigation of the Charges, Settlement Agreements.

After the filing of the charge in the N.L.R.B. regional office, the charging party has seventy-two hours to provide several items of required information to support the charge, including names and addresses of possible witnesses, documents or other tangible evidence which support the charge, and an affidavit in which the charging party's version of all the relevant facts is presented in detail. While failure to meet the seventy-two hour deadline may result in the dismissal of the charge, the Regional Director has the discretionary authority to extend the deadline upon a showing of good cause.

Once the necessary supporting material has been provided, the charge is assigned to a Board agent for impartial investigation to "ascertain, analyze, and apply the relevant facts in order to arrive at the proper disposition of the case." (*N.L.R.B. Casehandling Manual, Part 1, Unfair Labor Practice Proceedings* ¶ 10050 (1975).) The case is established through interviews with the charging party, named witnesses, and other persons with possibly pertinent information as suggested by the charging party or independently developed by the agent. (*N.L.R.B. Casehandling Manual, Part 1, Unfair Labor Practice Proceedings* ¶ 10056 (1975).) The Board has established various rules regarding the presence of the charged party's counsel at interviews, permissible use of solicited as opposed to volunteered information, and other evidentiary questions, all of which must

37

be taken into account when preparing the general case. (*See N.L.R.B. Casehandling Manual, Part 1, Unfair Labor Practice Proceedings* ¶ 10056.5 (1975).)

The future progress of each case depends in great part on the results of this investigation. Even though the inquiry is restricted to the events set forth in the charge, evidence of other unfair labor practices or other parties to be charged is sometimes discovered. The agent will so inform the charging party, who then may amend the charge if the six-month statute of limitations does not bar the amendment. On the other hand, if the charge proves to have no merit, an informal disposition may be made by the examiner's requesting or the charging party's volunteering to withdraw the charge. If the charging party refuses to withdraw a meritless charge, the Regional Director will refuse to issue a complaint, in effect dismissing the charge.

A valid charge does not always result in formal litigation, for the unfair labor practice may be voluntarily adjusted by the parties in a settlement agreement. Before allowing a voluntary withdrawal of a charge pursuant to such an agreement, the Regional Director will investigate the settlement to ascertain whether it will serve the best interests of both the parties and the general public. If the agreement is approved as a proper remedy of the unfair labor practice, it is reduced to writing and becomes binding on the parties.

A Regional Director and the charged party may even agree to a settlement over the protests of the charging party. In *George Ryan Co. v. NLRB*, 609 F.2d 1249 (7th Cir. 1979), the Seventh Circuit held that the Board did not abuse its discretion by approving a settlement agreement over the objections of the charging party. The agreement may establish a *quid pro quo*. For example, in *Coca Cola Bottling Co. of Los Angeles*, 101 LRRM 1456, 243 N.L.R.B. No. 89 (1979), the Board upheld a settlement agreement in which a suspended employee was reinstated on the condition that he withdraw his unfair labor practice charge.

Once a settlement agreement is achieved, any violation will cause the Board to issue a complaint. In *NLRB v. All Brand Printing Corp.*, 594 F.2d 926 (2d Cir. 1979), the court found an employer committed an unfair labor practice when the company failed to abide by a settlement agreement entered into with the union whereby the union had agreed to withdraw its charge in return for the employer's agreeing to bargain. The settlement agreement has a "definite legal effect," for even though it does not constitute an admission of past liability, it does provide a basis for future liability.

The first case dealing with this situation and formulating a policy on the legal effect of a settlement agreement was *Poole Foundry & Machine Co. v. NLRB,* 192 F.2d 740 (4th Cir. 1951), *cert. denied,* 342 U.S. 954 (1952). The more recent case of *NLRB v. Vantran Electric Corp.,* 580 F.2d 921 (7th Cir. 1978), upheld the reasoning and result in *Poole.* In *Vantran Electric,* the fact that the employer's agreement to bargain was not a *quid pro quo* for the union's withdrawing its unfair labor practice charge led the Board to conclude that the intent of the parties was not clear enough to enforce the settlement. Thus, intent, even trade within the settlement, as established in *Poole,* is the key to the Board's issuing a complaint after a charge has been withdrawn pursuant to an approved settlement agreement.

§ 1-2(B)(4). The Complaint and Answer.

If no voluntary settlement of the unfair labor practice dispute can be reached as a result of the field examiner's investigation, then formal litigation commences. The Regional Director, on behalf of the General Counsel, issues and serves an official complaint and notice of hearing on the charging party, respondent, and all other interested parties.

These other additional parties could include, for example, all signatures to an allegedly unlawful contract, all parties involved in a company-dominated labor organization, or every contending union in a jurisdictional dispute. The complaint, often likened to an indictment, must contain a clear statement of the facts establishing the authority of the Board over the case and a clear statement of the acts claimed to be unfair labor practices. This second statement should include as many precise names, dates, and places as possible, for the respondent is entitled to as much specificity in the charges as possible in order to prepare a proper answer.

The answer, which must be filed by the respondent within ten days of receipt of the complaint, should be constructed as a direct response to each allegation in the complaint, either admitting or denying and then explaining each response and providing supporting facts for the defense. When the answer is filed, copies are served on all the parties who were served with the complaint, and a date is confirmed for a hearing before the Administrative Law Judge (ALJ). The failure to file a timely answer or to provide the required specificity will result in the Board's finding that the respondent has admitted the allegations of the complaint, unless a strong showing of good cause can be made. "If a party charged with an unfair labor practice in a complaint does not file an answer within the time and in the manner prescribed . . . , all allegations in the complaint shall be deemed to be admitted as true and judgment may be rendered on the basis of the complaint alone." (*Neal B. Scott Commodities, Inc.,* 238 N.L.R.B. 32 (1978).) Rules and Regulations, 29 CFR § 102.20 (1979) and the *N.L.R.B. Casehandling Manual, Part 1, Unfair Labor Practice Proceedings* ¶ 10208.1 (1975).) The entry of a summary judgment in favor of the plaintiff in such a case has been specifically upheld in *NLRB v. Aaron Convalescent Home,* 479 F.2d 736 (6th Cir. 1973).

The authority of the General Counsel over the complaint phase of an unfair labor practice proceeding is based on the statutory language of 29 U.S.C. § 153(d) (1970) and § 3(d) of the National Labor Relations Act: "[The General Counsel] shall have final authority, on behalf of the Board, in respect of the investigation of charges and issuance of complaints. . . ." Even before the position of General Counsel was created, the Court of Appeals for the Third Circuit in *Jacobsen v. NLRB,* 120 F.2d 96 (3d Cir. 1941), interpreted as absolute the original Board discretion to cause a complaint to issue. When the position of General Counsel was created in 1947, cases which soon followed, such as *Lincourt v. NLRB,* 170 F.2d 306 (1st Cir. 1948), and *Haleston Drug Stores, Inc. v. NLRB,* 187 F.2d 418 (9th Cir. 1951), confirmed that the same unreviewable authority had been transferred from the Board and was now vested in the new position. This interpretation was tacitly accepted in dictum by the Supreme Court in *Vaca v. Sipes,* 386 U.S. 171 (1967).

The unreviewable, discretionary control of the General Counsel over unfair labor practice complaints has significant impact at three distinct steps in the litigation procedures of the N.L.R.B. First is his decision whether or not to issue a complaint at all. Second is his power to control the scope of the complaint in response to evidence produced during discovery and elicited during the hearing. Third is his ability, after the issuance of the complaint and even after the commencement of the hearing, to effect a settlement of a labor dispute without the agreement of the charging party.

The unappealable authority of the General Counsel over the issuance of a complaint is based on the fundamental principle that the purpose of the Labor Management Relations Act is to protect the public interest. This protection is to be accomplished by promoting the free flow of commerce and by providing peaceful procedures by which to deal with interferences "inimical to the general welfare. . . ." LMRA, § 1, 29 U.S.C. § 141 (1970). This language has consistently been interpreted to mean that since congressional intent was to establish a single agency through which to develop a national labor policy, no private causes of action were permissible in unfair labor practice disputes because they could lead to conflicting interpretations of the law. Any individual right to appeal a no-issuance decision would, in effect, acknowledge a private right of action to overcome the General Counsel's estimation that no public interest would be served by issuance of that particular complaint.

Only two types of exceptions to this otherwise blanket policy are recognized. First, LMRA §§ 301 and 303 specifically provide for private rights of action for breaches of collective bargaining agreements and for secondary boycott activity. Second, the District of Columbia Court of Appeals in *Hourihan v. NLRB*, 201 F.2d 187, 188 n. 4 (D.C. Cir. 1952), specifically reserved the question whether the courts have power to correct an "abuse of discretion by the General Counsel in failing to issue a complaint." The lower federal courts, although generally unreceptive to suits challenging the General Counsel's refusal, have recognized narrow exceptions in specific representation situations, namely (1) if the plaintiff nonfrivolously asserts that his constitutional rights have been infringed, *Fay v. Douds,* 172 F.2d 720 (2d Cir. 1949), (2) if the N.L.R.B. action has violated a specific statutory provision, *Leedom v. Kyne,* 358 U.S. 184 (1958), and (3) if prompt judicial review is necessary to prevent possible international complications, *McCulloch v. Sociedad National de Marineros de Honduras,* 372 U.S. 10 (1963). To date, however, no such exceptions have been allowed in unfair labor practice proceedings. *Hennepin Broadcasting Associates, Inc. v. NLRB,* 408 F. Supp. 932 (D. Minn. 1975), indicated that some extreme case might exist where a district court would have the power to compel the N.L.R.B. to issue or to reconsider issuing an unfair labor practice complaint; however, only in a situation in which it was readily apparent that inadequate consideration had been given to the plaintiff's charges would the court intrude on the Board's exclusive jurisdiction.

The second step over which the General Counsel exerts non-reviewable influence is in determining the final scope of the complaint. Under fairly specific conditions, the complaint may be broadened beyond the charges originally filed. Evidence of additional unfair labor practices, parties to be charged, or parties aggrieved often will be uncovered during either the first field investigation or during discovery in preparation for the hearing. If the additional charges are closely related to the subject matter of the complaint, *Ackerman Manufacturing Co.,* 241 N.L.R.B. 621 (1979), or if the complaint includes a catch-all phrase such as "by the above and other acts," *Gulf State Manufacturers, Inc.,* 230 N.L.R.B. 558 (1977), the General Counsel may expand the scope of the original charge to include these further allegations in the formal complaint. *NLRB v. Kohler Co.,* 220 F.2d 3 (7th Cir. 1955). This authority to expand the complaint has definite limitations, however, for an Administrative Law Judge may not grant the General Counsel's motion to add allegations during the course of the hearing if the new charges have no connection with the original complaint. In *R.J. Causey Construction Co.,* 241 N.L.R.B. 1096 (1979), for example, the General Counsel was not permitted to add charges of failure to pay contractually required fringe benefits to an original complaint which dealt only with unlawful discharges.

Further charges may be added, however, even without a close relationship to the original complaint or an appropriate catch-all phrase if the additional charges are fully litigated at the hearing before the Administrative Law Judge. In *Alexander Dawson, Inc. v. NLRB,* 586 F.2d 1300 (9th Cir. 1978), the court of appeals held that an N.L.R.B. finding of illegal surveillance by the employer, despite the lack of such a charge in the complaint, did not deprive the employer of any due process rights because the surveillance issue had been fully litigated during the hearings. Likewise, in *Montefiore Hospital & Medical Center,* 102 L.R.R.M. 1121, 243 N.L.R.B. No. 106 (1979), the N.L.R.B. upheld the General Counsel's refusal to dismiss a portion of the complaint based on a charge that had been withdrawn. New repetitions of the allegedly unlawful conduct, unavailable as evidence when the charge was withdrawn, constituted new evidence, thus authorizing the General Counsel to litigate that issue and proceed on a previously withdrawn charge.

This "fully litigated" means of expanding a complaint has a significant restriction. In *Jasta Manufacturing Co.,* 102 L.R.R.M. 1610, 246 N.L.R.B. No. 16 (1979), although all the facts necessary to establish an unlawful discharge were placed in evidence, the facts were offered bit by bit by the General Counsel for other relevant purposes. At no time during the hearing was the employer put on notice that an unlawful discharge was being alleged, so the employer never put forth a defense to that charge. In this situation, the Board held that although all the relevant evidence had been presented, the issue itself had never been litigated.

The third stage at which the unreviewable discretion of the General Counsel has significant impact on the complaint is in the achievement of a settlement after a complaint has issued. If the charging party refuses to join in the settlement, his ability to object depends upon whether the settlement is formal or informal. In a formal settlement agreement, the parties waive their right to a hearing and agree that the N.L.R.B. may both issue an appropriate remedial order and apply for a court decree enforcing its order. The charging party may then file written objections with supporting reasons within five days after the service upon him of the proposed agreement. The settlement agreement, the objections, and the Regional Director's advisory statements are then submitted to the General Counsel in Washington, D.C. for review. His approval, in turn, must be submitted to the Board for final approval, at which time the charging party may file further objections. Most courts acknowledge that a formal postcomplaint settlement agreement may be entered into without the charging party's consent. (*NLRB v. Oil, Chemical & Atomic Workers International Union,* 476 F.2d 1031 (1st Cir. 1973).)

In the case of an informal settlement agreement, however, the courts are in disagreement over whether the charging party's consent is necessary. The First, Second, Fifth, and D.C. Circuits, hold that the charging party's consent is not necessary, basing their position on the fact that the General Counsel represents the public interest and that the actual dispute is between the Regional Director, as agent of the General Counsel, and the charged party. "The selection of cases to be pursued to the end through adversary proceedings is a responsibility of the Board," which also "has the power to settle controversies within its jurisdiction." *Textile Workers Union v. NLRB,* 294 F.2d 738 (D.C. Cir. 1961).

In contrast, the Third and Eighth Circuits have held that no formal postcomplaint settlement agreement may be entered into without the charging party's consent. The strongest statement upholding this point of view was made in *Leeds & Northrup Co. v. NLRB,* 357 F.2d 527 (3d Cir. 1966), in which the court labeled as faulty the reasoning behind the unreviewability of the General Counsel's decision to approve an informal settlement over the charging party's objections. While all parties agree that a formal order is final and therefore appealable, the Board contends that informal settlements are not final dispositions and are therefore unappealable. The *Leeds & Northrup* court labeled this distinction as "overtechnical" and held that the informal settlement may not be used to "thwart the statutory machinery," which contemplates Board action. "Anything less, such as informal actions of its agents in dismissing such complaints over the objection of the charging party, is arbitrary and capricious. . . . [I]f an amicable adjustment of a labor dispute cannot be brought about through informal negotiations with the consent of all the parties, after the issuance of a complaint, then such informal proceedings must be formalized for Board action within the statutory scheme, thereby creating a record for judicial review." This position, that an informal settlement which adjusts the conflicting interests of the parties and remedies the underlying labor dispute lies within the review provisions of NLRA § 10(f), was affirmed in *International Ladies' Garment Workers' Union v. NLRB*, 501 F.2d 823 (D.C. Cir. 1974).

This controversy among the various circuits is further complicated by the issue of whether the charging party has a right to an evidentiary hearing before the Regional Director and the charged party enter into an informal settlement agreement without the charging party's consent. In this situation, the circuits significantly realign, and only the Second Circuit denies the charging party any right to an evidentiary hearing. The Third Circuit has consistently held that once a complaint has issued, the charging party is entitled to an evidentiary hearing before either a formal or informal settlement agreement. The remainder of the circuits which have considered this issue maintain a middle ground. Even in those circuits upholding the validity of a settlement without the charging party's consent, the

46

necessity of an evidentiary hearing to settle material issues of disputed fact has been upheld by the First, Fifth, Seventh, and Ninth Circuits, although the same right would not result when the charging party objects only to the terms of the proposed settlement.

The statutory basis of this nationwide disagreement lies in the language of NLRA § 10(b), which specifically grants a hearing in an unfair labor practice case only to the party charged. The purpose of the NLRA and its administering agency is to protect the public. The refusal to recognize the right of a private party to enforce or challenge an N.L.R.B. order was upheld by the Supreme Court in *Amalgamated Utility Workers v. Consolidated Edison Co.*, 309 U.S. 261 (1940), when it stated that "[t]he Board as a public agency, not any private [individual] . . . is chosen as the instrument" by which to settle unfair labor practices. The granting of a general private right of action was specifically denied in the legislative history of the Act. Because the N.L.R.B. acts only on behalf of the public, "private rights must give way when the Board reasonably determines that the purposes of the Act are best served by settlement." *Local 282, International Brotherhood of Teamsters v. NLRB*, 339 F.2d 795 (2d Cir. 1964).

Recent scholarly attacks on the unreviewable discretion of the General Counsel has been totally deprived of his cause of action, no matter how valid or how devastating to his personal economic stability. If the case is arguably within the jurisdiction of the Board, the plaintiff is also deprived of any state court relief. In addition, the possibility of abuse of authority by the General Counsel, not necessarily by intent but by the restrictions of manpower and budget, will of necessity increase, most predictably in the automatic dismissal of borderline cases. Other arguments in favor of a private right of action point to the fact that a uniform body of substantive law has been developed and

47

judges have ample precedent by which to decide private wrongs; no longer dominant is the pressure to develop a uniform, consistent body of case law. Several labor reform bills have recently been introduced, and although none has succeeded thus far, the possibility of significant changes in this area of labor law should not be dismissed lightly.

§ 1-2(B)(5). The Unfair Labor Practice Hearing.

§ 1-2(B)(5)(a). Prehearing Procedures.

Before the opening of the hearing, the parties may file various motions and applications with the Regional Director, all of which must contain detailed grounds for the action. Either the Regional Director or the administrative law judge, if one has already been assigned to the case, rules on motions to intervene and extend the various dates and deadlines assigned to the hearing. All motions pertaining to the conduct of the hearing except those for summary judgment are referred to the administrative law judge. Each ruling is made in writing and is served on all parties. (29 C.F.R. § 102.25.) On the other hand, in cases where no answer or a defective answer to the complaint has been filed, motions for summary judgment are filed directly with the Board by counsel for the General Counsel. (29 C.F.R. § 102.24.)

Rules governing prehearing discovery by subpoena or deposition may vary widely from circuit to circuit depending upon which procedure is requested. Witnesses and pertinent documents are made available at the hearing through subpoenas *ad testificandum* or *duces tecum,* which are issued by the Board on a non-discretionary basis at the request of any party. (29 U.S.C. § 1161 (1).) The General Counsel is a "party" in unfair labor practice cases and therefore also may request issuance of subpoenas. (*NLRB v.*

Duval Jewelry Co., 357 U.S. 1 (1958).) Applications for either type of subpoena are filed with either the Regional Director or the administrative law judge, depending upon the stage of the case.

The subpoenas themselves are issued in blank and contain only the name and address of the requesting party, who in turn designates the particular witness whose attendance and testimony are required as well as the particular documents to be produced. If the person served with a subpoena does not intend to comply, he has five days after service in which to file a written petition with the Regional Director or the administrative law judge to have the subpoena revoked. (29 C.F.R. § 103.31(b).) The Regional Director or administrative law judge must then give notice of the petition to revoke to the party originally requesting the subpoena.

Power to revoke a subpoena lies with either the Board or the administrative law judge, who will grant the petition to revoke if the evidence sought is irrelevant to the matter under investigation, if the subpoena does not describe the desired evidence with sufficient particularity, or if "enforcement . . . would be inconsistent with law and with the policies of the Act." (29 C.F.R. § 102.31(d); *NLRB v. Adrian Belt Co.,* 578 F.2d 1304 (9th Cir. 1978).) Although the administrative law judge must state the grounds for his ruling on the petition to revoke, the petition itself, any answer filed by the party who requested the subpoena, and the ruling are not made part of the record except on the request of the aggrieved party. (29 C.F.R. § 102.31(b).)

If a person served with a subpoena refuses to comply and either does not petition for a revocation or has his petition refused, any proceedings to enforce the subpoena must be instituted by the General Counsel, not by any of the private parties involved. (*NLRB ex rel. International Union of Electrical, Radio & Machine Workers v. Dutch-Boy, Inc.,* 606

F.2d 929 (10th Cir. 1979).) This limitation on enforcement of subpoenas stems from the fact that although the district court does have jurisdiction to enforce subpoenas issued in connection with proper Board investigations and hearings, jurisdiction attaches only "upon application of the Board." (29 U.S.C. § 161(2), NLRA § 11(2).) However, the General Counsel applies for enforcement as a matter of course upon the request of a private party.

The only significant limitation on the enforcement of issued subpoenas arises in situations in which the party subpoenaed may legitimately claim a privilege against testifying, or the policies of the Act would be violated. For example, the Board refused to seek judicial enforcement of a subpoena requiring a labor mediator to testify about bargaining sessions. (*NLRB v. Joseph Macaluso, Inc.,* 618 F.2d 51 (9th Cir. 1980).) Also, NLRB investigators usually may not be required to testify about the Board's investigation and trial preparation procedures, *Stephens Produce Co. v. NLRB,* 515 F.2d 1373 (8th Cir. 1975), and Board employees may not testify or produce evidence concerning knowledge gained in their official capacity without the written consent of the Board. (29 C.F.R. § 102.118(a)(1). *See NLRB ex rel. International Union of Electrical, Radio & Machine Workers v. Dutch-Boy, Inc.,* 606 F.2d 929 (10th Cir. 1979).)

However, rule 102.118 cannot by itself create a recognized evidentiary privilege under which to revoke a properly issued subpoena. (*NLRB v. Seine & Line Fisherman's Union of San Pedro,* 374 F.2d 974 (9th Cir. 1967). *See P.S.C. Resources, Inc. v. NLRB,* 576 F.2d 380 (1st Cir. 1978).) Evidence otherwise admissible under general rules of evidence may not be excluded purely on the basis of the rule. (*General Engineering, Inc. v. NLRB,* 341 F.2d 367 (9th Cir. 1965).) This restriction on the Board's power to withhold information from a hearing is based on 5 U.S.C. § 22 (1958), which permits the heads of certain executive departments to regulate both their personnel and the distribution and use of all property of the department but specifically refuses to authorize the withholding of information or records from the public.

If a petition to revoke a subpoena based on inadmissibility of evidence is filed by the General Counsel, the party requesting the subpoena may counter with a showing of "good cause" based on general relevance and reasonable scope. The requested material claimed to be protected by privilege is then examined *in camera* by the administrative law judge, who may excise protected information and admit the remainder. Although the Board may decline to produce any evidence in its possession, it cannot enter an enforcement order in a case in which it withheld admissible evidence. (*NLRB v. Robbins Tire & Rubber Co.*, 437 U.S. 214 (1978).)

Unlike the liberal policy governing applications for subpoenas, the Board's rule 102.30 (29 C.F.R. § 102.30) governing depositions is quite restrictive. An application for a deposition, made to either the Regional Director or the administrative law judge depending upon the stage of the case, must state with particularity the reasons why the deposition is necessary and the subjects about which the witness is expected to testify. All parties are permitted to examine and cross-examine the witness, (29 C.F.R. § 102.30(c)), and objections must be made at the time of the examination and transcribed into the record of the deposition. The witness then signs his testimony, copies are sent to the Regional Director or the administrative law judge, who then rules on the admissibility of all or part of the deposition.

In the Second Circuit, depositions may be taken only " 'upon good and exceptional cause for the purpose of obtaining and preserving evidence for trial, not for the purpose of discovery.' The Board ... has construed the Rule as requiring more than a showing that the taking of depositions would aid counsel in the preparation of his case for trial." (*NLRB v. Interboro Contractors, Inc.*, 432 F.2d 854, 857-58 (2d Cir. 1970).)

An even more restrictive view has been adopted by the Ninth Circuit, which stated in *Harvey's Wagon Wheel, Inc. v. NLRB*, 550 F.2d 1139, 1141 (9th Cir. 1976), "Under Board rules, all disclosure is expressly forbidden except certain public documents of witnesses (provided only after the witness has testified) and requests cognizable under the Freedom of Information Act." (29 C.F.R. §§ 102.30, 102.117, 102.118.) A slightly less restrictive view is held by the Fifth and Sixth Circuits, in which Board discretion controls the granting of permission to conduct pretrial discovery. Unless prejudice is shown, the Board's ruling will not be disturbed. (*NLRB v. W.R. Bean & Sons, Inc.*, 450 F.2d 93 (5th Cir. 1971); *NLRB v. Valley Motel Co.*, 530 F.2d 693 (6th Cir. 1976).) However, discovery may be allowed to protect the rights of parties as long as "good cause" is shown; although what constitutes "good cause" has not been specified, the extent to which a party needs the information and the prejudice it would suffer without the discovery appear to be the determining factors. (*NLRB v. Rex Disposables, Div. of DHJ Industries, Inc.*, 494 F.2d 588 (5th Cir. 1974).) In practice, "good cause" amounts to the otherwise total unavailability of the witness and is limited to situations of a witness' illness or his extreme distance from the location of the hearing. (*See NLRB v. Globe Wireless, Ltd.*, 193 F.2d 748 (9th Cir. 1951).)

§ 1-2(B)(5)(b). The Prehearing Conference.

Prior to the hearing, the parties have a right to a conference with the administrative law judge either at their own request or by the decision of the judge himself. (*NLRB*

Casehandling Manual, Part I, Unfair Labor Practice Proceedings ¶ 10381 (1975).) The purpose of the prehearing conference is to avoid surpise and confusion during the hearing by defining and simplifying issues, thereby eliminating the need for evidence on undisputed but relevant matters. As a result, parties have an opportunity to stipulate to the facts of the case and waive the hearing, instead of submitting the undisputed facts to the administrative law judge or the Board for a decision. (*NLRB Casehandling Manual, Part I, Unfair Labor Practice Proceedings* ¶ 10284 (1975).) All alleged discriminatees must join in the stipulation and must fully understand the consequences of waiving the hearing. However, any party's right to a review of a decision based on stipulated facts is not altered. (*NLRB Casehandling Manual, Part I, Unfair Labor Practice Proceedings* ¶ 10286, ¶ 10288 (1975).)

§ 1-2(B)(5)(c). The Unfair Labor Practice Hearing.

The basic structure of an unfair labor practice hearing is similar to that of a criminal rather than a civil trial. Instead of the charging and charged parties being the plaintiff and defendant, the adversaries are the General Counsel, representing the charging party, and the charged party, or respondent. However, unlike the complaining witness in a criminal trial, the person or organization filing the unfair labor practice charge also is a "party" and thus has the right to fully participate during the hearing. (*John L. Clemmy Co.,* 118 N.L.R.B. 599 (1957).)

The hearing is conducted before an administrative law judge designated by the chief administrative law judge in Washington, D.C. or the associate chief administrative law judge in San Francisco, California. The judge assigned to conduct the hearing may be changed at any time, or the case may be ordered transferred to the Board or any NLRB member rather than another administrative law judge. (29 C.F.R. § 102.50.)

The administrative law judge is responsible for assuring in an impartial manner that all pertinent evidence is made part of the record. He must see that each party clearly and fully develops his own case and therefore has the duty to require full presentation of all facts underlying the complaint. For example, in *NLRB v. Doral Building Services, Inc.,* 666 F.2d 432 (9th Cir. 1982), the judge's refusal to allow counsel for Doral to use unofficial English translations of Spanish language affidavits by witnesses or to provide for official translations was considered reversible error since all cross-examination was thereby prevented and a complete record impossible to make.

The order of evidence in an unfair labor practice hearing is the same as that in a trial. The General Counsel presents its case, the charged party then puts on a defense, and the General Counsel concludes with a rebuttal. Following the presentation of all the evidence, each party, including the charging party, has the right to argue orally. (29 C.F.R. § 102.42.) Alternatively, parties may request permission to file written briefs to illustrate a crucial point or to bring new facts to the attention of the administrative law judge. (*NLRB Casehandling Manual, Part I, Unfair Labor Practice Proceedings* ¶ 10410 (1975).)

All parties in an unfair labor practice hearing may call and examine witnesses, introduce evidence, submit briefs, propose findings to the administrative law judge, and engage in oral argument. The counsel for the General Counsel must "introduce admissible evidence which will support the allegations of the complaint" issued at the request of the General Counsel. (*NLRB Casehandling Manual, Part I, Unfair Labor Practice Proceedings* ¶ 10380 (1975).) Similarly, counsel for the charging party may participate in the hearing by calling witnesses and engaging in cross-examination and oral argument subject only to the discretion of the administrative law judge. (*Spector Freight System, Inc.,* 141 N.L.R.B. 1110 (1963).) Finally, the respondent presents his case and the General Counsel concludes with rebuttal.

Pursuant to his statutorily required duty "to inquire fully into the facts," the administrative law judge may himself question witnesses and even produce witnesses of his own. (29 C.F.R. § 102.35; *NLRB v. Seafarers International Union,* 496 F.2d 1363 (5th Cir. 1974).) In addition to the powers discussed above concerning subpoenas, depositions, and pretrial conferences, the administrative law judge rules on offers of proof and admissibility of evidence, regulates the progress of the hearing, rules on all motions, dismisses unsupported complaints or portions of complaints, takes any other action concerning stipulated facts, requests statements of each party's position on each issue, and any other matters authorized under the NLRB Rules and Regulations. (29 C.F.R. § 102.35.) Because the guiding rule of the hearing is the fair, impartial, and unbiased development of a complete record through the actions of the administrative law judge, hearings characterized by bias, suppressive rulings, or a general pattern of actions designed to reach a predetermined conclusion will be set aside and a new hearing ordered. (*A.O. Smith Corp. v. NLRB,* 343 F.2d 103 (7th Cir. 1965).) However, even a judge's expressed feelings against one of the parties will not automatically disqualify him if the development of the evidence and his decision show impartiality. (*NLRB v. Taxicab Drivers Union,* 340 F.2d 905 (7th Cir. 1964).) Nevertheless, a remand will be ordered if a judge's inexcusable and injudicious attacks on a witness deprive a party of a fair hearing. (*NLRB v. Aluminum Cruiser, Inc.,* 620 F.2d 116 (6th Cir. 1980).)

All rulings by the administrative law judge are subject to review by the Board, either before or after the judge issues his decision; while the Board has discretion to grant an appeal before the final decision is announced, the parties have an absolute right of appeal after the decision is issued. In addition, any party may request the administrative law judge to withdraw from the case on the grounds of personal bias or disqualification; an affidavit describing in detail the reasons believed to warrant removal must accompany the request. (29 C.F.R. § 102.37). The judge may respond either by disqualifying himself and withdrawing from the case or by ruling against the request on the record, stating the grounds for his ruling, and then proceeding with the hearing. (29 C.F.R. § 102.37.)

The passage of the Taft-Hartley Amendments of 1947 authorizing application of the federal rules of evidence to Board hearings caused two major changes in the conduct of the hearings. First, the only significant limitation placed on any party's right to participate in the hearing, was the administrative law judge's new power to sequester witnesses, including parties, in order to preserve the credibility of the hearing. While the new amendment specifically ordered the application of the federal rules to labor hearings, the administrative law judge, thus given the discretionary power to exclude witnesses, usually did not exercise this power against witnesses who were also discriminatees, for as charging parties, they had the right to be present. (*Rickert Carbidge Die, Inc.*, 126 N.L.R.B. 757, n. 3 (1960); 29 C.F.R. § 102.8.) However, the 1976 revision of the federal rules of evidence, specifically rule 615, provided that a party may request the court to exclude witnesses to prevent their hearing the testimony of other witnesses. The new federal rule, therefore, changed the standard of the original application of the rules from the broad guideline "so far as practicable," 29 U.S.C. § 160(b), to one supporting "exclusion demandable as of right except for the listed exceptions. Eliminating the courts' discretion emphasizes the degree of importance placed upon 'the rule's' utility by Congress. . . . [W]e cannot deny the exclusion process its deserved prominence as a vehicle for ascertaining truth," *i.e.,* minimizing fabrication, perjury, and inaccuracy, and increasing the possibility of detecting false and inconsistent testimony. (*Unga Painting Corp.,* 237 N.L.R.B. 1306, 1306-07 (1978).) Consequently, even discriminatees are now excluded from hearings during testimony about events to which they themselves will testify unless the administrative law judge determines that special circumstances warrant their unrestricted presence. (*See NLRB v. Stark,* 525 F.2d 422 (2d Cir. 1975).)

The second major impact of the federal rules of evidence on Board hearings resulted from application of the rules governing admissibility of evidence. "The original Act gave the Board great latitude in choosing the evidence it would believe and giving great effect to findings that rested on that evidence, the . . . [result being] what the courts had described as 'shocking injustices' in the Board's rulings." (Annot., 32 A.L.R. Fed. 838, *NLRB Proceeding—Rules of Evidence,* § 3, at 845.) Thus, under the revised rule, hearsay is excluded unless the Board provides an adequate explanation for admitting otherwise inadmissible hearsay. (*Teamsters Local Union v. NLRB,* 532 F.2d 1385 (D.C. Cir. 1976).) Findings against a labor union based on improperly admitted hearsay will be rejected. (*NLRB v. Amalgamated Meat Cutters & Butcher Workmen,* 202 F.2d 671 (9th Cir. 1953).) On the other hand, in *NLRB v. Capitol Fish Co.,* 294 F.2d 868 (5th Cir. 1961), the exclusion of a Board attorney's evidence on the ground he had allegedly tainted the credibility of several other witnesses was reversed by the district court. Although the Board had refused permission for the attorney to testify, the district court found no privilege justifying exclusion of the evidence.

It is clear from an examination of several cases dealing with admissibility of evidence that unjustified or improper *exclusion* of evidence will necessitate a reversal of an administrative law judge's decision whereas improper *admission* of evidence, although discouraged, is not as prejudicial unless the record reveals that the improperly admitted evidence was the basis of the decision. (*NLRB v. West Side Carpet Cleaning Co.,* 329 F.2d 758 (6th Cir. 1964); *NLRB v. W.B. Jones Lumber Co.,* 245 F.2d 388 (9th Cir. 1957).) Because no jury is involved in an administrative hearing, the judge is presumed to rely only on proper evidence. However, the presumption can be overcome and an NLRB decision reversed if the record reveals that the Board relied on incompetent evidence and excluded competent evidence. (*International Union, United Auto v. NLRB,* 459 F.2d 1329 (D.C. Cir. 1972).) Even with this liberal policy toward admissibility of evidence, the Board may nevertheless exclude evidence if other objectives of the Act would be contravened. For example, secretly made tape recordings supporting § 8(b)(1)(A) charges were held admissible in *NLRB v. Plasterer's Local 90,* 606 F.2d 189 (7th Cir. 1979) but inadmissible in *Carpenter Sprinkler Corp. v. NLRB,* 605 F.2d 60 (2d Cir. 1979). The crucial difference was that the recordings in *Carpenter Sprinkler* were made during on-going contract negotiations, and the Board's policy protecting "the willingness of the parties to express themselves freely ... [during] collective bargaining" took precedence over the admitted relevance of the contents of the recordings. (*Carpenter Sprinkler,* 605 F.2d 60, 66.)

Evidence at an unfair labor practice hearing usually is given through the oral testimony of witnesses and their production of pertinent documents. (29 C.F.R. § 102.38.) Although pretrial discovery, as discussed earlier, is severely curtailed in an unfair labor practice hearing, parties have an absolute right to obtain copies of pretrial statements made by witnesses. The Board has adopted the position that the *Jencks* rule, derived from the holding in *Jencks v. United States,* 353 U.S. 657 (1957), providing for the right of counsel in a criminal trial to examine pretrial statements of witnesses called by the government, must be observed in Board proceedings. If the pre-trial statement is requested at the end of the witness' direct testimony, it must be produced or the Board will strike the witness' testimony from the record. (*Harvey Aluminum, Inc. v. NLRB,* 335 F.2d 749 (9th Cir. 1964); 29 C.F.R. § 102.118(b)(1).) The only exceptions are (1) proof of a good faith but unsuccessful effort made to obtain copies of lost or inadvertently destroyed statements, *Killian v. United States,* 368 U.S. 231 (1961), and (2) requests made after completion of cross-examination because the purpose of the rule is to aid preparation for cross-examination. (*Army Aviation Center Federal Credit Union,* 216 N.L.R.B. 435 (1975).)

The burden of establishing commission of an unfair labor practice always rests on the General Counsel, who must prove his case by a preponderance of the evidence. (*International Tel. & Tel. Corp. v. International Brotherhood of Electrical Workers,* 419 U.S. 428 (1975); 29 C.F.R. § 101.10(b).) The filing of a charge or the issuance of a complaint creates no presumption of a violation. (*Boeing Airplane Co. v. NLRB,* 140 F.2d 423 (10th Cir. 1944).) Once the General Counsel has made out a *prima facie* case, however, the burden of producing evidence to the contrary shifts to the respondent, for he has better access to evidence establishing any affirmative defense. (*NLRB v. Great Dane Trailers, Inc.,* 388 U.S. 26 (1966).) The burden then shifts back to the General Counsel to overcome the charged party's evidence.

No unfavorable inferences may be drawn from the respondent's failure to present any evidence countering the charges; the General Counsel's burden of putting on sufficient evidence to establish a *prima facie* case remains undiminished. In order for the findings of fact made by the administrative law judge or the Board to be conclusive, they must be supported by substantial evidence on the record as a whole. (29 U.S.C. § 160(e).) This requirement has been interpreted to mean sufficient evidence to provide a substantial basis of fact from which reasonable inferences may be drawn. (*Radio Officers Union of Commercial Telegraphers v. NLRB*, 347 U.S. 17 (1954).)

The only exception to the rule demanding substantial evidence to support an inference occurs when one party fails to produce relevant evidence known to be within its control. In such situations, the Board, when reviewing the record, applies the "adverse inference rule," (*International Union, United Auto., etc. v. NLRB*, 459 F.2d 1329 (D.C. Cir. 1972)), and permissibly infers that the missing evidence is unfavorable to the party who could produce it but refuses. (*Crow Gravel Co.*, 168 N.L.R.B. 1040 (1967).) The same adverse inference may be drawn against the General Counsel litigating a discriminatory discharge case if he fails to produce evidence known to be available and relevant to proof of the employer's motivation. (*NLRB v. Ford Radio & Mica Corp.*, 258 F.2d 457 (2d Cir. 1958).)

§ 1-2(B)(6). The Administrative Law Judge's Decision.

Following the close of the hearing and the receipt of any brief, the administrative law judge issues a report containing his findings of fact, conclusions of law, and the reasons for his decisions on all pertinent issues. His report concludes with recommendations on the disposition of the case, including suggestions concerning corrective actions to be required of a respondent found to have committed an unfair labor practice. (29 C.F.R. § 101.11(a).) The decision may sustain all or part of the complaint or dismiss it in whole or in part. The decision is filed with the Board, and copies are served on each of the parties. (29 C.F.R. § 102.45(a).) Finally, an order is entered and served on all parties automatically transferring the case to the Board.

The administrative law judge is the agent of the Board charged with the responsibility of gathering facts and making findings and recommendations to the Board in the form of an intermediate report, which is merely advisory and may be accepted or rejected by the Board. (*NLRB v. Botany Worsted Mills*, 133 F.2d 876 (3d Cir. 1943).) The Board, not the administrative law judge, is vested with the responsibility for determining whether an unfair labor practice has been committed. (*Universal Camera Corp. v. NLRB*, 340 U.S. 474 (1951).) While the administrative law judge's estimation of the credibility of witnesses should be given great weight by both the Board and a reviewing court, his determinations are not final. (*NLRB v. Hamilton Plastic Molding*, 312 F.2d 723 (6th Cir. 1963).)

The significance of the administrative law judge's report depends largely on the importance of credibility in the particular case; his decisions are of greater consequence to the extent that material facts in any case depend on the determination of the credibility of witnesses as shown by their demeanor or conduct at the hearing. (*Universal Camera Corp. v. NLRB*, 340 U.S. 474 (1951).) Indeed, the Board may adopt the administrative law judge's credibility determinations and findings of fact but still draw different conclusions of law. (*Paintsmiths, Inc. v. NLRB*, 620 F.2d 1326 (8th Cir. 1980).) Thus, the Board need not follow the administrative law judge's findings even though they were not erroneous; the only requirement is that there be substantial evidence to support the Board's determination, whether or not substantial evidence also supports the judge's contrary decision. (*NLRB v. Treasure Lake, Inc.,* 453 F.2d 202 (3d Cir. 1971).)

§ 1-2(B)(7). Exceptions Filed With the Labor Board.

If none of the parties wishes to challenge the administrative law judge's decision and instead they elect to comply with his recommendation, the ALJ's recommended order becomes the order of the Board without review, and the case is concluded. (*W.T. Grant Regional Credit Center,* 225 N.L.R.B. 881 (1976).) In such cases, all exceptions or objections to any part of the ALJ's report are waived. (29 C.F.R. § 102.46(h).) However, a dissatisfied party may obtain a review of any part of the ALJ's report by filing exceptions to the decision or any ruling with the Board within 20 days after the service of the order transferring the case to the NLRB. (29 C.F.R. §§ 101.41(b), 102.46(a).) An exception challenges the correctness of a particular portion of the decision; it must state specifically which ruling, conclusion, or underlying policy is being questioned, the exact pages of the record believed to support a contrary view, and a statement of the precedential authority supporting each exception. (29 C.F.R. § 102.46(b).)

The ultimate result of failing to file exceptions or filing them improperly is that the Board and therefore a federal court are precluded from reviewing the decision. (*Barton Brands, Ltd. v. NLRB,* 529 F.2d 793 (7th Cir. 1976).) Despite these consequences, however, general objections to each finding and recommendation of the ALJ are not regarded as proper exceptions. (*Marshall Field & Co. v. NLRB,* 318 U.S. 253 (1943).) The Board recommends restraint in the filing of exceptions, the guideline being whether they have reasonable possibilities of success. Credibility findings are difficult to upset unless the ALJ himself has stated that they were based on "logical analysis" of the facts presented in testimony rather than on demeanor, or where demeanor findings are mutually inconsistent with logic, pattern, or themselves. (*NLRB Casehandling Manual, Part I, Unfair Labor Practice Proceedings* ¶ 10438.3 (1975).)

Each party filing exceptions may also present arguments and authority in a supporting brief. Opposing parties then have 10 days in which to file answering briefs either opposing the exception or, rarely, supporting the ALJ's decision. (29 C.F.R. § 102.46(c), (d)(1).) The NLRB also has discretion to hear oral argument if a timely written request is made at the time the statement of exceptions is filed. (29 C.F.R. § 102.46(i); *Consolidated Edison Co. v. NLRB,* 305 U.S. 197 (1938).) However, reviewing courts have held that the NLRB does not deprive a party of due process of law by refusing to hear oral argument and requesting a written brief instead. (*NLRB v. Allied Distributing Corp.,* 297 F.2d 679 (10th Cir. 1961).)

§ 1-2(B)(8). Labor Board Decisions in Unfair Labor Practice Cases.

Once all exceptions and briefs are filed and oral argument, if granted, is heard, the Board may (1) render a decision in the case, (2) reopen the record and take further evidence before a Board member, agent, or agency, or (3) otherwise dispose of the case, including adopting the ALJ's recommendations. (29 C.F.R. § 102.48(b).) Although the Board's policy is to sustain an ALJ's credibility findings unless those findings are, by a preponderance of the evidence, clearly incorrect, the Board may reject his findings when, for example, he specifically ignores pertinent evidence. (*NLRB v. Interboro Contractors, Inc.,* 388 F.2d 495 (2d Cir. 1967).) Until a case is filed in a reviewing court, the Board may also modify or set aside any part of its decision or order. (29 C.F.R. § 102.48(d)(1).)

The only limitation placed by the Act on the Board's discretion in rendering a decision is that it must be based on the "preponderance of the testimony taken" at the hearing. (29 U.S.C. § 160(c); *NLRB v. Ellis & Watts Products, Inc.*, 344 F.2d 67 (6th Cir. 1965).) Another rule limiting the Board's latitude is that findings must be based on charges known to the respondent, either through the complaint or through full litigation of the issue at the hearing. (*Electri-Flex Co. v. NLRB*, 570 F.2d 1327 (7th Cir. 1978).)

If the ALJ's decision is adopted in its entirety, the Board must consider all the exceptions but need not specify its own finding on each point raised. (*NLRB v. Process Corp.*, 412 F.2d 215 (7th Cir. 1969).) Alternatively, the Board may issue a fully detailed decision complete with a thorough consideration on all material issues raised. (NLRB Statements of Procedure, 29 C.F.R. § 101.12(a).)

After the Board has issued its decision and a remedial order, if appropriate, a party may move promptly for reconsideration, rehearing, or reopening of the record. Reconsideration is requested if a party feels the Board has made a material error in its findings. Similarly, a motion for a rehearing must allege that a specific error caused prejudice to the moving party and requires a new hearing to correct the mistake. (29 C.F.R. § 102.48(d)(1).)

A motion to reopen the record is made by a party wishing to add additional evidence into the record. Such motions must identify the evidence, explain why it was not presented earlier, and prove how the evidence, if found credible, would alter the result of the hearing. (*NLRB v. Arrow Elastic Corp.*, 573 F.2d 702 (1st Cir. 1978).) If the Board grants the motion, it will hear only that evidence which has been newly discovered, made available since the close of the hearing, or should have been admitted at the hearing. (29 C.F.R. § 102.48(d)(1).)

If the Board's final determination is that an unfair labor practice has been committed, it will issue an order in two parts. First is the "cease and desist" portion requiring the respondent to stop its unlawful activity; this portion of the order is mandatory. (*Eichleay Corp. v. NLRB,* 206 F.2d 799 (3d Cir. 1953).) Second is the affirmative portion requiring the respondent to take certain remedial measures to correct the effect of the unfair labor practice on the charging party and the public. (N.L.R.A. § 10(c), 29 U.S.C. § 160(c).) Unlike the mandatory cease and desist order, however, the Board has some discretion to decide what corrective action would be appropriate in a given situation. The order may also require the respondent to make periodic reports demonstrating compliance. (29 U.S.C. § 760(c).)

The Board has considerable control over the scope of the cease and desist order issues and may not only prohibit the respondent from engaging in the activity but also determine the extent of the respondent's operations to which the order applies. (*Florida Steel Corp.,* 102 L.R.R.M. 1181, 244 N.L.R.B. No. 61 (1979).) The scope of the remedial portion of the order also is within the control of the Board, subject to the limitations that the order must effect a remedy, not a punishment of the respondent, and it must not contravene other policies of the Act. (*Republic Steel Corp. v. NLRB,* 311 U.S. 7 (1940).)

CHAPTER 2

BARGAINING UNITS

§ 2-1. General Principals Governing Unit Appropriateness Decisions.

Section 9(b) of the Act provides that "[t]he Board shall decide in each case whether, in order to assure to employees the fullest freedom in exercising the rights guaranteed by this Act, the unit appropriate for the purpose of collective bargaining is the employer unit, craft unit, plant unit, or subdivision thereof ...." (29 U.S.C. § 159(b) (1974).) Although section 9(b) and (c) contain several limitations on the NLRB's authority to make unit appropriateness determinations, the Labor Board's discretion in this area is generally considered to be quite broad. (*See* Nash & Blake, Appropriate Units for Collective Bargaining (1979).) Moreover, the Board's decision, "if not final, is rarely to be disturbed." (*Packard Motor Co. v. NLRB,* 330 U.S. 485, 491 (1947).)

In *NLRB v. Hearst Publications, Inc.,* 322 U.S. 111, 134 (1944), the United States Supreme Court recognized that

> [w]ide variations in the forms of employee self-organization and the complexities of modern industrial organization make difficult the use of inflexible

66

rules as the test of an appropriate unit. Congress was informed of the need for flexibility in shaping the unit to the particular case and accordingly gave the Board wide discretion in the matter.

In view of the diversity of employment circumstances extant in the various industrial settings, the Labor Board has rejected a clear or simple test in favor of a more flexible, but less predictable approach for determining whether a unit is appropriate. (*See, e.g., Libbey-Owens-Ford Co. v. NLRB,* 495 F.2d 1195 (3d Cir. 1974), *cert. denied,* 419 U.S. 998 (1975); *NLRB v. Krieger-Ragsdale & Co.,* 379 F.2d 517 (7th Cir. 1967), *cert. denied,* 389 U.S. 1041 (1968); *Mueller Brass Co. v. NLRB,* 180 F.2d 402, 404 (D.C. Cir. 1950).) The Board instead applies a case by-case test in which it considers "all relevant factors." (*Mallinckrodt Chemical Works,* 162 N.L.R.B. 387, 389 (1966).)

The Labor Board has long held the view that more than one unit may be appropriate in any given case. (*General Instrument Corp. v. NLRB,* 319 F.2d 420 (4th Cir. 1963), *cert. denied,* 375 U.S. 966 (1964); *cf. Local 627, IUOE v. NLRB,* 595 F.2d 844, 848 (D.C. Cir. 1979), *enforcing* 231 N.L.R.B. 76 (1977) (the determination that two businesses are "single employer" does not necessarily render the employer wide unit appropriate).) Its institutional responsibility is merely to determine whether the requested unit is "an" appropriate one for collective bargaining, not whether it is the "best or most" appropriate unit for that purpose. (*See Vicksburg Hospital, Inc. v. NLRB,* 653 F.2d 1070, 1073-75 (5th Cir. 1981), *enforcing* 251 N.L.R.B. (1980); *Alaska Statebank v. NLRB,* 653 F.2d 1285, 1287 (9th Cir. 1981), *enforcing* 250 N.L.R.B. (1980); *Wheeler-Van Label Co. v. NLRB,* 408 F.2d 613 (2d Cir. 1969), *enforcing* 172 N.L.R.B. (1968); *Morand Bros. Beverage Co.,* 91 N.L.R.B. 409 (1950), *enforced,* 190 F.2d 576 (7th Cir. 1951).) In addition, to set aside a Board certified unit, the employer must establish that the designated unit is clearly not appropriate. (*NLRB v. J.C. Penney Co.*, 559 F.2d 373, 375 (5th Cir. 1977).)

Section 9(c)(5) of the act precludes the Board from considering "the extent to which employees have organized" as controlling. In other words, the Board cannot find appropriate a unit corresponding to the union's successful organizational efforts where other indications of community interest are not present. (29 U.S.C. § 159(c)(5) (1974); *NLRB v. Western & Southern Life Insurance Co.*, 391 F.2d 119, 121-22 (3d Cir. 1968), *cert. denied*, 393 U.S. 978 (1968); *accord NLRB v. Southern Metal Service, Inc.*, 606 F.2d 512 (5th Cir. 1979); *Szabo Food Services, Inc. v. NLRB*, 550 F.2d 705 (2d Cir. 1976).) The United States Supreme Court, however, has held that section 9(c)(5) does not prohibit the Board from considering the extent of organization "as one factor" when determining unit appropriateness. (*NLRB v. Metropolitan Life Insurance Co.*, 380 U.S. 438 (1965).)

Although the Board's case-by-case and all the circumstances test renders near impossible a definitive analysis of Board law governing unit appropriateness determinations, several experts have attempted to provide a more detailed analysis than that provided herein. (*See generally* Ferrick, Baer & Anfa, *NLRB Representation Elections — Law, Practice and Procedure* (1979); Nash & Blake, *Appropriate Units for Collective Bargaining* (1979); Abodeeley, *The NLRB and the Appropriate Bargaining Unit* (1971).) Without presuming to duplicate or approach the depth of those efforts, this section will highlight the more frequently recited factors which have traditionally influenced the Board's unit appropriateness determinations.

§ 2-1(A). Community of Interest Factors.

The primary consideration in unit appropriateness determinations is the degree of common interests held by the employees involved. (*Peter Kiewit Sons' Co.*, 231 N.L.R.B. 76 (1977).) The ultimate determination is resolved by evaluating the various factors relevant to the employees' community of interests. (*Id.* at 77.) The rationale behind the community of interests doctrine is to insure cohesion among the employees in the unit and thereby enhance efficient collective bargaining. (*Allied Chemical & Alkali Workers v. Pittsburgh Plate Glass Co.*, 404 U.S. 157 (1971).)

§ 2-1(A)(1). Single-Plant v. Multi-Plant Units.

The National Labor Relations Board has consistently held that "a single-plant unit is presumptively appropriate absent a bargaining history in a more comprehensive unit or a functional integration so severe as to negate the identity of a single-plant unit." (*Black & Decker Mfg. Co.*, 147 N.L.R.B. 825, 828 (1964). *Cf. Orkin Exterminating Co.*, 258 N.L.R.B. 773 (1981) (functional integration so substantial that it negated separate identity).) This presumption has been applied with court approval to retail chain operations. (*NLRB v. Lerner Stores Corp.*, 506 F.2d 706 (9th Cir. 1974); *Sav-On Drugs, Inc.*, 138 N.L.R.B. 1032 (1962)); the insurance industry (*State Farm Mutual Automobile Insurance Co. v. NLRB*, 411 F.2d 356 (7th Cir. 1969), *cert. denied*, 396 U.S. 832 (1969); *Metropolitan Life Insurance Co.*, 156 N.L.R.B. 1408 (1966); bank branches (*Alaska Statebank v. NLRB*, 653 F.2d 1285 (9th Cir. 1981); and health and day care centers (*NLRB v. Living & Learning Centers, Inc.*, 652 F.2d 209 (1st Cir. 1981); *National G. South, Inc., d/b/a Memorial Medical*, 230 N.L.R.B. 976 (1977).)

The presumption favoring single-plant units, though not conclusive, is difficult to rebut. (*Victoria Station, Inc. v. NLRB*, 586 F.2d 672 (9th Cir. 1978).) When evaluating the circumstances surrounding the operations of an employer with many plants or a chain of retail stores, the Board considers various factors which may weigh against the single-plant presumption.

§ 2-1(A)(2). Geographic Proximity.

The distance between the employer's various plants is quite significant in evaluating whether the presumption favoring single-operation units should be adhered to. The courts have recognized two practical effects which geographic proximity has on the union's collective bargaining efforts. One concern is that employees should not be overly inconvenienced, if not totally prohibited, by being forced to attend union meetings one hundred miles away. (*Alaska Statebank v. NLRB,* 653 F.2d 1285, 1288 (9th Cir. 1981).) In addition, differences in economic and social concerns among geographic regions may hinder the union's efforts to fairly represent all members of the bargaining unit. (*Id. See also Automobile Club of Michigan v. NLRB,* 631 F.2d 82, 85 (6th Cir. 1980).)

Thus, the Board has generally held that where a plant or store is geographically isolated from other locations owned by the employer, the presumption favoring single-plant units is reinforced. (*Compare Capital Bakers, Inc.,* 168 N.L.R.B. 904 (1967) *with Cheney Bigelow Wire Works, Inc.,* 197 N.L.R.B. 1279 (1972).) On the other hand, if the employer operates a number of retail outlets within a geographic area, interchange of merchandise, personnel, and employee opinions is more likely and the multi-facility unit may be deemed appropriate notwithstanding the presumption. (*ITT Continental Baking Co.,* 231 N.L.R.B. 326 (1977). *Cf. Lawson Milk Company Division, Consolidated Foods Corp.,* 213 N.L.R.B. 360 (1974).)

Geographic proximity, however, is not determinative.

(*Orkin Exterminating Co., Inc.,* 258 N.L.R.B. 773, 108 L.R.R.M. 1170 (1981); *NCR Corporation,* 236 N.L.R.B. 215 (1978).) Even where the geographic distance among the employer's various operations favor the presumption, other important factors may militate against single-plant unit and render geographic distance much less significant. (*Orkin Exterminating,* 108 L.R.R.M. at 1171, 258 N.L.R.B. at 773; *NCR Corp.,* 236 N.L.R.B. at 215.) Moreover, the Sixth Circuit has denied enforcement of the Board's unit determination where geographic proximity was overemphasized, evidencing an arbitrary or unreasonable unit. (*N.L.R.B. v. Pinkerton's, Inc.,* 428 F.2d 479 (6th Cir. 1970).)

§ 2-1(A)(3). Interchange of Employees.

Another relevant consideration impacting on the presumption of single-plant unit appropriateness is the employer's transfer of employees from operation to operation. (*See generally* Abodeeley, *The NLRB and the Appropriate Bargaining Unit,* 48-53 (1971).) If there is no significant interchange between employees from facility to facility, the presumption is reinforced. (*See, e.g., Penn Color, Inc.,* 249 N.L.R.B. 1117, 1119 (1980); *Angelus Furniture Mfg. Co.,* 192 N.L.R.B. 992 (1971).) Local recruitment of personnel likewise supports the presumption (*Capitol Bakers, Inc.,* 168 N.L.R.B. 904 (1967)), even if the ultimate hiring decisions are made by a centralized office. (*Cf. Penn Color, Inc.,* 249 N.L.R.B. at 1119, n. 9 (1980).)

A high percentage of work force transfers, on the other hand, provide probative evidence of functional integration. As employees become more familiar with one another, they exchange views more frequently, thus promoting shared interests. (*Petrie Stores Corp.,* 212 N.L.R.B. 130 (1974).) The development of this "community of interest" militates against the presumption. *Id.*

71

In determining whether the transfer of employees is significant, the Board often looks to whether the interchange is temporary or permanent, or made because of an emergency at a particular plant. (*See e.g., Bud's Food Stores, Inc. d/b/a Bud's Thrift-T-Wise,* 236 N.L.R.B. 1203, 1204 (1978); *Razco Inc. d/b/a Hit 'n Run Food Stores,* 227 N.L.R.B. 1186, 1187 (1977); *Liebmann Breweries, Inc.,* 142 N.L.R.B. 121 (1963). *But see Black & Decker Mfg. Co.,* 147 N.L.R.B. 825 (1964).) Likewise transfers created by the opening or closing of a plant, or done for the personal convenience of the employee "[are] not entitled to too much weight in determining the scope of the appropriate unit." (*Renzetti's Market, Inc.,* 238 N.L.R.B. 174, n. 8 (1978). *See also Penn Color, Inc.,* 249 N.L.R.B. 1117, 1119 (1980); *Pneumo Corp. d/b/a P & C (Cross Co.),* 228 N.L.R.B. 1443 (1977).) Moreover, the "subjectivity" of the standard itself has led one commentator to note that the Board is more likely to use this factor "as support for its decisions rather than reasons for them." (Abodeeley, The NLRB and the Appropriate Bargaining Unit, 53 (1971).)

§ 2-1(A)(4). Centralized Administration.

Prior to the Board's recognition of the presumptive appropriateness of a single-store unit in *Sav-On Drugs, Inc.,* 138 N.L.R.B. 1032 (1962), the single most decisive factor in determining bargaining unit questions was the employer's administrative divisions. (*Paxton Wholesale Grocery Co.,* 123 N.L.R.B. 316 (1959).) In *Paxton,* the Board held that "[i]n view of the highly centralized administration of all the Employer's stores, ... we find that ... a companywide unit is alone appropriate." (*Id.* at 317.) *Sav-On* and its progeny (*see e.g., Dixie Belle Mills, Inc.,* 139 N.L.R.B. 629 (1962)), redefined administrative division as merely one factor to be considered. (*See also Howell Refining Co. v. NLRB,* 400 F.2d 213 (5th Cir. 1968).)

The Board has occasionally hinted that the centralization of the employer's administrative functions, in terms of bookkeeping, purchasing, merchandising, etc., are "of little significance in determining the question" of an appropriate unit. (*Haag Drug Co.,* 169 N.L.R.B. 877, 879 (1969).) Rather, "the degree of autonomy at the . . . [local] store level is critical to the unit issues. . . ." (*ITT Continental Baking Co.,* 231 N.L.R.B. 326, 328 (1977).) In this regard, the NLRB appears particularly concerned with the day-to-day impact upon the employees, as opposed to the "policy decisions" of labor relations. For example, in *ITT Continental,* the Board highlighted the centralized authority over hiring, discharge, merit increase, and discipline. (*Id.* at 327-28.)

Central administration of day-to-day labor matters, however, is not of itself sufficient to rebut the presumption favoring single-plant units. (*See NLRB v. Living & Learning Centers, Inc.,* 652 F.2d 209 (1st Cir. 1981). *Cf. American Automobile Ass'n,* 242 N.L.R.B. 722, 724 (1979) (administrative organization not so compelling as to require multi-district unit).) On the other hand, where the single-store unit corresponds with the employer's administrative division, the presumption is reinforced. (*Wyandotte Savings Bank,* 245 N.L.R.B. 943, 944 n. 9 (1979).)

§ 2-1(A)(5). Previous Bargaining History.

One of the most important factors in resolving virtually all labor relations disputes is the concept of past practice. In making unit appropriateness determinations, the Board often looks to the prior bargaining history between the practice in the industry or within the geographic area. *See Fraser & Johnston Co.,* 189 N.L.R.B. 142, 151, n. 50 (1971); *Transcontinental Bus Systems, Inc.,* 178 N.L.R.B. 712 (1969). *But see Buckeye Village Market, Inc.,* 175 N.L.R.B. 271 (1969). Successful bargaining in a certain unit shows a

73

workable relationship, continuation of which undoubtedly supports the Congressional policy of promoting industrial peace. (Abodeeley, *The NLRB and the Appropriate Bargaining Unit* 54-55 (1971).) Conversely, a prior history of unsuccessful systemwide bargaining reinforces the presumptive appropriateness of single-store units. (*Bowman Transportation Co.*, 166 N.L.R.B. 982 (1967).)

Although previous bargaining history is not controlling, it is often said that only compelling circumstances would cause the Board to deviate from past practice. (*See, e.g., Crown Zellerbach Corp.*, 246 N.L.R.B. 202 (1979).) It is likewise well settled that the Board accords substantial weight to prior bargaining history and will not disturb such bargaining unless repugnant to Board policy. (*Fraser & Johnston Co.*, 189 N.L.R.B. 142, 151, n. 50 (1971).) But where all the relevant factors support a single-plant unit, the Board will disregard prior history of multi-plant bargaining. (*Crown Zellerbach*, 246 N.L.R.B. at 202-03.) In addition, changes in technology or economic conditions may render the past bargaining history less significant. (*Calpine Containers, A California Corp.*, 251 N.L.R.B. 1509 (1980).)

§ 2-1(B). Craft Unit Certification and Severance.

One of the most difficult issues facing the Labor Board in unit appropriateness cases is the choice between smaller craft units comprised solely of skilled workers and more integrated plant or industry units. The question can arise in one of two ways. The first is during an initial organizational campaign where a craft union, seeking to represent the skilled workers in a plant, challenges the industrial union contending for plantwide representative status. (*See e.g., E.I. du Pont de Nemours & Co.*, 162 N.L.R.B. 413 (1966).) The second situation raising this issue is craft severance, where a group of skilled workers, constituting a definable craft, seeks to secede from the union representing both them and a larger group of less skilled workers, and establish separate representation. (*See generally* Abodeeley, *The NLRB and the Appropriate Bargaining Unit,* 89 n. 3 (Philadelphia: Industrial Research Unit, Wharton School of Finance & Commerce, University of Pennsylvania 1971).)

The difficulty surrounding this issue results from the conflicting interests involved between craft workers, the total plant work force, and the employer. Skilled workers are, more often than not, minorities in industrial plants, and tend to feel that their particular interests are ignored in plantwide units. (*Id.* at 87.) By the same token, their skills make them integral parts of industrial processes, and job action on their part could adversely affect the unskilled workers in the business enterprise. (*Id.*) Separation of employees into different units may well lead to animosity between groups, thereby counteracting the Act's policy of promoting industrial harmony. (*Id.*)

Under the Wagner Act, the NLRB was considerably more receptive to requests from skilled craftsmen for separate representation when made during an initial organizational campaign. (*See Globe Machine & Stamping Co.,* 3 N.L.R.B. 294 (1937). *Cf. American Can Co.,* 13 N.L.R.B. 1252 (1939).) In "appropriate circumstances," employees in the craft were allowed through self-determination elections to choose between contending unions. (*Globe Machine & Stamping Co.,* 3 N.L.R.B. 294 (1937).) Severance petitions, however, were summarily denied on the ground that the Act did not authorize splitting a previously determined appropriate unit, *American Can Co.,* 13 N.L.R.B. at 1256, unless the craftworkers demonstrated that they were more than a mere dissident faction and had actually maintained a separate identity despite inclusion in the comprehensive unit. (*General Electric Co.,* 58 N.L.R.B. 57, 59 (1944); *Allied Chem. & Dye Corp.,* 71 N.L.R.B. 1217 (1946).)

75

In the Taft-Hartley Amendments, Congress added Section 9(b) (2) which provides that "the Board shall not . . . decide that any craft unit is inappropriate for [the purposes of collective bargaining] on the ground that a different unit has been established by a prior Board determination, unless a majority of the employees in the proposed craft unit votes against separate representation. . . ." (29 U.S.C. § 159(b)(2) (1974).) Thus, the Board was prohibited from disallowing severance of a craft unit on the sole ground that it had previously found the more comprehensive unit appropriate. (*National Tube Co.*, 76 N.L.R.B. 1199, 1205-08 (1948).) This conclusion is consistent with the admonition that the Board's duty is merely to select an appropriate unit and that it may select from among several appropriate units in deciding which best fosters the purposes of the Act. (*International Union of Operating Engineers v. NLRB*, 595 F.2d 844 (D.C. Cir. 1979).) In *National Tube*, the Board found that consideration must be given to the functional integration of the employer's operations and the relevant bargaining history. (76 N.L.R.B. at 1207-08.) The presence of these factors could warrant the disallowance of craft severance. (*Id. See also Corn Products Refining Co.*, 80 N.L.R.B. 362 (1948) (functional integration in wet milling industry); *Weyerhaeuser Timber Co.*, 87 N.L.R.B. 1076 (1949) (integrated timber industry); *Permanente Metals Corp.*, 89 N.L.R.B. 804 (1950) (aluminum industry). *See generally* Abodeeley, *supra*, at 106 (steel, wet milling, timber and aluminum later became the "four favored" industries exonerated from the *American Potash* ruling).)

In 1954, the NLRB decided *American Potash & Chemical Corp.*, 107 N.L.R.B. 1418 (1954), and liberalized its policy toward craft severance. Craft workers would be granted self-determination elections, provided the petitioning union proved two elements. First, the departmental group had to consist of a true craft (*id.* at 1424), which later cases defined as skilled workmen with identifiable interests. (*Diamond T. Utah, Inc.,* 124 N.L.R.B. 966 (1959).) Second, the union had to be a traditional representative of the craft; one "devoted . . . to serving the special interest of the employees in question." (*American Potash & Chemical Corp.,* 107 N.L.R.B. at 1424.) The Board's ruling was the first in a craft severance situation to emphasize the craft workers freedom of choice in selecting their bargaining representative over the interests of the employer and plantwide work force in avoiding disharmony. (*Id.* at 1422-23.) It likewise created an anomaly by affording exemptions to the *National Tube* industries based solely on the time of its ruling. (*Id.* at 1422.)

American Potash was strongly criticized by the Court of Appeals for the Fourth Circuit in *NLRB v. Pittsburgh Plate Glass Co.,* 270 F.2d 167 (4th Cir. 1959). The court found that by enacting Section 9(b)(2), Congress did not command that the Board allow craft severance. (*Id.* at 172.) It also noted that the Board's emphasis of craft self-determination over the interests of the other employees and the employer ran counter to the NLRB's statutory responsibility. (*Id.* at 174.) Instead, the Board was required to decide, as in other unit appropriateness cases, whether craft severance and two units would effectuate the purpose of the Act. (*Id.* at 172-74.) Moreover, the court found that exclusion of the *National Tube* industries created an arbitrary and unreasonable result since the glass industry was functionally identical to those industries.

Seven years later, in *Mallinckrodt Chemical Works,* 162 N.L.R.B. 387, 396 (1966), the Board majority used this same rationale in overruling *American Potash* and formulating a policy aimed at consideration of the interests of the other employees and the employer:

> [U]nderlying such determinations is the need to balance the interest of the employer and the total

employee complement in maintaining the industrial
stability and resulting benefits of an historical plant
wide bargaining unit as against the interest of
[craftworkers] . . . in having an opportunity to vote . . .
for separate representation. (*Id.* at 392.)

The Board then identified relevant factors to be considered
in determining craft severance questions; factors which
were drawn from case law both before and after the enact-
ment of Section 9(b)(2).

The first factor is an expanded version of the concept of a
"true craft" enunciated in *American Potash.* The Board
must determine whether the proposed unit consists of a
homogeneous group of skilled journeymen *or* a distinct
departmental unit working in trades which have
traditionally been afforded separate representation. (*Id.* at
397. *See United States Plywood-Champion Papers, Inc.,* 174
N.L.R.B. 292 (1969); *cf. Timber Products Co.,* 164 N.L.R.B.
1060 (1967) (group of merely "specialized workmen").) Second, *Mallinckrodt* revitalized the importance of the bargaining history of the employees involved, the stability
established thereunder and the potential disruption of
stability which severance might cause. (*Mallinckrodt
Chemical Works,* 162 N.L.R.B. at 397.) Third, the Board's
opinion resurrects the *General Electric* "craft-identity"
factors of a group of skilled workers maintaining a separate
identity despite inclusion in the broader unit, and not being
adequately represented by the industrial union. (*Id.*)
Fourth, the pattern of collective bargaining in the industry
is relevant to determining the appropriateness of craft severance. (*Id.*) Fifth, the Board would look to the relationship
between the craft function and the production process, and
the degree of functional integration in the plant. (*Id. See
also National Tube Co.,* 76 N.L.R.B. 1199 (1948).) Sixth, the
Board would examine the petitioning union's experience in
representing the particular craft, though it no longer

needed to qualify as a "traditional representative." (*Mallinckrodt Chemical Works,* 162 N.L.R.B. at 397. *See also American Potash & Chemical Corp.,* 107 N.L.R.B. 1418 (1954).)

Although the Board's opinion identifies the six factors, its decision emphasizes the heightened importance of three: (1) the high degree of functional integration between mechanics and the production process; (2) a twenty-five year bargaining history; and (3) adequate representation by the industrial union for the craftsmen's interests. (*Mallinckrodt Chemical Works,* 162 N.L.R.B. at 399.) In applying the *Mallinckrodt* factors to recent cases, the Board has continued to emphasize these same considerations, particularly a stable effective bargaining history. (*See, e.g., Continental Can Co.,* 217 N.L.R.B. 316 (1975); *Jordan Marsh Co.,* 174 N.L.R.B. 1265 (1969); *Radio Corp. of America,* 173 N.L.R.B. 440 (1968).) These cases demonstrate the Board's reluctance to grant severance except in connection with initial organization campaigns. (*Precision Cast Parts Corp.,* 224 N.L.R.B. 382 (1976); *Monsanto Research Corp., Mound Laboratory,* 185 N.L.R.B. 137 (1970); *E.I. du Pont de Nemours & Co.,* 162 N.L.R.B. 413 (1966). *But see Allied Gear & Machine Co.,* 250 N.L.R.B. 679 (1980). *See also Bendix Corp.,* 227 N.L.R.B. 1534, 1538 n. 10 (1977)), or where no stable history of bargaining in a plantwide unit existed. (227 N.L.R.B. at 1535 nn. 6-7. *See also Boise Cascade Corp.,* 238 N.L.R.B. 1022 (1979); *Continental Can Co.,* 217 N.L.R.B. 316 (1975).)

As previously mentioned, *Mallinckrodt* extended severance to groups that otherwise did not constitute "true crafts." (*See United States Plywood-Champion Papers, Inc.,* 174 N.L.R.B. 292 (1969).) To qualify as a craft, however, the employees must not merely be engaged in "the repetitive predefined performance of limited special skills particularly adapted to the Employer's productive process...."

(*Monsanto Co.*, 172 N.L.R.B. at 1462 (1968).) By the same token, a formalized journeyman/apprentice system of training is not required to create "craft" status. (*Precision Cast Parts Corp.*, 224 N.L.R.B. 382 n. 5 (1976). *But see Allied Gear & Machine Co.*, 250 N.L.R.B. 679, 680-81 (1980).) Departmental units must be separated from the remaining work force not only in supervision, but also in terms and conditions of employment, otherwise they do not possess sufficiently separate community of interest from production employees. (250 N.L.R.B. at 681 n. 6.)

A stable and substantial history of bargaining on a plantwide basis has been recognized as sufficient to justify a refusal to sever crafts from the broader unit. (*See, e.g., La-Z-Boy Chair Co.*, 235 N.L.R.B. 77, 78 (1978); *Bendix Corp.*, 227 N.L.R.B. 1534, 1539 (1977); *Dow Chemical Co., Rocky Flats Division*, 202 N.L.R.B. 17, 20 (1973); *Jordan Marsh Co.*, 174 N.L.R.B. 1265 (1969); *Allied Chemical Corp.*, 165 N.L.R.B. 235 (1967).) Likewise, a history of bargaining as separate units, particularly when predicated by industry patterns, outweighs the functional integration of the employer's operations. (*Continental Can Co.*, 217 N.L.R.B. 316, 317 (1975); *Buddy L Corp.*, 167 N.L.R.B. 808 (1967).)

Recent cases have also demonstrated the importance of inadequate representation by the industrial union. (*See, e.g., Boise Cascade Corp.*, 238 N.L.R.B. 1022, 1023 (1979); *Bendix Corp.*, 227 N.L.R.B. 1534, 1535 (1977).) One of the few cases approving craft severance, *Jay Kay Metal Specialties Corp.*, 163 N.L.R.B. 719 (1967), did so on the ground that craft employees had individually negotiated with the employer. (*Id.* at 720-21.) In *Bendix*, the incorporation of union members directly from the craft groups into the union bargaining committee was an important factor in denying severance. (*The Bendix Corp.*, 227 N.L.R.B. at 1535-36.)

Functional integration, though not determinative, is a severance factor in some cases. (*See La-Z-Boy Chair Co.,* 235 N.L.R.B. 77, 78 (1978).) Thus, in *Eaton Yale & Towne, Inc.,* 191 N.L.R.B. 217 (1971), the Board permitted severance where the employer contracted out some of the work performed by the crafts, thereby showing that production was not dependent on craft work. (*But see E.I. du Pont de Nemours & Co.,* 162 N.L.R.B. 413 (1966) (the Board discounted functional integration in allowing self-determination elections during an initial campaign).)

The clear thrust of the Board's decisions in this area has been to promote craft worker's freedom of choice whenever it does not seriously endanger industrial harmony and bargaining stability. Although its approach has been severely criticized by craft unionism supporters, the *Mallinckrodt* doctrine is consistent with the Board's responsibility under Section 9 and the purposes of the Act.

§ 2-2. Multi-Employer Bargaining Units.

Before passage of the National Labor Relations Act, employers sometimes organized in associations for the purpose of bargaining over terms and conditions of employment. (*See NLRB v. Truck Drivers Union (Buffalo Linen Supply),* 353 U.S. 87 (1957).) This practice existed predominately in industries such as stevedoring and construction where employees changed employers on a week-to-week basis. (*Id.* at 94.) With the passage of the Wagner Act in 1935 and the unionization of small manufacturing and retail operations, other employers sought to join together to match the increased bargaining strength of labor. (*Id.* at 94-95.) In recent years, multi-employer bargaining has become an increasingly important aspect of labor relations. During 1978, for example, nearly half of all major collective bargaining agreements, those covering

1000 or more employees, were negotiated by multi-employer associations. (Dep't of Labor, Bur. Labor Stat., *Characteristics of Major Collective Bargaining Agreements* — 1978, Bull. No. 2065 at 12.) Over three million employers were represented in these negotiations. (*Id.*)

Neither the original Act nor its various amendments expressly sanction multi-employer bargaining. However, the ability of employers to form a cohesive bargaining group arises in part from their protected right to designate the bargaining representative of their choice. (29 U.S.C. § 158(b)(1)(B).) In addition, the Board has recognized that such industry-wide bargaining within a geographic area often fosters stability in labor relations. (*Retail Associates, Inc.,* 120 N.L.R.B. 388 (1958).) For these reasons, the Board allows employers to voluntarily agree to bargain together, but prevents a union from coercing an employer into such negotiations. (*Id. See, e.g., Southern California Pipe Trades,* 120 N.L.R.B. 249 (1958). *But see NLRB v. Amax Coal Co.,* 453 U.S. 322 (1981) (union may strike to compel employer participation in multi-employer pension and health fund).)

§ 2-2(A). Formation of the Unit.

Employers generally bind themselves to multi-employer bargaining by indicating from the outset an unequivocal intention to delegate authority to the group to bargain with the union representing their employees and by notifying the union thereof and receiving its assent. (*Weyerhaeuser Co.,* 166 N.L.R.B. 299 (1967), *enf'd,* 398 F.2d 770 (D.C. Cir. 1968). *Accord Komatz Construction, Inc. v. NLRB,* 458 F.2d 317 (8th Cir. 1972).) "Absent such an unequivocal commitment ... an employer is free to withdraw from group contract." (*Charles D. Bonanno Linen Service, Inc. v. NLRB,* 102 S. Ct. 720, 729 (1982) (Stevens, J., concurring).

See also Ruan Transport Corp., 234 N.L.R.B. 241 (1978).)

It is not necessary that the association be formally established or that a written agreement be signed by the employers. (*Tobey Fine Papers,* 245 N.L.R.B. 1393, n. 1 (1979). *Cf. NLRB v. Sightseeing Guides & Lecturers Union, Local 20076,* 310 F.2d 40, 42 (2d Cir. 1962).) The unequivocal intention to participate in multi-employer bargaining may be established from past practice of negotiations and a particular employer's participation. (*See, e.g., Local 19 International Brotherhood of Longshoremen,* 125 N.L.R.B. 61 (1959), *enf'd,* 286 F.2d 661 (7th Cir. 1961). *Accord NLRB v. Gottfried Baking Co.,* 210 F.2d 772 (2d Cir. 1954). *But see Gordon Electric Co.,* 123 N.L.R.B. 862 (1959).) For example, in *Local 19, International Brotherhood of Longshoremen,* the Board held that the twenty-year practice of Chicago stevedoring companies who met prior to negotiations to formulate a joint proposal and appoint a bargaining spokesperson evinced an intent to be bound to multi-employer bargaining. (125 N.L.R.B. at 65, *citing United Productions of America,* 111 N.L.R.B. 390, 393; *Atlas Storage Division,* 112 N.L.R.B. 1175; *American Publishing Corp.,* 121 N.L.R.B. 115, 286 F.2d at 662. *See also McAx Sign Co. v. NLRB,* 576 F.2d 62 (5th Cir. 1978) (the Board found multi-employer bargaining where individual proposals were not consolidated into a joint offer until after negotiations started).)

The Supreme Court has reiterated the principle that Congress, while not expressly providing for multi-employer units, left the Board free to certify such units where appropriate. (*Charles D. Bonanno Linen Service, Inc. v. NLRB,* 102 S. Ct. at 723-724. *See also Buffalo Linen Supply,* 353 U.S. at 96.) In determining the appropriateness of multi-employer units, the most important factor considered by the Board is the prior history of bargaining in a unit of that scope for a substantial period of time. (*American*

Publishing Corp., 121 N.L.R.B. 115, 121 (1958) citing *Arden Farms,* 117 N.L.R.B. 318, *Cleveland Builders Supply Co.,* 90 N.L.R.B. 923; *Dittler Bros., Inc.,* 132 N.L.R.B. 444 (1961); *Belleville Employing Printers,* 122 N.L.R.B. 350 (1958).) That bargaining history must include the specific employees sought within the certification. (*Macy's San Francisco,* 120 N.L.R.B. 69, 71 (1958).) Additionally, the Board will examine, at the time the petition is filed, whether the employer has shown a desire to be bound in the future by multi-employer bargaining. (*American Publishing,* 121 N.L.R.B. at 121 *citing Chicago Metropolitan Home Builders Ass'n,* 119 N.L.R.B. 1184. See also *Krist Gradis,* 121 N.L.R.B. 601 (1958). *Accord NLRB v. Southwestern Colorado Contractors Ass'n,* 379 F.2d 360 (10th Cir. 1967). *But see Dittler Bros.,* 132 N.L.R.B. 444, 447 (1961) (Fanning, dissenting).) Moreover, the Board will only certify the unit after the employers involved have unequivocally signified their approval of group bargaining. (*American Publishing,* 121 N.L.R.B. at 121.)

Even where there has been a history of multi-employer bargaining, various factors may militate against finding that unit appropriate if it is contested. (*Chicago Metropolitan Homebuilders Ass'n,* 119 N.L.R.B. 1184 (1957).) These factors include: (1) a long history of bargaining on a single-employer basis predating the multi-employer negotiations; (2) length of time in which multi-employer bargaining has occurred — a short period militating against the unit; (3) the absence of a contract of substantial duration; (4) the absence of a prior Board determination that such a unit is appropriate; and (5) the existence of special problems not shared by other members in the group. (*Id.* at 1186. *See also NLRB v. Sheridan Creations, Inc.,* 357 F.2d 245 (2d Cir. 1966); *Highway Transport Ass'n,* 116 N.L.R.B. 1718 (1956); *Miron Building Products Co.,* 116 N.L.R.B. 1406 (1956).) While the NLRB's discretion in making unit appropriateness decisions is generally quite broad, nowhere is this principle better demonstrated than in certifications of multi-employer units. (*See Tennessee Products & Chemical Corp. v. NLRB,* 423 F.2d 169 (6th Cir. 1973); *NLRB v. Sheridan Creations Inc.,* 357 F.2d 245 (2d Cir. 1966); *NLRB v. Porter County Farm Bureau Cooperative Ass'n,* 314 F.2d 133 (7th Cir. 1963).)

§ 2-2(B). Withdrawal from the Unit.

While multi-employer bargaining is completely voluntary in its inception, the Board has placed some restrictions on the parties' ability to withdraw from that relationship once it is established. (*Retail Associates, Inc.,* 120 N.L.R.B. 388, 393-94 (1958).) Since multi-employer bargaining rests upon the notion that it fosters stability in labor relations, "the stability requirement ... dictates that reasonable controls limit the parties as to the time and manner that withdrawal will be permitted. . . ." (*Id.* at 393.)

It should be noted that the NLRB, with some strong dissent, has given the union the right to withdraw under the same guidelines as are applicable to an employer's right to separate from the group. (*See Pacific Coast Ass'n of Pulp & Paper Mfrs.,* 163 N.L.R.B. 892 (1967); *Hearst Consolidated Publications, Inc.,* 156 N.L.R.B. 210 (1965), enf'd sub nom. *Detroit Newspapers Ass'n v. NLRB,* 372 F.2d 569 (6th Cir. 1967).) From the union's point of view, however, this right is somewhat illusory. Employers must, of course, honor the union's timely withdrawal and negotiate on an individual basis. (*Detroit Newspapers Ass'n v. NLRB,* 372 F.2d at 571.) By the same token, there is nothing to prevent an employer from selecting the association as its individual representative, a choice protected by Section 8(b)(1)(B). (*Id.* at 572.)

Prior to the commencement of negotiations, an employer is free to withdraw from multi-employer bargaining provided it gives unequivocal notice to the union. (*Retail Associates, Inc.,* 120 N.L.R.B. at 393-94. *See also Associated General Contractors, Inc.,* 238 N.L.R.B. 156 (1978); *Carvel Co. & C & D Plumbing & Heating Co.,* 226 N.L.R.B. 111 (1976). *Cf. Northern Petroleum Equipment Corp.,* 244 N.L.R.B. 685 (1979) (where the employer merely notified the union that its attorney would represent it without expressly stating its intention to withdraw).) The Board has construed the unequivocal requirement strictly, and has considered the sequence of notice and proposals important in resolving the question of timeliness. (*Northern Petroleum Equipment Corp.,* 244 N.L.R.B. at 687. *See also Associated General Contractors, Inc.,* 238 N.L.R.B. 156 (1978).) Moreover, "[t]he decision to withdraw must contemplate a sincere abandonment . . . of the multi-employer unit and the embracement of . . . bargaining on an individual . . . basis." (*Retail Associates,* 120 N.L.R.B. at 394.) Thus, where the withdrawal is used solely as a temporary expedient to avoid certification of the multi-employer unit, or a strategic action in bargaining, or if the employer fails to commence single employer negotiations, the attempted withdrawal is not unequivocal. (*Id. Accord NLRB v. Southwestern Colorado Contractors Ass'n,* 379 F.2d 360 (10th Cir. 1967). *See also Michael J. Bollinger Co.,* 252 N.L.R.B. 406 (1980); *Lyons Van & Storage,* NLRB Advice Mem., Case No. 31-CA-9204, 102 L.R.R.M. 1675 (1979). *But see Pacific Coast Ass'n of Pulp & Paper Mfrs.,* 163 N.L.R.B. at 895.)

After negotiations have begun, withdrawal is permissible only where there is mutual consent of all the parties, or unusual circumstances justifying disturbance of the stable unit. (*Retail Associates,* 120 N.L.R.B. at 395.) The union's consent to withdrawal need not be expressed and may be implied from the union's conduct. But "if the union's consent is to be implied, the [u]nion's conduct must involve a course of *affirmative action* which is clearly antithetical to the . . . claim that the employer has not withdrawn. . . ." (*Preston H. Haskell Co.*, 238 N.L.R.B. 943, 948 (1978) (emphasis added) citing *I.C. Refrigeration Service, Inc.*, 200 N.L.R.B. 687.) Failure to immediately object or a delayed request to sign the contract is insufficient to constitute implied consent. (*Id. See also I.C. Refrigeration Service, Inc.*, 200 N.L.R.B. 687 (1972); *Reliable Roofing Co.*, 246 N.L.R.B. 716 (1979).)

The Board has generally limited the unusual circumstances exception to cases where "the very existence of the employer as a viable business . . . is about to cease," (*Hi-Way Billboads, Inc.*, 206 N.L.R.B. 22, 23 (1973)), or where the bargaining unit has become so fragmented through consensual withdrawals that it would be harmful to the collective bargaining process not to allow the remaining employers to withdraw. (*Connell Typesetting Co.*, 212 N.L.R.B. 918 (1974). *See generally Charles D. Bonanno Linen Service, Inc.*, 243 N.L.R.B. 1093 (1979), *Supp.* 229 N.L.R.B. 629 (1977).) Several appellate courts have also found unusual circumstances where the negotiating committee has not fairly represented the individual employer's interests. (*See, e.g., NLRB v. Siebler Heating & Air Conditioning, Inc.*, 563 F.2d 366 (8th Cir. 1977); *NLRB v. Unelko Corp.*, 478 F.2d 1404 (7th Cir. 1973).)

With respect to the first situation, the Board requires extreme financial hardship. (*See United States Lingerie Corp.*, 170 N.L.R.B. 750 (1968) (employer's economic difficulties which eventually led to its status as debtor in possession under the Bankruptcy Act). *See also Spun Jee Corp.*, 171 N.L.R.B. 557 (1968); *Atlas Electrical Service Co.*, 176 N.L.R.B. 827 (1969). *But see Universal Insulation Corp.*, 149 N.L.R.B. 1397 (1964), *enf'd,* 361 F.2d 406 (6th Cir. 1966) (economic hardship from terms of the multi-employer agreement is not grounds for withdrawal).) The hardship, however, need not entail the employer's total operations. Where the economic condition of one of the employer's plants meets the Board's criteria, the employer may withdraw the single plant and leave within the unit those plants which are functioning economically. (*North American Refractories Co.*, 238 N.L.R.B. 480 (1978).)

The second circumstance justifying an otherwise untimely withdrawal, fragmentation of the bargaining unit, has generated a great deal of litigation which culminated in the Supreme Court's recent decision in *Charles D. Bonanno Linen Service, Inc. v. NLRB*, 102 S. Ct. 720 (1982). *Bonanno* resolved a conflict between the Board and several reviewing courts regarding whether impasse, alone or combined with the execution of an interim agreement between the union and one or more member employers, is a fragmentation of the unit justifying withdrawal. (*See, e.g., Charles D. Bonanno Linen Service, Inc.*, 243 N.L.R.B. 1093 (1979), *enf'd*, 630 F.2d 25 (1st Cir. 1980); *Associated Shower Door Co.*, 205 N.L.R.B. 677 (1973), *enf'd on other grounds*, 512 F.2d 230 (9th Cir. 1975); *Hi-Way Billboards*, 206 N.L.R.B. 22 (1973), *enf'g denied*, 500 F.2d 181 (5th Cir. 1974).)

The Supreme Court upheld the Board's view that impasse is merely a temporary deadlock in negotiations which is almost always broken and is often brought on purposely by one of the parties as a bargaining tactic. (*Charles D. Bonanno Linen Service, Inc.*, 102 S. Ct. 720, 725 (1982), citing *Charles D. Bonanno Linen Service*, 243 N.L.R.B. 1093, 1093-94 (1979).) The Supreme Court also concurred with the Board's conclusion that the possibility of strikes and the execution of interim agreements did not justify withdrawal. (*Id.* at 726.) Rather than fragmenting the multi-employer unit, "interim agreements, on balance, tend

88

to deter . . . fragmentation since they preserve a continuing mutual interest by all employers in a final association-wide contract." (*Id.* at 727.) Signing interim agreements is no more disruptive of the unit's bargaining force than a refusal to participate in a defensive lockout. (*Id.* at 726-27.) Moreover, the majority approved the Board's distinction between truly interim agreements and separate contracts which were to remain in full force and effect regardless of the result of the association-wide negotiations. (*Id.* at 726; *Compare Sangamo Construction Co.,* 188 N.L.R.B. 159 (1971), *Plumbers & Steamfitters Local 323 (P.H.C. Mechanical Contractors),* 191 N.L.R.B. 592 (1971) *with Typographic Service Co.,* 238 N.L.R.B. 1565 (1978), *Teamsters Union, Local 378 (Olympia Automobile Dealers Ass'n),* 243 N.L.R.B. 1086 (1979).) The execution of separate agreements which allow the employer to escape the binding effect of the multi-employer contract is itself an unfair labor practice which the remaining member employers may challenge. (*Olympia Automobile Dealers Ass'n,* 243 N.L.R.B. 1086, 1089, n. 4.) Thus, it appears that only where separate agreements follow consensual withdrawals that substantially weaken the unit will the Board permit late withdrawal from the multi-employer group. (*See Bonanno Linen Service, Inc.,* 243 N.L.R.B. at 1096; *Tobey Fine Paper,* 245 N.L.R.B. 1393, 1396 (1979) (the Board will take notice of the final agreement in light of the proposals and negotiations which preceded it to determine strength of the unit).)

The Supreme Court likewise found that the Board's rejection of impasse, coupled with selective strikes, as justifying withdrawal, to be a permissible balance of the respective rights of employers and employees. (102 S. Ct. at 727.) Selective strikes against individual members of the multi-employer unit are, of course, aimed at manipulating the competitive status of member employers, and causing capitulation. (*See NLRB v. Brown,* 380 U.S. 278, 284-86

(1965); *Buffalo Linen Supply,* 353 U.S. 87, 90-91 (1957).) This tactic, commonly referred to as "whipsawing," is a legitimate economic weapon to assert pressure on multi-employer associations. (*Buffalo Linen Supply,* 353 U.S. at 90, n. 7.)

Furthermore, employers were not without effective defensive measures of their own. In *Buffalo Linen* the Supreme Court affirmed a Board holding that a selective strike against one employer carried with it an implied threat of successive strikes and justified a resort to a defensive lockout by the remaining members. (*Id.* at 91.) The Court later found this arsenal to include the use of permanent replacements by the struck employer and temporary replacements by the non-struck members as a necessary corollary to lockout. (*NLRB v. Brown,* 380 U.S. at 285-86.) These defensive actions are permissible efforts to preserve the integrity of multi-employer bargaining, provided they are not combined with union animus. (*Id.* at 286-88.) In *Bonanno,* the Court emphasized that Congress had entrusted the Board with the responsibility of balancing the conflicting interest of employers in preserving the integrity of multi-employer units and the right of employees to exert economic pressure in support of their demands. (102 S. Ct. at 724, 727, *citing Buffalo Linen Supply,* 353 U.S. at 96.) It therefore refused to disturb the Board's approach. (*Id.* at 727.)

CHAPTER 3

EMPLOYER UNFAIR LABOR PRACTICES

§ 3-1. The Dangers of Premature Recognition.

Collective bargaining relationships normally arise out of either a Board certification, or as the result of a Board remedial order following a finding of an unlawful refusal to bargain, or a settlement agreement, or from voluntary recognition of a majority union. When a collective bargaining relationship arises from an employer's voluntary recognition of a union, there is always a danger that the union may not actually represent a majority of the employees. A labor organization may be recognized as bargaining representative for all employees only when it has been "designated or selected for the purposes of collective bargaining by the majority of the employees in a unit appropriate for such purposes." (29 U.S.C. § 159(a).) Therefore, if an employer recognizes a union that actually represents a minority of the unit employees and deals with this union as the exclusive employee representative, the employer interferes with the employees' rights to bargain collectively through representatives of their own choosing, or to reject collective bargaining. (29 U.S.C. § 158(a)(2).)

As a result of premature recognition, where the union is a minority, the employer may be found to have committed an unfair labor practice. In *International Ladies' Garment Workers' Union, AFL-CIO v. NLRB,* 366 U.S. 731 (1961), the Supreme Court addressed the issue of whether it was an unfair labor practice for both employer and union to enter into an agreement in which the employer recognized the union as the exclusive bargaining representative of certain of his employees, although in fact, only a minority of the employees had authorized the union to represent their interests. The Supreme Court held that the employer and the union invaded employees' rights under the Act in violation of Section 8(a) (1), (2) and (b) (1) (A) by granting exclusive recognition to the union at a time when it did not represent a majority of the employees. Premature recognition gives a minority union the appearance of employee support, thereby inducing employees to join the union. A union that is granted exclusive recognition without a majority is given an advantage over any other union since the recognized union is afforded a "deceptive cloak of authority." (*Id.* at 736.)

The employer in *International Ladies' Garment Workers' Union, AFL-CIO,* signed a "memorandum of understanding" recognizing the union as the exclusive bargaining representative. The union representative asserted that the union's comparison of the employee authorization cards indicated that the union in fact secured such cards from a majority. Neither the company nor the union checked the cards to ascertain whether the union's assertion was correct. Rather, the employer and the union believed there was a majority on a "good faith" assumption. At the time of recognition the union did not enjoy majority status, but by the time the parties executed a collective bargaining agreement the union had a majority. The Court held the parties' good faith, yet mistaken, belief in the union's majority was no defense to the unfair labor practices. The Court noted that the statutory language of the Act does not require "scienter" as an element of the Section 8(a) (1), (2) or (b) (1) (A) unfair labor practices. Section 8(a) (2) makes it unlawful for an employer to support a minority union. Accordingly, prohibited conduct cannot be pardoned by a showing of good faith.

The Board has extended the holding in *International Ladies' Garment Workers' Union AFL-CIO* further and held that a good faith fear by the employer that a refusal to recognize the union would result in the filing of a Section 8(a) (5) charge against the employer is not a defense to recognition of a minority union. In *Kenrich Petrochemicals, Inc.,* 149 N.L.R.B. 910 (1964), the company violated Section 8(a) (1), (2) and (3) of the Act by executing and maintaining a collective bargaining agreement containing a union security clause with a union which was not the representative of the majority of the employees covered by the agreement at the time of the execution. When the company relocated

93

its plant, it replaced four of its seven employees. The replacements were not required to join the union, although the union's contract imposed such a requirement. When the union sought to renegotiate its contract with the company, the company questioned the union's majority, and the union filed a refusal to bargain charge against the company. The company feared that the Board might find that although the union had no majority in fact, it had a majority in law because the union's loss of de facto majority was due to employer unfair labor practices. The Board cited the *International Ladies' Garment Workers' Union AFL-CIO* case and reiterated the Supreme Court's finding that the company's good faith was immaterial and no defense to the unfair labor practice.

One month after the decision in *Kenrich,* the Board in *Ellery Products Manufacturing Co.,* 149 N.L.R.B. 1388 (1964), was faced with a similar issue. In *Ellery,* the union lacked majority status when it was accorded exclusive recognition and thereafter entered into a collective bargaining contract containing union security provisions. The General Counsel proved that valid authorization cards obtained in advance by the union fell short of establishing its majority status. The company argued that it was under a threat of strike which it could not endure, and therefore, it entered into the contract relying upon a clause in which the union "warranted" its majority status.

The Board held that even a good faith but erroneous belief by the company that the union represented a majority constituted no defense, and the fact that the union "warranted" its majority status did not justify or mitigate the unfair labor practice. The clause was not a proper alternative to proof of the union's claim. The Board further emphasized that the company had a definite duty to resist union demands if there was an improper demonstration of majority, notwithstanding the union's threat to strike.

Although premature recognition of a minority union is an unfair labor practice, the charge is barred if it does not meet the six-month statute of limitations contained in Section 10(b) of the National Labor Relations Act. (*Machinists Local v. NLRB,* 362 U.S. 411 (1960).)

In *Machinists Local,* Bryan Manufacturing Company and the International Association of Machinists, AFL, entered into a collective bargaining agreement on August 10, 1954. The agreement contained a recognition clause and a union security clause. On August 30, 1955, a new agreement was entered into, replacing the old agreement. When the original agreement was executed on August 10, 1954, the union did not represent a majority of the employees covered. Ten to twelve months after the original agreement, charges were filed with the Board against the company alleging the union's lack of majority status. The Supreme Court held that the unfair labor practice occurred at the time of the illegal recognition, and the passing of six months from that date will bar an unfair labor practice charge. The fact that the agreement continued until the date the charge was filed did not make the violation a continuing one. The Court further noted that the legislative history contains affirmative evidence that Congress was specifically advertent to the problems of agreements with minority unions. Congress wished to protect such agreements from belated attack and therefore enacted Section 10(b).

As an effect of the foregoing decisions, the employer should take great pains to authenticate the union's majority claim prior to recognition. However, if the employer chooses to check the union's majority status by way of a poll or interrogation, then the employer will be under a duty or obligation to bargain with the union if the union truly has a majority. Under those circumstances, failure to bargain will result in a violation of Section 8(a)(5). (*Sullivan Electric Co.,* 199 N.L.R.B. 809 (1972).)

Generally, the remedy, for premature recognition is an order instructing the employer to cease and desist and to withdraw all recognition until a Board-conducted election certifies the union.

As previously mentioned, an employer's voluntary recognition of a majority union imposes a bargaining duty. This duty also arises when an employer enters into a settlement agreement.

In either case, the Board has held that the parties can rely on the continuing representative status of the lawfully recognized union for a "reasonable period of time." (*Keller Plastics Eastern, Inc.*, 157 N.L.R.B. 583 (1966); *Poole Foundry & Machine Co. v. NLRB*, 192 F.2d 740 (4th Cir. 1951).) As a result, election petitions are barred for a reasonable period of time.

The question arises as to what is a "reasonable period of time"? The court in *NLRB v. Frick Co.*, 423 F.2d 1327 (3d Cir. 1970), addressed the issue of whether the rules of the Board relating to the withdrawal of recognition from a certified union, after the one-year certification period, may be applied to the withdrawal of recognition from a voluntary recognized union after the passage of a reasonable time. In *Frick*, the employer agreed to recognize the union on April 1, 1965. From April 5th to May 14th, the parties met to work on a collective bargaining agreement. They reached impasse on May 17th, and the union called an economic strike. During the strike, the company engaged in unfair labor practices, violating Section 8(a) (1), converting the strike into an unfair labor practice strike. While the strike was in progress, the company advised the union that they were withdrawing recognition. Meetings were held to explore possible settlements. However, on June 1, 1966 the company informed the union that they did not believe the union represented a majority of the employees and would not engage in further meetings. The Board found that the company violated Section 8(a) (1) and (5).

96

The court of appeals first noted that the Board's holding that the company violated the Act when it withdrew recognition rested on the rules of the Board respecting the establishment and continuance of bargaining relationships. When a bargaining relationship has been openly established by Board certification or voluntary recognition, there is an irrebuttable presumption that majority status continues for a reasonable time. In regard to a certified union, there is an irrebuttable presumption of majority status that continues for one year. (*Brooks v. NLRB,* 348 U.S. 96 (1954).) At the end of the year, even though the presumption of majority status still exists, it becomes rebuttable. (*Orion Corp. v. NLRB,* 515 F.2d 81 (7th Cir. 1975).) The employer may refuse to bargain without violating the Act if and only if he has a good faith, reasonable doubt as to the union's majority. However, the employer must provide objective evidence casting doubt as to the union's majority.

The court of appeals held that the Board may, within its authority, properly apply the same rebuttable presumption of continued majority status to unions which have been certified and to unions which have been recognized voluntarily. The court noted that the area involves a weighing of conflicting goals of labor policy: preservation of employees' free choice of bargaining representatives and providing stability for established bargaining relationships. The Board must strike a balance between the two, and to do so must be free to utilize its administrative expertise.

The court in *Frick* established that after a reasonable time, an employer may properly rebut the presumption that a union continues to have majority status. However, the question still remains as to what constitutes a "reasonable time"? The court in *Ruffalo's Trucking Service, Inc.,* 114 N.L.R.B. 1549 (1955), noted that a reasonable time must be determined under the particular circumstances of each case. What may be deemed reasonable in one case may not be so in another case.

In *Aero Engineering Corp.*, 177 N.L.R.B. 176 (1969), the union exhibited to the company a number of authorization cards it claimed had been signed by a majority of the employees in an appropriate unit. Thereafter, on September 11, 1967, the company signed a recognition agreement according the union recognition as the sole collective bargaining agent. No bargaining transpired, and the union filed charges against the company for failure to bargain. Thereafter, on February 21, 1968, the company entered into a settlement. The company and the union met in collective bargaining sessions in March, May, and July. On August 5, 1968, the company questioned the majority status of the union and the appropriateness of the unit, and refused to bargain. The union then alleged that the company violated Section 8(a) (1) and (5).

The Board held that the company's recognition of the union, its execution of the settlement agreement, and the subsequent actual bargaining, established a presumption of the union's majority which the company failed to rebut. The Board reasoned that allowing an employer to raise a belated challenge to a union's majority, eleven months after granting recognition and after a settlement agreement, would be a destabilizing factor in bargaining. To permit this type of challenge with no supportive evidence to rebut the presumption would unnecessarily undermine the settlement agreement and would promote "gamesmanship." This would not be within the policy of the Labor Act.

In *Aero*, the employer failed to make a good faith showing of evidence to rebut the presumption of the union's majority status. In contrast, the union in *Poole Foundry & Machine Co. v. NLRB*, 192 F.2d 740 (4th Cir. 1951), clearly did not represent a majority of the employees, yet the court of appeals enforced a settlement agreement. In *Poole*, a consent election was held on November 27, 1946. The union was certified as the bargaining representative for Poole's employees, and on April 16, 1947, a one-year collective bargaining agreement was executed. After the contract expired, bargaining was continued but no new agreement was reached. Subsequently, Poole was charged with a Section 8(a) (5) violation. Thereafter, Poole and the union entered into a settlement agreement which specified that Poole would bargain collectively upon the union's request. On March 9, 1950, 61 out of 66 of Poole's employees in the bargaining unit filed a decertification petition; Poole would not bargain with the union until the union proved that it actually represented a majority.

The court reasoned that a settlement agreement manifests an administrative determination by the Board that some remedial action should safeguard the public interest intended to be protected by the Act. The settlement agreement represented an agreement by the employer to undertake remedial action set out in the agreement rather than to litigate. Accordingly, the court said that if a settlement agreement is to have any real force, a reasonable time must be afforded under which the status fixed by the agreement is to operate. Otherwise, these agreements would have no effect as an amicable and judicious means to expeditious disposal of disputes arising under the Labor Act. In light of this view, the three and one-half months after the agreement was not considered a reasonable time even though the union clearly no longer had a majority.

In *Poole,* the court reasoned that even though the union clearly no longer maintained a majority, three and one-half months after the settlement agreement, a chance to work out a bargaining agreement must take priority over the employees' selection privileges. However, the Board in *Ruffalo's Trucking Service,* 114 N.L.R.B. 1549 (1955), held that where an employer carried out its obligation to bargain in good faith under a settlement agreement, and the parties reached impasse in their negotiations through no fault of the employer, the settlement agreement, unlike a certification, was no bar to an election.

In contrast to *Ruffalo's,* the Board in *N.J. MacDonald & Sons, Inc.,* 155 N.L.R.B. 67 (1965), held that a six-month period after a settlement was not considered to be a reasonable period. In *MacDonald,* the union had never been certified as bargaining representative of the employees of the unit. However, on May 18, 1964, a majority of the unit employees designated the union as their collective bargaining representative, and on May 19th, requested recognition and bargaining. After unfair labor practice charges were filed against MacDonald, the Regional Director approved a settlement agreement on August 13, 1964. Bargaining commenced, and on January 20, 1965, MacDonald submitted a written contract to the Regional Director. Four days later, the employees presented a petition to MacDonald stating that they no longer wished the union to represent them, and MacDonald informed the union that it would no longer bargain because the union did not represent a majority of the employees.

The Board found that the parties, having never negotiated before, met nine times over six months and executed a written contract. At the time of the refusal to bargain, there was no indication of an impasse in negotiations. Therefore, to hold that six months was a reasonable time would ignore the fruitful negotiations.

In sum, premature recognition by an employer may interfere with important employee Section 7 rights. Therefore, when an employer is presented with claims of majority status by a union or rival unions, a question of representation is raised, and the employer should either refuse to bargain with any union, poll to establish the truth of a majority, or petition for an election by the Board.

Once a majority union has been recognized voluntarily or by a settlement agreement, it is important for an employer to keep in mind that the Board wishes to stabilize collective bargaining relationships. Accordingly, a reasonable time must pass in order to give bargaining a chance. Depending upon the circumstances of each particular case, a reasonable time will vary. Keeping all this in mind, an employer should give serious consideration and forethought prior to voluntarily recognizing a union.

§ 3-2. Employer Conduct During the Selection Process.

§ 3-2(A). Employer Statements During the Campaign.

During a union's campaign to become the employees' bargaining representative, the employer may make statements which on their face or within their context potentially interfere with the employees' statutory freedom to select a labor organization. Whether given statements are either unfair labor practices, objectionable conduct, or both usually depends on a balancing of interests by the National Labor Relations Board. The Board can regulate employer as well as union statements in two ways, through the unfair labor practice proscriptions and through the representation election process. In the latter case, the Board regulates conduct and statements by setting aside elections when it determines that a party, or sometimes an outsider, or Board agent has disturbed the laboratory conditions sought to be maintained before the election. The material which follows explains how this is done.

§ 3-2(A)(1). The Laboratory Conditions Standard and the Critical Period.

Prior to the holding of a representation election, the

101

Labor Board seeks to maintain an atmosphere free of coercion and confusion in which the employees may freely exercise their statutory right to choose a bargaining agent or reject representation. In *General Shoe Corp.*, the Board stated:

> In election proceedings, it is the Board's function to provide a laboratory in which an experiment may be conducted, under conditions as nearly ideal as possible, to determine the uninhibited desires of the employees. It is our duty to establish those conditions; it is also our duty to determine whether they have been fulfilled. When, in the rare extreme case, the standard drops too low, because of our fault or that of others, the requisite laboratory conditions are not present and the experiment must be conducted over again. (77 N.L.R.B. 124, 127 (1948).)

Under this highly restrictive standard, the Board has held that any violation of Section 8(a)(1) falling within the critical period preceding the representation election is, *a fortiori*, objectionable conduct which warrants setting aside the election. (*Dal-Tex Optical Co.*, 137 N.L.R.B. 1782 (1962).) But the laboratory conditions test for objectionable conduct is considerably more sensitive than the unfair labor practice provisions. Accordingly, conduct that may not constitute an unfair labor practice may nonetheless interfere with the election atmosphere, leading the Board to invalidate the election. (*General Shoe Corp.*, 77 N.L.R.B. 124, 126 (1948).)

The Board has held that conduct falling within the "critical period" may be considered objectionable and may warrant setting aside an election. This critical period begins to run at the time the petition is filed and ends when a valid election is held. (*Ideal Electric & Manufacturing Co.*, 134 N.L.R.B. 1275 (1961).) Generally, the Labor Board will not consider pre-petition conduct when determining whether election results are reliable. However, exceptions have been forged for "egregious" pre-petition misconduct and other special situations. (*See Catholic Medical Center v. NLRB,* 589 F.2d 1166, 1170-71 (2d Cir. 1978).)

Prior to 1941, the Board required strict neutrality of an employer during the campaign of a union. (*W.A. Jones Foundry & Machine Co.,* 30 N.L.R.B. 809 (1941).) This doctrine was based upon two notions. First, every anti-union statement violated the act because such statements created the fear of economic reprisals in the minds of the voters. (*Southern Colo. Power Co.,* 13 N.L.R.B. 699, 711 (1939).) Second, since the selection of a bargaining representative was the exclusive right of the employees, the employer's interest was held to be insufficient to infringe upon this exclusive right. (*Mellin-Quincy Mfg. Co.,* 53 N.L.R.B. 366, 367 (1943).)

In 1941 the Supreme Court recognized the employer's first amendment right of free speech. (*NLRB v. Virginia Electric & Power Co.,* 314 U.S. 469 (1941).) However, the Court restricted this right to situations where, after consideration of all the facts and circumstances, the total activities of an employer did not restrain or coerce his employees in the exercise of their free choice. (*Id.* at 477.) Despite this limitation placed upon the "strict neutrality" doctrine, the Board continued to limit employer speech, (*Monumental Life Ins. Co.,* 69 N.L.R.B. 247 (1946)), and Congress reacted in 1947 by enacting Section 8(c) of the National Labor Relations Act. Section 8(c) became known as the free speech provision since it ensures both the employer and the union the right to express their views regarding unionization, so long as their statements do not constitute threats of reprisal or promise of benefits. Section 8(c) provides:

> The expression of any views, argument, or opinion, or the dissemination thereof, whether in written, printed,

103

graphic, or visual form, shall not constitute or be evidence of an unfair labor practice under any of the provisions of this Act, if such expression contains no threat of reprisal or force or promise of benefit. (29 U.S.C. § 158(c) (1976).)

The Board responded to the mandate which Congress expressed in Section 8(c) by adopting a less restrictive view toward employer campaign statements. However, the Board limited the application of Section 8(c) and its free speech provision to unfair labor practice cases. (*Dal-Tex Optical Co.*, 137 N.L.R.B. 1782, 1787 (1962); *General Shoe Corp.*, 77 N.L.R.B. 124 (1948).) Thus, the Board may set aside elections based upon speech which would otherwise be protected under Section 8(c). This approach raises a fundamental distinction between objectionable conduct and unfair labor practice violations.

§ 3-2(A)(2). Lawful Predictions Distinguished from Unlawful Threats.

While Section 8(c) is not applicable in representation cases, the same distinction made in unfair labor practice cases between lawful predictions and unlawful threats or promises of benefits is applied in representation cases. In *NLRB v. Gissel Packing Co.,* the Supreme Court held that an employer may state his opinions regarding a union or unionization in general as long as his remarks do not contain a threat of reprisal or a promise of benefits. (395 U.S. 575, 618 (1969).) He may even make a prediction as to the precise effects of unionization on his company, but the employer must phrase the prediction in terms of objective facts which lead to the belief of demonstrably probable consequences beyond his control, or state a previously arrived at management decision to close the plant in the event of unionization.

The Court described the distinction between a lawful prediction and an unlawful threat in these terms:

> If there is any implication that an employer may or may not take action solely on his own initiative for reasons unrelated to economic necessities and known only to him, the statement is no longer a reasonable prediction based on available facts but a threat of retaliation based on misrepresentations and coercion, and as such without the protection of the First Amendment. (*Id.*)

In balancing the interest of the employer against the interest of the employees, the economic dependence of the employees must be considered in determining the effect of the employer's speech. The Court stated:

> Any balancing of those rights must take into account the economic dependence of the employees on their employers, and the necessary tendency of the former, because of that relationship, to pick up intended implications of the latter that might be more readily dismissed by a more disinterested ear. (*Id.* at 617.)

The Court recognized the Board's competence to control employer speech, and cautioned employers to avoid making statements which may mislead employees. The Court made it clear that it will not hesitate to find a violation by an employer who engages in brinkmanship. (*Id.*)

Following the *Gissel* decision, the Board and the courts developed specific guidelines to distinguish between protected speech and threats or promises of benefits which violate Section 8(a) (1) and warrant setting aside an election. In examining and classifying statements by an employer during a representation campaign, all the circumstances surrounding the employer's speech are examined. (*NLRB v. Kaiser Agricultural Chems.*, 473 F.2d 374, 381 (5th Cir. 1973); *NLRB v. Sinclair Co.*, 397 F.2d 157, 160 (1st Cir. 1968); *NLRB v. Gissel Packing Co.*, 395 U.S. 575, 617

(1969).) These circumstances include not only what the employer intended to imply, but also what the employee might reasonably infer from the employer's statements. (*NLRB v. Kaiser Agricultural Chems.*, 473 F.2d 374, 381 (5th Cir. 1973); *NLRB v. Roselyn Bakeries, Inc.*, 471 F.2d 165, 167 (7th Cir. 1972).) Even if the employer's statements are innocuous on their face, these statements may restrain or coerce employees in the exercise of their rights when the employer's total conduct is considered. (*NLRB v. Kaiser Agricultural Chems.*, 473 F.2d 374, 381 (5th Cir. 1973).)

The fact that an employer has the ability to control the consequences of a prediction is a factor considered by the Board and the courts. (*Id.*) Campaign statements in which an employer states that unionization will cause the closing or moving of a plant, (*Stride Rite Corp.*, 228 N.L.R.B. 224 (1977); *Monroe Auto Equipment Co.*, 230 N.L.R.B. 742 (1977)) or the loss or withholding of wage increases and other benefits (*Plastronics, Inc.*, 233 N.L.R.B. 155 (1977); *Coach & Equipment Sales Corp.*, 228 N.L.R.B. 440 (1977)) are subject to close scrutiny by the Board. These types of statements may be violations of Section 8(a)(1) and constitute grounds for setting aside an election when they are not made "on the basis of objective fact to convey an employer's belief as to demonstrably probable consequences beyond his control." (*Honeywell, Inc.*, 225 N.L.R.B. 617 (1976), *quoting NLRB v. Gissel Packing Co.*, 395 U.S. 575, 618 (1969).) The reasonableness of an employer's predictions must also be examined. Predictions may be so outrageous that employees may be deemed to have taken them as threats since the events depicted would not be likely to occur unless the employer acted to fulfill the prediction. (*NLRB v. Golub Corp.*, 388 F.2d 921 (2d Cir. 1967).)

Threats

The laboratory conditions are destroyed by threats which have "a tendency to affect or interfere with the employees' actions at the polls." (*Westside Hosp.,* 218 N.L.R.B. 96 (1975); *Great Atlantic & Pacific Tea Co.,* 177 N.L.R.B. 942 (1969).) The source of the threat may be irrelevant. The most important factor is whether the threats or coercive conduct precluded the employees from exercising a "free and untrammeled choice of representatives contemplated by the act." (*Diamond State Poultry Co.,* 107 N.L.R.B. 3, 6 (1953).)

Some threats which occur during the critical period may not interfere with the employees' free choice in the election. For the threats to trigger the setting aside of an election, the objectionable conduct (threats) must have affected the outcome of the election. (*NLRB v. Zelrich Co.,* 344 F.2d 1011 (5th Cir. 1965); *Westside Hosp.,* 218 N.L.R.B. 96 (1975).) Threats of a relatively minor nature or isolated threats which do not affect the employees' free choice will not be violations of Section 8(a)(1) nor warrant overturning an election. (*Hecla Mining Co. v. NLRB,* 564 F.2d 309 (9th Cir. 1977); *NLRB v. Bostik Div.,* 517 F.2d 971 (6th Cir. 1975); *Rock Island Franciscan Hosp.,* 226 N.L.R.B. 291 (1976); *Owens-Corning Fiberglass Corp.,* 179 N.L.R.B. 219, 223 (1969).) However, where an election is close, the Board and courts may scrutinize minor threats more carefully. (*United Steelworkers v. NLRB,* 496 F.2d 1342, 1347 (5th Cir. 1974); *Dresser Indus., Inc.,* 231 N.L.R.B. 591 (1977).) Whether the election results were affected and the employees' rights interfered with depends upon the character and circumstances surrounding the alleged objectionable conduct. (*United Steelworkers v. NLRB,* 496 F.2d 1342, 1346 (5th Cir. 1974); *Steak House Meat Co.,* 206 N.L.R.B. 28, 29 (1973).)

107

Serious threats made by an employer to only one employee may violate Section 8(a)(1) and constitute grounds for setting aside an election. (*Custom Recovery*, 230 N.L.R.B. 247 (1977).) The Board will not consider these serious threats as isolated since the Board presumes that such threats are the subject of discussion and publication among the fellow employees. (*Montgomery Ward & Co.*, 232 N.L.R.B. 848 (1977); *Coach & Equipment Sales Corp.*, 228 N.L.R.B. 440 (1977).) In *Montgomery Ward & Co.*, the Board set aside an election where a supervisor threatened 4 out of 254 employees with discharge. (232 N.L.R.B. 848 (1977).) The presumption is that if the threat is serious, it can be expected to be published and spread throughout the work place. Other than the threat of discharge, statements regarding changes in work conditions, loss of benefits, and loss of jobs are expected to be the subjects of employee discussion. (*Super Thrift Markets, Inc.*, 233 N.L.R.B. 409 (1977); *Coach & Equipment Sales Corp.*, 228 N.L.R.B. 440 (1977); *General Stencils, Inc.*, 195 N.L.R.B. 1109 (1972).)

Under the Board's objective test, an employer's statements regarding future collective bargaining with a union, such as "bargaining starts at zero," may be unlawful and objectionable conduct. The Board established its rule in *Plastronics, Inc.*, where the employer made a "bargaining from scratch" threat. (*Plastronics, Inc.*, 233 N.L.R.B. 155 (1977).) The Board stated:

> Such statements are objectionable when, in context, they effectively threaten employees with the loss of existing benefits and leave them with the impression that what they may ultimately receive depends in large measure upon what the union can induce the employer to restore. On the other hand, such statements are not objectionable when additional communication to the employees dispels any implication that wages and/or benefits will be reduced during the course of bargaining and establishes that any reduction in wages or benefits

108

will occur as a result of the normal give and take of collective bargaining. (*Id.* at 156.)

In the *Plastronics* case, the Board held that, under the circumstances of the case, the employer's statements interfered with the outcome of the election, and a second election was ordered. (*Id.*)

In *Host International, Inc.,* the Labor Board held that "bargaining from scratch" statements did not destroy the laboratory conditions surrounding the election. (195 N.L.R.B. 348 (1972).) The statement in that case was made by the employer's general manager to an employee who testified he was told that "wage negotiations would start at the federal minimum wage" and that "he (the general manager) could not guarantee all the benefits we have now." The Board held that there was no evidence that the employer gave a threatening color to his remarks, overruling the objections to the election and certifying the election result. (*Id.* at 348.)

The employer's ability to control the consequences of his threatening statements may also justify the setting aside of an election. Examples of statements within the control of the employer are, that unionization will result in a loss or withholding of benefits, a curtailment of operations, or a halt in wage increases. (*Marathon Metallic Bldg. Co.,* 224 N.L.R.B. 121 (1976); *Parke Coal Co.,* 219 N.L.R.B. 546 (1975); *Gary Aircraft Corp.,* 193 N.L.R.B. 108 (1971).) Despite the seriousness of these types of threats and the employer's ability to control the consequences, the statements must be shown to have interfered with the employees' free choice before an election can be set aside.

The threat of a plant closing is also a basis for setting aside an election. (*Royal Typewriter Co. v. NLRB,* 533 F.2d 1030 (8th Cir. 1976); *NLRB v. Kaiser Agricultural Chems.,* 473 F.2d 374 (5th Cir. 1973).) In *Paoli Chair Co.,* the Board set aside an election where the president of the company gave a speech, telling his employees that the union was telling them only half truths about the law as it relates to plant closings. (231 N.L.R.B. 539 (1977).) He referred to specific circumstances under which a plant had closed after a union had won an election. The president also stated that the employees had "a lot to lose and nothing to gain" by electing a union, because the company was paying all it could afford. The Board held that the president's speech had constituted implicit threats to close the plant. (*Id.* at 540.)

In *Stride Rite Corp.,* the Board examined statements made by the employer which threatened curtailment of operations and unemployment. (228 N.L.R.B. 224 (1977).) In that case, the employer related to his employees' the inability of the union to prevent a plant shutdown, and the company's own ability to cancel its lease on thirty days notice. His reasons for a shutdown were vague economic consequences of unionization. The Board upheld the Regional Director's finding that the vague economic reasons were not lawful predictions, and concluded the employer had threatened to use tactics solely within his control.

Constant references to strikes and the consequences of strikes may lead the Board to set aside an election. In *Thomas Products Co.,* the Board held that an employer may describe the strike as a union's chief economic weapon, and tell employees that a strike would cause certain consequences. (167 N.L.R.B. 732 (1967).) The Board cautioned, however, that

> [w]hen the employer additionally warns that he stands ready to demand a reduction in employee benefits in exchange for security measures which the union might request, the employees can well believe that the employer has decided in advance to refuse to accord to the union in bargaining the good faith and open mind that the law requires. (*Id.* at 733.)

110

Based on the *Thomas* decision, statements that a strike is a result of unionization interfere with employee's free choice when the statements indicate the employer's intent to refuse to bargain in good faith. However, where an employer merely states that he will not yield to a union's pressure in collective bargaining, the election will be allowed to stand. (*J.R. Wood, Inc.,* 228 N.L.R.B. 593 (1977).)

In *Honeywell, Inc.* the employer's general manager made a statement including the expression of the need to recall 10 employees because of customer demands. (225 N.L.R.B. 617 (1976).) He told the employees that these efforts would be wasted as "the interference of a labor union would only hinder our chances of further recovery." The Board set aside the election finding the general manager's statements were objectionable conduct which interfered with the employees' free choice. The basis for finding objectionable conduct was the Board's holding that the employer was required to explain his statements based upon objective considerations. (*Id.* at 618.) The holding of the Board in *Honeywell* may be in conflict with the Board's holding in *Oxford Pickles.* (190 N.L.R.B. 109 (1971).)

In *Oxford Pickles* the employer stated that he did not have to agree to union demands, he did not have to sign a contract with the union, bargaining would start from scratch, the union's only lever was the strike, that he controlled the wages, that in the event of a strike the employees would not receive worker's compensation, that he could hire replacements, and that he might be forced to move. The majority of the Board refused to set aside the election, stating that an employer cannot be penalized for accurate statements of law and facts. (*Id.* at 110.) The Board has recently cited *Oxford Pickles* with approval. (*St. Francis Hospital,* 263 N.L.R.B. No. 109, sl. op. 8 (1982).)

In sum, the Board and courts will find a violation of Section 8(a)(1) of the Act and set aside an election if an employer makes a pre-election statement which employees would reasonably interpret as threatening retaliation should they select a labor organization to represent them. However, employer predictions as to the consequences of employee selection of a union are protected by Section 8(c) of the Act and are lawful if based on demonstrably objective facts outside the employer's control. Since the Board and courts consider the totality of the conduct when examining such employer statements, it is often difficult to discern the difference between an illegal threat and a lawful prediction. Although the Board decisions are somewhat inconsistent, an employer who strays too close to the brink of violation will not be saved if he falls over and commits the unfair labor practice. (*Turner Shoe Co.,* 249 N.L.R.B. 144, 146 (1980).)

§ 3-2(B). Rules Restricting Access to Outsiders.

An employer's rule which prohibits union organizers from entering onto its property during a union organizing campaign is presumed lawful so long as other reasonable means of communicating to employees are available to them. This is the essence of the rule laid down by the Supreme Court in *NLRB v. Babcock & Wilcox Co.,* 351 U.S. 105 (1956).

The facts in no-access cases are of critical importance in determining whether an employer rule violates Section 8(a)(1). In *Babcock & Wilcox* the employer had a plant on a 100-acre tract of land situated about one mile from a town of 21,000 people. Approximately 40 percent of the employees lived in the nearby town, while the other 60 percent lived within a 30-mile radius. Over 90 percent of all the employees drove to work, parked in a company parking lot, and entered via the privately owned driveway. The only nearby public area was a public right-of-way which crossed the driveway.

Union organizers sought to distribute literature in the company parking lot, claiming that the public area was unsafe. The Board held that the employer violated Section 8(a)(1), reasoning that union difficulties in communicating with employees would ultimately impede the employees right to self-organization. The court of appeals refused to enforce the Board's order holding it did not have authority to impose a servitude on an employer's property where no employee was involved. The United States Supreme Court affirmed the court of appeals by making an important distinction between the access rights of employees versus those of non-employees. The Board had applied its reasoning in *LeTourneau Co. of Georgia*, 54 N.L.R.B. 1253 (1944) in which it held that an employee's right to self-organize is superior to the employer's rights to property. However, the Supreme Court pointed out that the union organizers in *Babcock & Wilcox* were not employees. The Court then considered the facts presented, balanced the interests, and found the scales tipped in favor of the employer.

> It is our judgment, however, that an employer may validly post his property against non-employee distribution of union literature if reasonable efforts by the union through other available channels of communication will enable it to reach the employees with its message and if the employer's notice or order does not discriminate against the union by allowing other distribution. In these circumstances the employer may not be compelled to allow distribution even under such reasonable regulations as the orders in these cases permit. (351 U.S. at 112.)

Fundamental to this holding is the availability of other methods of communication and the nondiscriminatory application of the no-access rule. Employers cannot deny access to union organizers while allowing parking lot access to church groups and other charities (*Priced-Less Discount Foods, Inc.*, 162 N.L.R.B. 872 (1976)). Likewise, employers

113

cannot deny access where no other reasonable means of communicating to employees exists. (*S & H Grossinger's, Inc.,* 156 N.L.R.B. 233 (1965), *enforced as modified,* 372 F.2d 26 (2d Cir. 1967).) The *Grossinger's* case is illustrative of the "reasonable" standard. There, the employer operated a resort hotel where approximately 60 percent of his employees lived and ate on the premises. The Board held that if denied access to the employer's property, the union would have no other effective means of discussing unionization with the employees. Thus, denial of access resulted in an interference with rights guaranteed by Section 7 and violated Section 8 (a)(1). However, not all hotel cases yield the same result. (*See, e.g., NLRB v. New Pines, Inc.,* 468 F.2d 427 (2d Cir. 1972).)

Each case must be decided on the basis of its own facts. As the Supreme Court pointed out in *Babcock & Wilcox,*

> [t]his is not a problem of always open or always closed doors for union organization on company property. Organization rights are granted to workers by the same authority, the National Government, that preserves property rights. Accommodation between the two must be obtained with as little destruction of one as is consistent with the maintenance of the other. The employer may not affirmatively interfere with organization; the union may not always insist that the employer aid organization. But when the inaccessibility of employees makes ineffective the reasonable attempts by nonemployees to communicate with them through the usual channels, the right to exclude from property has been required to yield to the extent needed to permit communication for information on the right to organize. (351 U.S. at 112.)

What constitutes a reasonable attempt to communicate is often difficult to identify. Such "reasonable attempts" sometimes include use of the mail, telephone, home visits, or meetings (*Monogram Models, Inc.,* 192 N.L.R.B. 705, 706

114

(1971)). The Board also differentiates "reasonable attempts" from "convenient attempts." In *Monogram Models, Inc.,* the Board explained that

> [t]he test established [in *Babcock & Wilcox*] was not one of relative convenience, but rather whether "the location of a plant and the living quarters of the employees place the employees beyond the reach of reasonable union efforts to communicate with them. . . ." (*Id.* at 706.)

For this reason, the Board declined to establish a "big city rule" which would allow access to an employer's property where the employees lived in different parts of a large metropolitan area.

> We do not believe it wise or proper to adopt a "big city rule" and a different "smalltown rule" in applying *Babcock and Wilcox,* or to attempt to determine how big a city must be to justify the proposed differing application. (*Id.*)

A related issue is raised by off-duty employees seeking access to the employer's property for the purpose of union organizing. This situation presents the problem of whether the off-duty employee should be considered an insider or an outsider for purposes of determining access. In a leading case on point, the union objected to an employer rule which stated, "an employee is not to enter the plant or remain on the premises unless he is on duty or scheduled to work." The Board upheld the employer's work rule, declaring it to be presumptively valid as long as there were other reasonable means of communication and as long as the rule was applied equally to all off-duty employees irrespective of their purpose (*G.T.E. Lenkurt, Inc.,* 204 N.L.R.B. 921 (1973)).

Several years later the Board retreated from this posture, holding that the *G.T.E. Lenkurt* rule should be narrowly construed. In *Continental Bus System, Inc.,* 229 N.L.R.B. 1262 (1977) and *Tri-County Medical Center, Inc.,* 222

N.L.R.B. 1089 (1976), the Board stated that an "off-duty no access rule" is valid only if:

(1) Access is limited solely to the internal plant and/or other work areas;

(2) The rule is clear and disseminated to all employees; and

(3) The rule applies equally to all employees for all purposes.

§ 3-2(C). Polling Employees.

In some cases an employer may wish to grant voluntary recognition to a union which claims to represent the majority of its employees. However, the grant of voluntary recognition must be approached with caution in order to avoid charges of employer interference in violation of Section 8(a)(1) and (2) through an inadvertent infringement of Section 7 guarantees. In such situations, methods of validating the union's claim are available to an employer. One such method is to conduct a poll of the employees. The poll itself, however, is fraught with dangers of infringing employee rights guaranteed by Section 7 and sanctioned by Section 8(a)(1). Certain measures must be taken in order to avoid the risks inherent in questioning employees about union preference.

The issue of polling employees and what constitutes lawful questioning has had an elastic judicial history. The *per se* approach as set out in *Standard Coosa-Thatcher Co.,* 85 N.L.R.B. 1358 (1949), was that all questioning of employees as to their union's sympathies violated Section 8(a)(1). The rigidity of the *per se* approach was abandoned by the Board in *Blue Flash Express, Inc.,* 109 N.L.R.B. 591 (1954), in favor of an "all of the circumstances" test. Here the Board held it was not a violation of the Act for the general manager of a company to call employees individually into his office and ask them if they had signed union cards in order to determine the validity of a union's claim of majority status. In deciding that such a poll did not violate Section 8(a)(1), the Board noted that there were several factors which insured a non-coercive atmosphere:

(1) The employer conducted the poll for a legitimate purpose to determine the validity of a union's claim that it represented a majority of the employer's employees;

(2) The employer informed the employees of its purpose in conducting the questioning;

(3) The employer assured the employees there would be no reprisals;

(4) The question occurred against a background free of employer hostility for the union.

Nevertheless, the Board emphasized that "the test is whether, under all the circumstances, the interrogation reasonably tends to restrain or interfere with the employees in the exercise of rights guaranteed by the Act." (*Id.* at 593.) Accordingly, the Board stated that in future cases other circumstances could be relevant in applying the test. These would include the time and place of the poll, the personnel involved, the information sought, the employer's conceded preference for or against the union, and if it occurs, the fact that the employees gave false answers when questioned.

For thirteen years following *Blue Flash,* there was considerable confusion among employers over which circumstances would satisfy the "all the circumstances" test for a permissible poll. This issue was faced head on by the Board in *Struksnes Construction Co.,* 165 N.L.R.B. 1062 (1967). On remand, the Board followed the directives set down by the United States Court of Appeals for the District of Columbia Circuit:

117

We think the Board should come to grips with this constantly recurring problem for the protection of the employees as to their section 7 rights and for that of an employer acting in good faith. It would seem that the Board could, in the exercise of its expertise, develop appropriate policy considerations and outline at least minimal standards to govern the ascertainment of union status, or even in given permissible situations, the desire of the employees respecting a contract with the Union. (*International Union of Operating Engineers, Local 49, AFL-CIO v. NLRB,* 353 F.2d 852, 856 (D.C. Cir. 1965).)

The general rule set out in *Struksnes* is that *any* attempt by an employer to ascertain an employee's union sympathy will be an infringement of Section 7 rights. The rationale is that fear of reprisal for an affirmative reply would inhibit union activities. The exception to this general rule is found where an employer carefully adheres to the following five safeguards specified in *Struksnes:*

Absent unusual circumstances, the polling of employees by an employer will be violative of Section 8(a)(1) of the Act unless the following safeguards are observed: (1) the purpose of the poll is to determine the truth of a union's claim of majority, (2) this purpose is communicated to the employees, (3) assurances against reprisal are given, (4) the employees are polled by secret ballot, and (5) the employer has not engaged in unfair labor practices or otherwise created a coercive atmosphere. (165 N.L.R.B. at 1063.)

The Board further indicated that a union's claim of majority would be a lawful purpose for a poll so long as a petition for an election has not been filed by either side. Where a petition has been filed, the poll would not serve any legitimate purpose that would not be better served by the election itself.

The *Struksnes* rule is generally applied by the Board in cases involving systematic and continued polling of

118

employees. It has also been applied where an employer involved in contract negotiations and facing a strike deadline, attached a questionnaire to its employment application form and inquired as to whether the applicant would cross a picket line in the event of a strike. The Board and Eighth Circuit held that inasmuch as the employer had given no assurance against reprisals, the questioning violated the *Struksnes* criteria. (*W.A. Sheaffer Pen Co. v. NLRB,* 486 F.2d 180 (8th Cir. 1973). *See also Preterm, Inc.,* 240 N.L.R.B. 654 (1979).)

Although *Struksnes* has become the general rule, neither the Board nor the Courts of Appeals have been inclined to apply it strictly. One line of cases suggests a return to the *Blue Flash* "all of the circumstances" test. They evince a disinclination to apply a mechanical formula without inquiring into the particular facts in each case. The factual inquiries often follow the line of questioning set forth in *Bourne v. NLRB,* 332 F.2d 47 (2d Cir. 1964). The *Bourne* court attempted to determine whether or not a reasonable employee, under the circumstances, would feel coerced and inhibited. The court stated that answers to the following questions would provide assistance:

1. Is there a history of employer hostility and discrimination?
2. Did the interviewer appear to be seeking information on which to base action against individual employees?
3. How high was the interviewer in the company hierarchy?
4. Was there an atmosphere of unnatural fear?

Another example of a return to the "all of the circumstances" test is presented in *Bushnell's Kitchens, Inc.,* 222 N.L.R.B. 110 (1976). There, employees striking for recognition were asked whether they wanted a union. The questioning came in a group meeting where the employees

119

were accompanied by both the union president and the union business agent. The Board held that given these circumstances, it would be unreasonable for the employees to fear reprisal. The Board cautioned:

> [t]he requirements of *Struksnes* have their place. But they are not a straightjacket to be applied in any and all circumstances. Where employees openly proclaim their adherence to a union and invite verification, we do not believe that the employer can be said to coerce employees by complying with their request. (*Id.* at 110.)

This reasoning is echoed in a recent case in which a foreman called fifty employees individually into his office to show them union cards and ask if they understood the cards' significance. Holding that this activity did not violate the Act, the Seventh Circuit Court of Appeals held:

> We join with other circuits, however, in declining to approve a *per se* rule and instead will look to the totality of the circumstances, including the purpose of the interview, the entire statement made to the employee, and the scope of the questioning. (*A & R Transport, Inc. v. NLRB,* 601 F.2d 311, 313 (7th Cir. 1979).)

Although there are differences of opinion extant between the Board and the appellate courts, they should not create serious difficulties for an employer deciding whether to poll. In most cases an employer who follows the stricter guidelines set down in *Struksnes* will avoid violation of the Act. However, where an employer does not comply with all the requirements of *Struksnes* in a case involving systematic polling and defends on the basis of the "all of the circumstances" test, he chances an unfavorable ruling by the Board and the court of appeals.

In a recent decision by the newly appointed Board, the NLRB adopted a test under which all of the circumstances

would be considered in determining whether an interrogation reasonably tends to restrain, coerce, or interfere with
statutory rights. (*Rossmore House,* 269 N.L.R.B. No. 198
(1984).

§ 3-2(D). Promises of Benefits and Conduct Relating to Benefits.

An employer may violate Section 8(a)(1) of the National
Labor Relations Act in a variety of ways through conduct
and/or announcements relating to benefits. Promises of
benefits calculated to persuade employees to vote against
the union in an upcoming election, actual grants of benefits
before an election, threats to withhold benefits, and actual
delays or withholdings of benefits may violate Section
8(a)(1) depending on their timing, coterminous employer
statements and actions, and other circumstances which
may reveal that employee exercise of Section 7 rights has
been impaired.

§ 3-2(D)(1). Employer Grants of Benefits.

An employer is not automatically prevented from making
adjustments in his employees' wages and benefits simply
because an election to decide union representation is
pending. The National Labor Relations Board has stated
that an employer is permitted to increase benefits during an
election campaign, "where the raise under consideration
was one which was regularly or periodically granted or one
which the employees normally expected to receive." (*Standard Coil Products, Inc.,* 99 N.L.R.B. 899, 903 (1952).) In
fact, the employer faced with a union organizational campaign should proceed as it would have, had the campaign
not occurred. (*Russell Stover Candies, Inc.,* 221 N.L.R.B.
441 (1975).) Examples of permissible increases during an
organizing campaign are: (1) the granting of holiday bene-

fits and higher wages based on an inflationary trend and not tied to statements relating to unionization. (*Simpson Electric Co.,* 654 F.2d 15 (7th Cir. 1981); *E-Z Mills, Inc.,* 101 N.L.R.B. 979 (1952)); (2) general wage increases based on economic considerations used in previous years, such as market conditions. (*Gillcraft Furniture Co.,* 103 N.L.R.B. 81 (1953)); (3) benefits introduced in order to compete with other companies in the industry for the labor force. (*NLRB v. May Department Stores Co.,* 154 F.2d 533 (8th Cir. 1946).)

It is a violation, however, when an employer grants benefits to his employees for the purpose of influencing them to vote against the union. (*NLRB v. Exchange Parts Co.,* 375 U.S. 405 (1964).) There are numerous decisions in which unilateral increases in benefits were found to constitute illegal interference with the employees' right to organize. The Supreme Court has said, "there could be no more obvious way of interfering with these rights than by grants of wage increases upon the understanding that the employees would leave the union in return." (*Medo Photo Supply Corp. v. NLRB,* 321 U.S. 678 (1944).)

§ 3-2(D)(2). Wage Increases.

A unilateral grant of wage increases during a union organizing campaign is regarded as a prime form of illegal interference with the employees' right to organize. It is relatively easy for the Board to find that an employer violated the Act when the granting of the wage increase is preceded or followed by anti-union statements. Where an employer does not make such statements, it is more difficult to determine if the employer acted with an anti-union motive. However, the Board may find a violation of Section 8(a)(1) when an employer grants wage increases during a union organizing campaign without expressly conditioning the increases upon the defeat of the union. The Board may presume an unlawful purpose or effect based on the timing of the employer's action, and shift the burden to the employer to show that the granting of the benefit was justified on other than anti-union motives.

The Supreme Court has approved this approach. (*NLRB v. Exchange Parts Co.*, 375 U.S. 405 (1964).) In *Exchange Parts*, an employer conferred unconditional economic benefits on his employees shortly before the representation election. It was no defense, the Court said, that the benefits were granted permanently and unconditionally and that there was no other interference with employees' rights. In a frequently quoted passage, the Court explained:

> The danger inherent in well-timed increases in benefits is the suggestion of a fist inside the velvet glove. Employees are not likely to miss the inference that the source of benefits now conferred is also the source from which future benefits must flow and which may dry up if it is not obliged. (*Id.* at 409.)

The Supreme Court emphasized the timing of the benefits. Although *Exchange Parts* seems to set up a *per se* rule based on the timing of the grant, the Board actually considers the variables surrounding the grant. The Board looks at the timing of the grant to determine whether the grant coincides with the employees' expectation of such a grant, whether it is strategically announced to interfere with the election, and whether the timing of the grant differs from customary practices. If these factors are present, the Board will find a violation. (*United Screw & Bolt Corp.*, 91 N.L.R.B. 916 (1950).)

§ 3-2(D)(3). Employer Promises of Benefits.

An employer promise of benefits, made at a crucial point in an organizing campaign, may have as harmful an effect on employee freedom of choice as actual grants of benefits. The Board has indicated that promises made during the pre-election period, whether made directly or indirectly to employees, are illegal if the employees have reasonable cause to believe that the promise was provoked by union activity. There is also a distinction made between explicit and implicit promises.

The promise of a benefit made to an employee contingent upon the union being defeated in an NLRB election constitutes an explicit promise interfering with the election and is unlawful. (*Howell Chevrolet Co. v. NLRB,* 346 U.S. 482 (1953).) Usually these types of cases provide the clearest examples of election interference. In *Paterson Fire Brick Co.,* the Board determined that it was unnecessary for the explicit promise to accomplish the intended result for it to be unlawful interference. (93 N.L.R.B. 1118 (1951).)

Some commentators believe that the Board should prevent explicit attempts to sway employee votes by promising benefits contingent upon the union's defeat. However, they also criticize the Board for exceeding the limits of sound regulatory policy by setting aside elections where promises were not contingent upon the election outcome, but were campaign statements protected by the right of free speech or else were replies to union assertions. (Williams, Janus, Huhn, *NLRB Regulation of Election Conduct,* Industrial Research Unit (1974).)

The Board may determine that a promise of a benefit could lead employees to believe that the benefit promised was conditioned upon the results of the election, even though there has been no explicit conditioning of the benefit upon the result of the election. In *Grandee Beer Dist., Inc. v. NLRB,* the court of appeals determined that the promises of benefits (increased wages and a health plan) were not expressly made dependent upon the employees' rejection of the union. (630 F.2d 928 (2d Cir. 1980).) The court further stated, "nevertheless, the timing of those offers indicated a coercive purpose and effect." (*Id.* at 932.) The court ruled that the employer failed to justify the timing of the promise and, therefore, could not avoid the inference of anti-union action.

In another case, the Court of Appeals for the Third Circuit held that the Board was warranted in finding that employer campaign promises violated Section 8(a)(1) of the Act. (*NLRB v. Garry Mfg. Co.,* 630 F.2d 934 (3d Cir. 1980).) There, during a union organizing campaign the employer listed its past benefits and promised to do even better in the future. It then stated that nobody would regret it if the union lost the representation election. The court agreed with the Board that these statements were implied promises of future benefits in exchange for the union's defeat. (*See also I.C. Refrigeration Service, Inc.,* 200 N.L.R.B. 687, 695 (1972). *Compare El Cid, Inc.,* 202 N.L.R.B. 1315 (1976).)

§ 3-2(D)(4). Employer Withholding of Promised Benefits.

An employer may be hesitant to announce or grant increases in benefits for fear that it would be interpreted as unlawfully influencing the employees to vote against a union. In order to protect itself, the employer may announce to the employees that it intends to postpone any increases until after the election. However, the employer must be careful not to make the postponement seem to be a form of punishment, since this would be a clear interference of the employees' protected rights. (*See Sugardale Foods, Inc.,* 221 N.L.R.B. 1228 (1975).)

In *Bonwit Teller, Inc.,* the Board found that the employer interfered in the employees' free choice by deferring wage increases until after the election. (96 N.L.R.B. 608 (1951).) On appeal, the Court of Appeals for the Second Circuit reversed the Board. (197 F.2d 640 (2d Cir. 1952).) The employer stated that it did not want to be accused of an unfair labor practice by granting the increases. The Board held that this delay in wage increases was illegal since the deferment tended to encourage votes against the union. However, the court concluded that the employer was merely indicating that the increases would follow in the ordinary practice and that therefore it fell short of being a threat of reprisal if employees voted in favor of the union.

In another case, the Court of Appeals for the Second Circuit upheld the Board's finding of a violation when an employer stated that an expected wage increase would be postponed until after the election. (*NLRB v. Porta Systems Corp.*, 625 F.2d 399 (2d Cir. 1980).) In *Porta*, the chief executive officer made speeches to employees notifying them of the suspension of routine raise increases two weeks before the election. The court said that the evidence was sufficient that the employer created an impression that the withholding of wage increases would be the fault of the union.

In addition to the postponement of benefit increases until after the election, an employer may also violate the Act by withholding benefits without regard to the election. In *G.C. Murphy Co. v. NLRB*, the employer cancelled previously prepared wage increase requisitions and refused to proceed with its annual employee wage review procedure because of the union's campaign. (550 F.2d 1004 (4th Cir. 1977).) This was done even though the union assured the employer that no unfair labor practice charges would be filed if it granted the increases. Accordingly, the employer had no ground to fear that granting wage increases at that time would provoke an unfair labor practice charge, and the court found that withholding the increase violated Section 8(a)(1) of the Act. (*See also Osco Drug, Inc.,* 237 N.L.R.B. 231 (1978).)

The Court of Appeals for the Ninth Circuit went further in its analysis in *Free-Flow Packaging Corp. v. NLRB*, 566 F.2d 1124 (9th Cir. 1978). That court reasoned that the focus of inquiry must be on the employer's true motive and not what employees might reasonably have assumed to be his motive. It is only when the focus is directed towards the employer does the question become one of anti-union intent. In *Free-Flow,* the court agreed with the Board that the employer withheld wage increases to discourage unionization.

§ 3-2(D)(5). Employer Threats to Reduce or Withhold Benefits.

To attempt during an organizing campaign to discourage employees from affiliating with a union by threatening to cut back certain of their benefits is also illegal under the Act. Statements that reasonably induce fear that the employee will be treated less favorably on the job are often sufficient to constitute a Section 8(a)(1) violation.

The list of what constitutes a violation is long in regard to employer threats. The employer in *NLRB v. Pilgrim Foods,* was found to violate the Act when his supervisor threatened an employee that the employer would cut his hours if the union won, and also cancelled the employee's promised raise because he participated in the election. (591 F.2d 110 (1st Cir. 1978).) In *NLRB v. Jamaica Towing, Inc.,* the Court of Appeals for the Second Circuit held that threatening employees with onerous working conditions and the loss of benefits if the union was successful in the representation election violated Section 8(a)(1). (602 F.2d 1100 (2d Cir. 1979).) In another case, the blanket assertion that unionization would be followed by worsening of conditions at the plant was held to be unlawful interference with employees' free choice. (*Lingerie, Inc.,* 101 N.L.R.B. 1374

(1952).) Also barred are threats to cut the piece-rate system and to eliminate overtime work if a union wins a pending election. (*Dovedown Hosiery Mills,* 102 N.L.R.B. 1592 (1953).)

§ 3-3. Discharges and Strikers' Rights.

§ 3-3(A). Pretext and Dual Motive Cases.

In resolving cases involving alleged violations of section 8(a)(3) it must be determined whether an employee's involvement in union or other protected activities has had an adverse effect on his or her employment conditions and, if so, whether the employer's action was motivated by such employee activities. In a typical section 8(a)(3) case the General Counsel will allege that the employee was discriminatorily discharged because of his or her protected union or concerted activity. The employer, on the other hand, will allege that the employee was discharged for legitimate business considerations. A question that has perplexed the courts for over a decade arises where the employer has "dual motives" for a discharge — one lawful and the other unlawful. What test should the Board or court apply in determining whether the discharge violates section 8(a)(3)?

Various tests have been used by the Board and the courts in answering the above question. Although each test proposed is different in some respect, they share a common denominator in that they all examine the concept of "causality," that is, the relationship between the employee's protected activities and the employer's actions which detrimentally affected employment. In *Wright Line, A Division of Wright Line, Inc.,* 251 N.L.R.B. 1083 (1980), the Board addressed the confusion and criticism concerning the test of causality in "dual motivation" cases, and set forth a formal test of causation that is to be applied in cases alleging section 8(a)(3) violations.

In *Wright Line,* the Board explained the distinction between pretext and dual motive cases, and discussed the various tests employed by the courts prior to the *Wright Line* decision.

§ 3-3(A)(1). The Distinction Between Pretext and Dual Motive Cases.

Rarely will an employer admit that an employee has been disciplined for engaging in union or other protected activities. Instead, the employer will allege that its action was justified by a legitimate business reason. However, the Board will examine the evidence to determine whether the reasons advanced by the employer to explain a discharge are the real reasons for the termination. If they are not, the employer's reasons for discharging an employee are said to be pretextual.

In dual motivation cases, on the other hand, the discharged employee has provided his employer with actual cause for disciplinary action. At the same time, however, the evidence indicates that the employer also had a discriminatory reason for discharging the employee. In such a situation the Board determines whether the unlawful reason played a part in the employer's decision.

Often it is difficult to discern the distinction between a pretext case and a dual motive case. However, the distinction may be more easily made if one views the employer's asserted justification as an affirmative defense. In a pretext case, the employer's affirmative defense has some merit, a "dual motive" may exist, and the question becomes whether there is sufficient proof necessary for the employer's affirmative defense to be sustained.

§ 3-3(A)(2). The "In Part" Test.

In the past, the Board applied the "in part" causation test

when dealing with dual motive cases. This test provides that if a discharge is motivated, "in part," by the protected activities of the employee, the discharge violates the Act even if the employer also relied upon a legitimate business reason. (*Youngstown Osteopathic Hospital Ass'n,* 224 N.L.R.B. 574, 575 (1976).) Various courts of appeals severely criticized this test for a number of reasons. Some critics asserted that rather than seeking to accommodate legitimate competing interests, the test went only half way, in that once it determined that an employee's protected rights were infringed, the Board's inquiry ended and the employer's plea of legitimate business justification was ignored. Others criticized the test because it forced an employer to take on the impossible burden of establishing that it did not even think about the employee's union activities in deciding on discipline. Despite such criticism, the Board continued to apply the "in part" test until it was finally replaced in the *Wright Line* decision.

§ 3-3(A)(3). The "Dominant Motive" Test.

In response to the enormous criticism leveled at the "in part" test, some of the circuit courts articulated a "dominant motive" or "but for" test. This test puts the burden on the General Counsel to establish not only that the employer had a discriminatory reason for the discipline, but also that the employee would not have been discharged "but for" his participation in protected activity. In other words, when both a legal and an illegal reason for the discharge exist, the burden is upon the General Counsel to establish that, in the absence of protected activities, the discharge would not have taken place. (*Coletti's Furniture, Inc. v. NLRB,* 550 F.2d 1292 (1st Cir. 1977).

§ 3-3(A)(4). The Mt. Healthy Test.

The conflict over which test to apply in dual motive cases led to continuing uncertainty and confusion in the courts. In *Wright Line,* the Board attempted to relieve some of the confusion by clarifying the analytical framework that should be applied in dual motivation cases. In so doing, the Board adopted the test of causality applied by the Supreme Court in *Mt. Healthy City School District Board of Education v. Doyle,* 429 U.S. 274 (1977).

In *Mt. Healthy,* an untenured teacher brought suit against the Mt. Healthy School Board, alleging that it had wrongfully refused to renew his contract and award him tenure. The school board cited the teacher's use of obscene language and gestures in the school cafeteria and his conveyance of a change in the school's policies to a local radio station as its reasons for not renewing his contract. In his suit, the teacher alleged that the refusal to renew his contract violated his rights under the first and fourteenth amendments. The district court found that of the two reasons cited by the school board, one involved unprotected conduct while the second was clearly protected by the first and fourteenth amendments. The district court reasoned that since protected activity had played a substantial part in the school board's decision, its refusal to renew the contract was improper and the teacher was, therefore, entitled to reinstatement and backpay. The court of appeals affirmed.

The Supreme Court reversed, rejecting the lower court's application of an "in part" test and ruling that the "school board must be given an opportunity to establish that its decision not to renew would have been the same if the protected activity had not occurred." (*Wright Line,* 251 N.L.R.B. at 1086.) The Court then fashioned the following test to be applied in a dual motivation context. Initially, the employee must establish that the protected conduct was a "substantial" or "motivating factor." When this is established, the burden shifts to the employer to demonstrate that it would have reached the same decision absent the protected conduct.

Mt. Healthy rejects an "in part" analysis which stops with the establishment of a prima facie case or at consideration of an improper motive. The "dominant motive" test is also done away with by the *Mt. Healthy* decision, even though it may appear that the two are similar. They are alike in that both reject a limited "in part" analysis and both require proof of how the employer would have acted in the absence of the protected activity. However, they are dissimilar in that they place the burden for this proof on different parties. Under the "dominant motive" test it is the *General Counsel* who has the burden of establishing a prima facie showing of unlawful motive, and of rebutting the employer's asserted defense by showing that the discharge would not have taken place in the absence of the employee's protected activities. The crucial distinction is that under the *Mt. Healthy* test, once the General Counsel makes out a prima facie case of employer reliance upon protected activity, the burden shifts to the *employer* to demonstrate that the decision would have been the same in the absence of the protected activity.

§ 3-3(A)(5). The Wright Line Test.

In *Wright Line,* the General Counsel alleged that the employer discharged Lamoureux, a shop inspector, in violation of section 8(a)(3) and (1). The employer denied the allegation, asserting that Lamoureux was discharged because he violated a plant rule against "knowingly altering, or falsifying production line reports, payroll records, and time cards."

At the time of his discharge, Lamoureux had been employed by the employer for over ten years. He had held the position of inspector for two years and was considered a better than average employee. On the day prior to his discharge, Lamoureux's supervisor, Forte, was instructed by the plant superintendent to check on Lamoureux. The next day, Forte discovered certain discrepancies in Lamoureux's timesheet. The timesheet indicated that Lamoureux had been working on certain jobs at the time when Forte had been looking for him the previous day, but Forte had been unable to find Lamoureux at his work station. Forte reported this finding to his own supervisor, and was told that "the offense was a dischargeable offense." Forte was instructed to ask Lamoureux for an explanation. Although Forte did so, the record revealed that Lamoureux's final check had already been prepared when Forte confronted him with the discrepancy. Forte then rejected Lamoureux's explanation. Lamoureux was promptly discharged, purportedly for violating a plant rule against "knowingly altering, or falsifying production time reports, payroll records, time cards." The employer conceded that Lamoureux was not discharged for being away from his work station or for not performing his assigned work.

In finding Lamoureux was illegally discharged, the Board adopted a two-part test adapted from the one used by the United States Supreme Court in *Mt. Healthy.* First, the General Counsel is required to make a prima facie showing sufficient to support the inference that protected conduct was a "motivating factor" in the employer's decision. Once that is established, the burden shifts to the employer to demonstrate that the same action would have taken place even in the absence of the protected conduct.

The General Counsel, the Board said, made a prima facie showing that union activity was the motivating factor in the employer's decision to discharge Lamoureux. The factors taken into consideration in reaching this decision were the employer's union animus, the fact that the discharge occurred shortly after an NLRB election, the fact that the employer departed from its usual practice of declining to discharge employees for the first violation of rules of this nature, and the employee had an admirable work record. As for the second part of the test, the Board found that the employer failed to demonstrate that it would have discharged the employee in the absence of his union activities. The discrepancies in the employee's work record were only discovered following a supervisor's directive to "check out the employee," even though the employer had no reason to believe that the employee was not trustworthy.

Wright Line clarifies rather than reformulates the traditional Board analysis in dual motivation cases. According to the Board, this case does not change the Board's traditional allocation of the burden of proof. Nor does it alter the standards by which the Board determines whether a litigant has carried its burden of proof. Rather, it sets forth more clearly the burden on each party, and it provides the Board with an analytical framework within which to discuss the extent to which the parties' respective burdens have been satisfied. It also eliminates the ambiguity that was once inherent in the Board's analytical process, giving both the courts and the parties a greater understanding of the processes that will eventually lead to a finding of whether or not a violation has occurred.

On the other hand, the *Wright Line* decision has brought about several significant changes from past practice. First, *Wright Line* purportedly rejects the "in part" test and substitutes a more precise analytical framework. The "in part" test was susceptible of loose application which created enforcement problems in the courts because, many times, the Board's inquiry went no further than determining that the employer's actions were motivated at least "in part" by an employee's protected activity. The new framework adopted by the Board will allow the Board to go one step further and determine whether, if the employer's action was in fact based in part on legitimate business reasons, the action would have been the same in the absence of protected activity. It is important to note that a mere showing that the employer would have come to the same conclusion is not sufficient. Rather, the employer must show that a decision would have been the same in the absence of protected activity.

In actual application the *Wright Line* test will be used in both pretext and dual motive cases. In both situations, the General Counsel must establish a prima facie case of discrimination. The employer will then present the affirmative defense, and the General Counsel may offer rebuttal. The Board will then look at all of the circumstances and make one of the following decisions: (a) there was no violation. Such a decision will occur if the General Counsel's prima facie case is rebutted by a showing that the employee's union involvement played no part in the employer's decision to dismiss the employee, or that the unprotected activities, by themselves, would have caused the employer's action; (b) there is a violation because the employer's reason for the action was not relied upon (*i.e.,* pretext case); or (c) there is a violation because the employer's reason for the action was relied upon in part, but the employer cannot show that reason alone would have caused his action (*i.e.,* dual motive case).

After the Board's decision in *Wright Line,* a number of courts of appeals accepted the *Wright Line* test and applied it in dual motivation cases. Adoption of this test has not been unanimous, however, as the following cases indicate.

In the first "dual motive" case to reach the Chicago appeals court after the Board's decision in *Wright Line,* the court said, "we have reviewed the decisions and have decided to follow the *Mt. Healthy/Wright Line* test in "dual motive" cases in this Circuit." (*Peavey Co. v. NLRB,* 648 F.2d 460, 461 (7th Cir. 1981).) In *Peavey,* the Board found that the employer violated section 8(a)(3) when it discharged an employee. The Administrative Law Judge found that the employee's discharge was motivated at least in substantial part by her protected activities. Affirming the Administrative Law Judge's conclusions of law, the Board labeled the employer's reason for the discharge a "pretext." The Board then found that the employee was discharged solely because of her concerted union activities. The employer claimed that legitimate business reasons justified the employee's discharge. On appeal, the court held that the employer met its burden under the *Wright Line* decision. The evidence showed that, although the employee in question was a good typist, she was a sloppy worker and had a history of disputes with her supervisors. The employer disciplined her in writing and advised her of a possible discharge unless her work record and attitude improved. The employee's discharge was ultimately prompted by her refusal to retype some poorly typed letters. The appellate court held that the employer's reasons for the discharge could not be labeled pretextual. The court agreed with the *Wright Line* holding that "a pretext can be found to exist when the purported rule or circumstances advanced by the employer did not exist, or was not, in fact, relied upon." (*Id.* at 462, quoting *Wright Line,* 251 N.L.R.B. at 1084.) Here, however, it was undisputed that the employee had been disciplined for cause prior to her contact with the union. Once the employer's reasons for the discharge are stripped of the label "pretext," it was clear that this employer met its burden under *Wright Line.* Even though the employee engaged in some protected activity, the employer showed that she would have been discharged even in the absence of the protected conduct.

136

The *Wright Line* test was again upheld by the Court of Appeals for the Seventh Circuit in three later decisions. (*NLRB v. Town & Country LP Gas Service Co.,* 111 LRRM 2196 (7th Cir. 1982); *Sioux Products, Inc. v. NLRB,* 111 LRRM 2077 (7th Cir. 1982); *NLRB v. Eldorado Mfg. Corp.,* 660 F.2d 1207 (7th Cir. 1981).) In *Town & Country,* the appellate court agreed with the Board's analysis of the evidence in accordance with the *Wright Line* decision, "which sets forth a bright line rule for resolving 'dual motive' discharge cases." (111 LRRM at 2198.) In *Sioux Products,* the appellate court noted that the burdens of proof assigned to the employer and the Board in this dual motive Section 8(a)(3) case, followed the *Peavey/Wright Line* standard. Under this standard, the Board, to establish a prima facie violation of Section 8(a)(3), must first show that the employee's protected activities were a motivating factor in the employer's discharge decision. The employer may rebut this prima facie showing with evidence indicating that the same action would have been taken in the absence of the employee's protected activities. The Board must then establish that the discharge was motivated by the employee's protected activities. The appellate court emphasized that even when using this analysis, a reviewing court is bound to a substantial evidence standard and may not reject, absent the most exceptional circumstances, properly supported findings of fact.

The San Francisco appeals court has held, "the rule articulated by the Board in *Wright Line* is a reasonably defensible interpretation of the Act, and is entitled to acceptance by the court." (*NLRB v. Nevis Industries, Inc.,* 647 F.2d 905, 909 (9th Cir. 1981) *citing Ford Motor Co. v. NLRB,* 441 U.S. 488, 497.) The *Wright Line* rule, it said, is consistent with the legislative history of the Act, which reveals an intent to require the employer to show that an employee was discharged for cause and with the reality that

137

the employer has the best access to proof of motivation. (*Nevis,* 647 F.2d 905.)

In *Nevis,* the Board found that the employer conditioned retention of one employee on his resignation from the local union. The employer contended that the findings were not supported by substantial evidence on the record as a whole. On appeal, the court adopted the *Wright Line* rule that the General Counsel has the initial burden of showing that protected conduct was "a motivating factor" in the decision to discharge an employee, and that the burden then shifts to the employer to show that it would have discharged the employee absent participation in protected activity. Here, the court found that the General Counsel carried its burden of showing that anti-union animus was a motivating factor in the decision not to retain the employee and that the employer failed to show that it would have acted as it did absent the protected conduct.

One year after the *Nevis* decision the Court of Appeals for the Ninth Circuit again accepted the Board's *Wright Line* test as a "reasonable interpretation of the Act consistent with its purposes." (*Zurn Industries v. NLRB,* 680 F.2d 683, 689 (9th Cir. 1982).) The court found support for its conclusion in the legislative history of the 1947 amendments to the Act, stating that, "this history, although not conclusive, places a sufficient gloss on Section 10(c) to sustain the Board's *Wright Line* rule." (*Id.* at 693.)

The Third Circuit Court of Appeals recently stated that the Board's *Wright Line* test which requires a determination that the employee would not have been discharged "but for" his protected activity substantively is correct, and "represents a substantial improvement over its prior practice and, except for its shifting burden of persuasion meets with our approval." (*Behring International, Inc. v. NLRB,* 675 F.2d 83, 90 (3d Cir. 1982).)

In *Behring,* the Philadelphia appellate court analyzed and elaborated on the *Wright Line* test. The court perceived that the *Wright Line* test has both substantive and procedural components. Substantively, it analyzed the connection between an employee's discharge and an employer's anti-union animus in terms of "but for" causation. The court condoned the Board's adoption of a "but for" test, stating that this test "satisfied this court's requirement that the Board seek the 'real motive' or 'real cause' for an employee's discharge." (*Id.* at 87.) The court, however, discerned that there are difficulties with the procedural aspect of the *Wright Line* rule. Once the General Counsel makes a prima facie showing sufficient to support the inference that protected conduct was a motivating factor in the employer's decision, the burden shifts onto the employer to demonstrate that the same action would have taken place even in the absence of the protected conduct. This shifting burden of persuasion undermines the "but for" test by relieving the General Counsel of his burden of proving that anti-union discrimination was the "real cause" of the employee's discharge. Instead, *Wright Line* only requires that the General Counsel show anti-union animus was "a" motivating factor in the employer's decision. If the employer then shows a legitimate reason for its action, but does not do so with enough weight to carry the burden of persuasion, the Board may rule that the Section 8(a)(3) violation has been proven, despite the fact that two factors have been advanced as causes, and the Board has never determined which was the real one. In this respect the Board failed to recognize that the General Counsel has the statutory burden to prove the unfair labor practice.

The Philadelphia court of appeals in *Behring* suggested its own formula. Once the General Counsel establishes a prima facie case of discriminatory discharge, the employer should rebut this evidence with a legitimate business reason for its action. The ultimate burden of proof does not shift from the General Counsel and does not go to the employer at any stage. Therefore, no violation may be found unless the Board determines that the General Counsel has proved by a preponderance of the evidence that the employer's anti-union animus was the real cause of the discharge.

The early cases in the Sixth Circuit Court of Appeals did not explicitly adopt *Wright Line,* but intimated that they might do so. (*Charge Card Ass'n v. NLRB,* 653 F.2d 272 (6th Cir. 1981); *NLRB v. Consolidated Freightways Corp. of Del.,* 651 F.2d 436 (6th Cir. 1981).) In *Charge Card,* the employees engaged in a protected walkout. Shortly thereafter, the employer placed several employees on probation and also suspended a number of other employees. Although not explicitly adopting *Wright Line,* the court of appeals held "under either the dominant motive test or the shifting burden as established in *Wright Line,* we conclude that there is not substantial evidence to support the conclusion that the reason for disciplining the employees was to punish them for engaging in a protected walk-out." (*Charge Card,* 653 F.2d at 275.)

Eventually, the Sixth Circuit Court explicitly adopted the *Wright Line* rule. In *NLRB v. Lloyd A. Fry Roofing Co. of Del.,* 651 F.2d 442 (6th Cir. 1981), the court explained the principles of the *Wright Line* test and applied those principles to the facts in the case, holding that the employee would not have been discharged but for his protected activity. In *Borel Restaurant Corp. v. NLRB,* 676 F.2d 190 (6th Cir. 1982), the court held where both a "good" reason, *i.e.,* violation of a company no-drinking rule, and a "bad" reason is alleged for an employee's discharge, the issue is resolved by applying the *Wright Line* test. An application of the *Wright Line* test to the factual situation in this case convinced the court that there was substantial evidence supporting the Board's decision finding a violation of Section 8(a)(3). The record clearly established that the employer failed to carry its burden of demonstrating that the discharge of the employee would have occurred in the absence of his union activity.

Initially, the Fifth Circuit Court of Appeals rejected the *Wright Line* test, reasoning that after the General Counsel has made out a prima facie case, only the burden of going forward is shifted to the employer, with the burden of ultimate persuasion remaining always with the General Counsel. (*TRW, Inc. v. NLRB,* 654 F.2d 307 (5th Cir. 1981).) Shortly thereafter, however, the Fifth Circuit Court accepted and applied the *Wright Line* test to cases coming before it, finding the test to be analytically sound. (*NLRB v. Robin American Corp.,* 654 F.2d 1022 (5th Cir. 1981); *NLRB v. Charles H. McCauley Associates, Inc.,* 657 F.2d 685 (5th Cir. 1981).)

In *McCauley,* an employee was discharged as a result of activity protected by the National Labor Relations Act. The employer alleged that the employee was discharged because of his tardiness record. The court held that the evidence supported a finding that Section 8(a)(1) and (3) was violated, reasoning that once the Board made out a prima facie case, the burden shifted to the employer to establish that the same action would have been taken in the absence of protected conduct.

In another case heard by the Fifth Circuit Court, the employer challenged the Board's *Wright Line* test in dual motive discharges as improperly requiring an employer to prove its innocence in derogation of the right of management to discharge employees for cause. The court rejected the employer's argument stating that another panel of this court had recently indicated no disapproval of the Board's use of the *Wright Line* test in determining whether, after a prima facie case of discharge for protected

141

activities has been established, the "good" cause assigned was indeed the real reason rather than a pretext for the discharge. The court further stated that there was substantial evidence in the present record to amply support the Administrative Law Judge's findings that the employee's growing propensity to engage in protected activity caught the attention of the employer's management, which was then motivated to engage in special surveillance of work performance and to seize upon her first alleged transgression as a pretext to terminate her. (*Red Ball Motor Freight, Inc. v. NLRB,* 660 F.2d 626 (5th Cir. 1981), *cert. denied,* 102 S. Ct. 2282 (1982).)

In the first case to reach the Second Circuit Court of Appeals after the Board's decision in *Wright Line,* the court stated "in reviewing the Board's findings we need not engage in the 'but for' analysis since the question before the Board was not the extent to which the company relied on valid grounds for its action, but whether the stated grounds were the real ones." (*NLRB v. Batchelder Co.,* 646 F.2d 33, 39 (2d Cir. 1981).) Even though *Wright Line* was referred to only in a passing way, it is important to note that the court was not dealing with a dual motive case here. Judge Newman, in his concurrence in *Batchelder,* stated that "when we say an employee has not sustained his burden under the 'but for' test, we mean that he has not proven that he would have acted the same way if only the valid ground had existed." (*Id.* at 42.) One year later a dual motive discharge case came before the Second Circuit Court which acknowledged the "but for" test to be the rule in that circuit. (*Consolidated Edison Co. of New York v. Donovan,* 673 F.2d 61 (2d Cir. 1982).)

The Court of Appeals for the Eighth Circuit has recently held that there is "a reasonable basis in law" for the Board's use of the *Wright Line* test, and that it may therefore be applied. (*NLRB v. Fixtures Mfg. Corp.,* 669 F.2d 547 (8th

Cir. 1982).) Any doubts as to whether the eighth circuit court would apply the *Wright Line* test in future dual motive cases were laid to rest in *NLRB v. Senftner Volkswagen Corp.*, 110 LRRM 3190 (8th Cir. 1982).

In *Senftner,* the union was certified as the bargaining unit at the company. The employee, then a mechanic in the service department and a member of the union's negotiating committee, was one of the signers of the agreement and thereafter served as assistant shop steward. His employer considered him an excellent mechanic and eventually offered him a service manager position. At that time the employer told the employee if he was not successful at the job or did not like it, he could return to the shop as a mechanic. The employee accepted the promotion, but within two months asked for his old job back. The employer promised the employee that a replacement would be found for him, but the replacement never was found. In the meantime the employee's job performance steadily deteriorated until he was eventually discharged. The principal question here was whether the employer was motivated by anti-union animus. The record indicated that the employee was quite active in the union before his promotion to service manager. It was also established that the employer asked the employee whether he would rejoin the union if he went back to the shop. The court held that this evidence was a prima facie showing sufficient to support the inference that the employee's union activity was a motivating factor in the employer's refusal to rehire him. Thus, under the *Wright Line* test, the company had the burden of demonstrating that it would not have rehired the employee if he had not participated in protected activity. The court found that the company failed to carry its burden here.

Although some of the courts of appeals were initially hesitant about accepting the *Wright Line* test, it now appears that the test has been adopted by eight of those courts, with the Fourth Circuit being the lone rejecter of the test. It is safe to assume that the *Wright Line* test will continue to be applied in future dual motive cases, unless, of course, the Board is able to formulate a more workable test for cases arising in this area. In any event, the United States Supreme Court has approved the Board's use of the *Wright Line* test in *NLRB v. Transportation Management Corp.,* 103 S. Ct. 2469 (1983).

§ 3-3(B). Strikers' Rights.

A striking employee's right to reinstatement, or conversely, an employer's right to replace the striker with a replacement employee is determined by whether the work stoppage engaged in was an economic strike or an unfair labor practice strike. (*NLRB v. Thayer Co.,* 213 F.2d 748, 752-53 (1st Cir.), *cert. denied,* 348 U.S. 883 (1954).) An economic strike is a work stoppage by employees to demonstrate either their support for the bargaining demands relating to wages and working conditions, or requests for union recognition by the employer. (R. Doherty & G. DeMarchi, *Industrial and Labor Relations Terms: A Glossary for Students and Teachers* 30 (3d ed. 1974). *See NLRB v. Herman Wilson Lumber Co.,* 355 F.2d 426, 430 (8th Cir. 1966).) This strike is neither prohibited by law nor by collective bargaining agreement nor caused by an employer's unfair labor practices. (*NLRB v. Transport Co. of Texas,* 438 F.2d 258, 262, n. 6 (5th Cir. 1971).) An unfair labor practice strike, however, is an employee work stoppage provoked not by economic concerns, but by the employer's unfair labor practices. (*NLRB v. Transport Co. of Texas, supra* at 262, n. 2; R. Gorman, *Basic Text on Labor Law, Unionization and Collective Bargaining* 339 (1976).)

Many strikes, however, contain a mixture of unfair labor practices and economic factors. A strike may be caused by both a bargaining impasse and the employer's unfair labor practice. A strike is termed an unfair labor practice strike unless the employer can demonstrate that the strike would have occurred absent any unfair labor practice. (*United Steelworkers of America, AFL-CIO v. NLRB*, 405 F.2d 1373, 1377 (D.C. Cir. 1968); *General Drivers & Helpers Union, Local 662 v. NLRB*, 302 F.2d 908, 911 (D.C. Cir.), *cert. denied*, 371 U.S. 827 (1962); *NLRB v. Wooster Div. of Borg Warner Corp.*, 236 F.2d 898, 907 (6th Cir. 1956), *modified on other grounds*, 356 U.S. 342 (1958).) The more common problem is not the mixture of factors, but the conversion of an economic strike to an unfair labor practice strike. This conversion occurs when an employer commits an unfair labor practice after the strike was initiated which has the effect of prolonging the strike. In *NLRB v. Crosby Chemicals*, 188 F.2d 91, 95 (5th Cir. 1951), the court stated the general rule that where a strike is initially undertaken for economic consideration but is prolonged by the employer's intervening unfair labor practices, "the employer is in the same position he would have been in had his unfair labor practice caused the strike in the first place." (*See, e.g., Local 833, UAW v. NLRB Kohler Case*), 300 F.2d 699 (D.C. Cir.), *cert. denied*, 370 U.S. 911 (1962), where a disagreement over contract terms initially caused the strike, but was prolonged by the employer's refusal to bargain. The strike converted from an economic nature to that of an unfair labor practice. *But see, e.g., Warehousemen & Mail Order Employees, Local No. 743 v. NLRB*, 302 F.2d 865 (D.C. Cir. 1962), where the employer did not convert an economic strike to an unfair labor practice strike. The employer advanced its own proposals when the union insisted that wage increases and cost of living clauses were still prime factors. The employer's discharge and refusal to reinstate employees did not convert the economic strike since its actions were not violative of the Act. *See generally*

Stewart, *Conversion of Strikes: Economic to Unfair Labor Practice: I & II,* 45 Va. L. Rev. 1322 (1959) and 49 Va. L. Rev. 1297 (1963) (initial article on strike conversion with update in light of important recent decisions).

As will be discussed, a striking employee has an absolute right to reinstatement when an unfair labor practice strike is terminated, but only a qualified right to reinstatement at the end of an economic strike. The employee may lose these rights, however, if he engages in strike violence and misconduct. The level of misconduct is necessarily more than "minimal," but how much more has caused courts much confusion.

§ 3-3(B)(1). Economic Strikers' Rights.

Economic strikers' rights to reinstatement of their jobs have developed over a thirty-year period. Initially, the employer's economic situation had controlling emphasis. An employer was permitted to hire permanent replacements during an economic strike and refuse to rehire the strikers. A permanent replacement, as opposed to a temporary, is hired to replace the economic striker permanently, notwithstanding the termination of the strike. A temporary replacement, however, forfeits his position to the economic striker once that striker unconditionally reapplies for his position. (*Compare NLRB v. Wells Fargo Armored Service Corp. of Puerto Rico,* 597 F.2d 7 (1st Cir. 1979) (employer can hire permanent replacements for economic strikers and is under no duty to discharge them and rehire strikers at end of strike), *with NLRB v. Mars Sales & Equipment Co.,* 626 F.2d 567 (7th Cir. 1980) (if employer hires replacements without a commitment or understanding that job is permanent and also discharges economic strikers, striker is entitled to displace the temporary replacement at the end of the strike).)

146

The leading Supreme Court case in this area of economic strikers and their replacements is *NLRB v. Mackay Radio & Telegraph Co.,* 304 U.S. 333 (1938). In *Mackay,* the company employed about 60 supervisors, operators and clerks, many of whom were members of a Local of the American Radio Telegraphists Association, a national union. After fruitless negotiations between the national union and Mackay's parent company, the national union called a "general strike" in which the Local participated. Mackay brought in employees from other offices to fill the strikers' places and continue business. The strike was unsuccessful, and Mackay told the strikers that they could return in a body, except for 11 men who would have to file applications for reinstatement. Only 5 replacements wished to remain, and 6 of the 11 special strikers were allowed to return to work. The Supreme Court found discrimination in the denial of reinstatement of the 5 special strikers, all prominent in union activities. The Court did, however, define the employer's replacement rights in an economic strike situation. The employer may protect and continue his business by filling places left vacant by strikers. He is not bound to fire these replacements to create places for the returning strikers if the employer has assured these replacements that their positions were "permanent." (*Id.* at 345-46.)

Strikers rights were further limited when the Court of Appeals for the Seventh Circuit recognized the employer's legitimate hiring needs. In *Chauffeurs "General" Local No. 200 v. NLRB,* 233 F.2d 233, 238 (7th Cir. 1956), the court held that where an economic striker's job had been abolished or absorbed by other employees for economic reasons when the striker applied for reinstatement, the employer's duty did not require that the employer seek out the applicant striker when a vacancy occurred three days later. The employer is merely required to refrain from discriminating

147

against the striker for his union activities if he made a request to fill a vacancy in the future. (*Id. See also Capitol-Husting Co. v. NLRB,* 671 F.2d 237, 247 (7th Cir. 1982) (economic strikers' reinstatement rights limited to employer's legitimate staffing requirements); *Atlas Metal Parts Co. v. NLRB,* 660 F.2d 304, 310 (7th Cir. 1981).)

More recently, emphasis has shifted from the employer's economic situation to that of the economic striker. In 1965, the Supreme Court in dictum stated that an employer's refusal to re-employ strikers may not be based upon anti-union animus. (*NLRB v. Brown,* 380 U.S. 278, 287-88 (1965).) Two years later, the Supreme Court held that an employer must rehire strikers as their jobs become available. (*NLRB v. Fleetwood Trailer Co.,* 389 U.S. 375 (1967).) In *Fleetwood,* the employer refused reinstatement of strikers because of a production cutback. Two months later, the employer increased production to prestrike levels but hired new replacements, even though the strikers had made known their continuing desire for reinstatement. The Supreme Court reasoned that a "striker" remains an "employee" under Section 2(3) of the Act until he has secured regular and substantially equivalent employment. Failure to reinstate these economic strikers was considered an unfair labor practice. (*Id.* at 378.) The employer need not rehire the strikers, however, if he can provide a showing of legitimate and substantial business justification, such as permanent replacement of all strikers or abolition or absorption of their jobs. (*Id.* at 380-81.)

The NLRB soon applied this rule enunciated in *Fleetwood* in *Laidlaw Corp. v. NLRB,* 171 N.L.R.B. 1366, 1369-70 (1968), *enforced,* 414 F.2d 99 (7th Cir. 1969), *cert. denied,* 397 U.S. 920 (1970). The employer in *Laidlaw* (1) threatened to deny employment forever to its employees if they struck and were replaced; (2) maintained an invalid no-distribution rule; (3) failed and refused to offer a replaced striker full reinstatement to his former job; (4) terminated employment status of many other replaced strikers following their unconditional offer to return to work; and (5) later failed and refused to offer those employees reinstatement. The Board found these to be unfair labor practices. It ruled that economic strikers who unconditionally apply for reinstatement when their positions are filled by permanent replacements remain employees for purposes of the Act and are entitled to reinstatement once vacancies occur unless the strikers have found regular and substantially equivalent employment, or failure to reinstate was for legitimate and substantial business reasons.

Thus, a consistent general rule for economic strikers' rights and their replacements has been established. Economic strikers who are not replaced or replaced temporarily are entitled to their previous positions upon an unconditional application for reinstatement, absent an employer's legitimate business reason for refusal. Permanently replaced economic strikers may make an unconditional application for reinstatement and are entitled to their previous positions upon departure of the permanent replacements unless they have found substantially equivalent employment elsewhere or the employer has legitimate business reasons for denying reinstatement.

§ 3-3(B)(2). Unfair Labor Practice Strikers' Rights.

In stark contrast, an unfair labor practice striker's right to reinstatement is absolute. (*Mastro Plastics Corp. v. NLRB*, 350 U.S. 270 (1956).) In *Mastro Plastics*, the employees struck even though a no-strike clause was contained in their contract. The strike was clearly precipitated by the employer's unfair labor practice. The Supreme Court rejected the employer's argument that the words "any

149

strike" necessarily includes all strikes. For economic issues and a relatively few less serious unfair labor practices, the employer's no-strike clause is binding. For serious unfair labor practices, however, the employee's right to strike is absolute. (*Id.* at 284.) When the unfair labor practice is sufficiently serious to undermine the basic collective bargaining process, and thus, infringe upon the employee's Section 7 rights, the employer commits an unfair labor practice, violating Section 8(a)(1) and (3), regardless of any contractual clauses.

If the strike is characterized as an unfair labor practice strike, the employees have an unconditional right to be reinstated if the unfair labor practice precipitated the strike to any degree, even if the practice was only one of multiple causes of the strike. (*NLRB v. Crystal Springs Shirt Corp.,* 637 F.2d 399, 404 (5th Cir. 1981).) These unfair labor practice strikers are entitled to immediate reinstatement upon their unconditional demand for reinstatement, even if this requires dismissal of replacements who have been hired to fill their jobs during the strike. (*George Banta Co. v. NLRB,* 604 F.2d 830 (4th Cir. 1979), *cert. denied,* 445 U.S. 927 (1980).) If the unfair labor practice striker's job is no longer in existence, he is still entitled to immediate reinstatement in a substantially equivalent position. (*NLRB v. Lyon & Ryan Ford, Inc.,* 647 F.2d 745, 754 (7th Cir.), *cert. denied,* 454 U.S. 894 (1981).) Displaced strike replacements may have civil causes of action for breach of contract and/or misrepresentation against an employer who has promised those replacement workers permanent employment. (*See Belknap, Inc. v. Hale,* 103 S. Ct. 3172 (1983).)

Thus, unfair labor practice strikers possess more expansive reinstatement rights than economic strikers. (*See generally* Note, *Replacement of Workers During Strikes,* 75 Yale L.J. 630 (1966).) The rights under both these categories, however, contain a proviso. Section 10(c) of the Act prohibits the NLRB from ordering the rein-statement of any employee discharged "for cause." (29 U.S.C. § 160(c) (1976).) There is no dispute that "cause" includes serious or violent striker misconduct, but how serious or violent is as yet unsettled.

§ 3-3(B)(3). Employee Misconduct During Strikes.

The reinstatement rights of a striker who has engaged in misconduct differ depending on the type of striker. Some misconduct remains protected concerted activity, and denial of reinstatement to either the economic or the unfair labor practice striker infringes on his Section 7 rights and would thus violate Section 8(a)(1) of the Act. If the miscon-duct is not protected concerted activity, the employer is free to deny the economic striker reinstatement because of that misconduct. For an unfair labor practice striker, however, the Board has the power to reinstate that striker even though his misconduct was not protected under his Section 7 rights. (*See Erickson, Forfeiture of Reinstatement Rights Through Strike Misconduct,* 31 Lab. L.J. 602, 603 (1980).) For these reasons, the misconduct of the economic versus the unfair labor practice striker must be discussed sepa-rately.

§ 3-3(B)(4). Economic Striker Misconduct.

For economic strikers, strike misconduct outside Section 7's protective scope constitutes sufficient cause for an employer to refuse reinstatement. In *Firestone Tire & Rubber Co. v. NLRB,* 449 F.2d 511 (5th Cir. 1971), the court agreed with a trial examiner's finding that an employee shouting obscenities and using vulgar hand signs during an economic strike intended a threat of physical harm suffi-ciently serious to warrant the employee's termination. The court also enumerated other acts of serious misconduct in refusing to enforce the reinstatement of that employee. In

151

W.J. Ruscoe Co. v. NLRB, 406 F.2d 725 (6th Cir. 1969), the court said that strikers may attempt to persuade nonstrikers to join their protest, but that throwing gravel and debris, and rocking and pushing an automobile so as to impede the ingress or egress from the plant, exceeded the reasonable limits of protected picket activity.

Both the *Firestone* and the *Ruscoe* cases indicate that the economic striker must confine his actions to reasonable limits to remain under protected strike activity. The appellate courts use the test of "substantial evidence in support of the NLRB's decision" to determine whether the employee is guilty of misconduct of sufficient gravity to justify the company's refusal to reinstate. (*Firestone,* 449 F.2d at 513; *Ruscoe,* 406 F.2d at 727. *See Universal Camera Corp. v. NLRB,* 340 U.S. 474 (1951), where the Supreme Court set the standard of whether there is substantial evidence as a whole to support the NLRB's findings.)

This standard must logically be applied to the specific facts of each case. The facts above amply demonstrate the strict limits placed on the economic striker for his unprotected actions. Thus, the issue is straightforward. If the conduct upon which the denial of reinstatement is premised is concerted activity under Section 7, then the striker is entitled to reinstatement. If the activity is outside the protected scope of Section 7, then the courts will easily find the misconduct of "sufficient gravity," and in most cases, support the employer's refusal to reinstate.

§ 3-3(B)(5). Unfair Labor Practice Striker Misconduct.

For an unfair labor practice striker whose activity causing dismissal is unprotected, the employer's denial of reinstatement must meet a two-prong test to be valid. Not only (1) must the strike conduct be the cause for discharge (as with an economic striker), but (2) under the circumstances of the strike, reinstatement would not further the policies of the Act. (*Mosher Steel Co. v. NLRB*, 568 F.2d 436, 441 (5th Cir. 1978).) This second factor, a balancing approach, has evolved as a limitation to the general rule.

The general rule, enunciated in *NLRB v. Fansteel Metallurgical Corp.*, 306 U.S. 240 (1939), indicated that any act of employee misconduct during a strike was a *per se* bar to reinstatment. In *Fansteel,* the strikers participated in a violent sit-down strike and were discharged. The employer subsequently offered to rehire some of them, but without union recognition. The Supreme Court, refusing enforcement of the Board's order for reinstatement, held that the "illegal" violence of the strikers provided an "independent and adequate basis" for discharge. (*Id.* at 255.) Implicit in this holding is the concept that if one adequate basis for discharge exists, all other inadequate bases become irrelevant since the striker no longer enjoys Section 7 protected status. (*See generally* Hart & Prichard, *The Fansteel Case: Employee Misconduct and the Remedial Powers of the National Labor Relations Board,* 52 Harv. L. Rev. 1275 (1939) (a strong and extensive criticism of the eloquent but broad, sweeping language of *Fansteel,* with suggestions for a more liberal handling of such situations).)

In spite of the generalized language in *Fansteel,* subsequent courts have seen the possibility of abuse in permitting employers to discharge strikers for minor incidents. By permitting reinstatement in cases of minor picket-line violence, while refusing reinstatement in serious incidents, these courts recognize that picket-lines and prolonged strikes are often highly emotionally-charged situations. In *Republic Steel Corp. v. NLRB,* 107 F.2d 472 (3d Cir. 1939), *modified on other grounds,* 311 U.S. 7 (1940), the court recognized that unlawful conduct of a serious nature, such as a sit-down strike which deprived the

153

employer of his plant, was sufficiently serious to deny reinstatement. The court, however, elaborated:

> We think it must be conceded, however, that some
> disorder is unfortunately quite usual in any extensive
> or long drawn out strike. A strike is essentially a battle
> waged with economic weapons. Engaged in it are
> human beings whose feelings are stirred to the depths.
> Rising passions call forth hot words. Hot words lead to
> blows on the picket line. The transformation from eco-
> nomic to physical combat by those engaged in the
> contest is difficult to prevent even when cool heads
> direct the fight. Violence of this nature, however much
> it is to be regretted, must have been in the contempla-
> tion of the Congress when it provided in [the Act] that
> nothing therein should be construed so as to interfere
> with or impede or diminish in any way the right to
> strike. If this were not so the rights afforded to
> employees by the Act would be indeed illusory. (*Id.* at
> 479.)

Thus, minor disorders are usually categorized as protected
activity, removing them from the scope of *Fansteel.*

Evaluating *Fansteel* and *Republic Steel,* one would
expect that a comprehensive definition of the phrase "for
cause" in Section 10(c) could be formulated. However, the
facts of each strike situation inevitably differ in some
important aspect. Two cases have made extensive attempts
to evaluate the meaning of the *Republic Steel* limitation.
They have given greater deference to protecting the
strikers' rights to engage in collective activity. Thus, the
employer's right of redress against violent strikers has been
limited.

In the first case, *NLRB v. Thayer Co.,* 213 F.2d 748 (1st
Cir.), *cert. denied,* 348 U.S. 883 (1954), the court looked to
specific incidents of individual employees to determine
whether their conduct barred reinstatement even though
the strike was clearly called because of the employer's
unfair labor practice. The *Thayer* court said that the NLRB
must weigh both the seriousness of the employer's unfair

labor practice and the gravity of the employee's misconduct in determining whether reinstatement would be consistent with the policies of the Act. This balancing approach has come to be known as the *Thayer* doctrine.

In the second case, *Local 833, UAW v. NLRB (Kohler Co.)*, 300 F.2d 699 (D.C. Cir.), *cert. denied*, 370 U.S. 911 (1962), the District of Columbia Court of Appeals gave new emphasis to the *Thayer* doctrine. The Board denied reinstatement to ninety strikers specifically discharged for misconduct, although some had not participated to any greater degree than 1700 other strikers in the frequent violent acts that scarred this long and bitter strike. The Board found that their presence during mass picketing contributed to the coercive effect and was no less serious than active violence. Relying on *Thayer*, the *Kohler* court remonstrated that the operative test for determining the validity of a strike discharge is balancing the employer's unfair labor practices against the strikers' misconduct.

Using this balancing approach, the employer has been allowed to refuse reinstatement where the employee caused property damage. (*See, e.g., NLRB v. Otsego Ski Club—Hidden Valley, Inc.*, 542 F.2d 18 (6th Cir. 1976) (employees spread nails in primary roadway of company and acted as lookouts while fellow picketers spread nails); *NLRB v. Juniata Packing Co.*, 464 F.2d 153 (3d Cir. 1972) (contemplated breaking of window, even though other picketers attempted to dissuade); *NLRB v. Hartmann Luggage Co.*, 453 F.2d 178 (6th Cir. 1971) (employee's act of damaging departing automobile during strike could easily have led to more serious consequences than mere flat tire); *NLRB v. Mt. Clemens Pottery Co.*, 147 F.2d 262 (6th Cir. 1945) (employee who was convicted in local court for malicious destruction of property by overturning a car of a non-striker denied reinstatement); *Standard Lime & Stone Co. v. NLRB*, 97 F.2d 531 (4th Cir. 1938) (conspiracy to

155

dynamite and dynamiting power lines leading to the plant sufficient to refuse reinstatement).) The Court of Appeals for the Fifth Circuit even allowed an employer to refuse to reinstate a striker whose acts could have precipitated future violent and dangerous consequences. (*Seminole Asphalt Refining, Inc. v. NLRB,* 497 F.2d 247 (5th Cir. 1974) (two employees tossed cherry bombs near employer's flammable petroleum storage tanks).)

The employer has also been allowed to refuse reinstatement where the strikers engaged in serious physical violence. (*See, e.g., Mosher Steel Co. v. NLRB,* 568 F.2d 436 (5th Cir. 1978) (threat uttered at picket line coupled with actual violent occurrence); *NLRB v. W.C. McQuaide, Inc.,* 552 F.2d 519 (3d Cir. 1977), *enforced after remand,* 617 F.2d 349 (3d Cir. 1980) (striker followed nonstriker to delivery area and said he would "get him," shook his fist at another worker, and shouted to cabdriver — "scab" — while partially blocking his egress were not merely spontaneous threats of picket line activity but threats which reasonably tended to coerce); *Oneita Knitting Mills, Inc. v. NLRB,* 375 F.2d 385, 392-93 (4th Cir. 1967) (employees physically prevented non-striking employee from crossing picket lines, evidenced in part by non-striker's blouse being torn from her shoulders); *Standard Lime & Stone Co. v. NLRB,* 97 F.2d 531 (4th Cir. 1938) (strikers' violently assaulting workers).) Serious threats of violence, if ambiguous, may not be sufficient to refuse reinstatement. (*See NLRB v. Moore Business Forms, Inc.,* 574 F.2d 835 (5th Cir. 1978) (striker's query to nonstriker's wife and children asking if they were safe, and then told the nonstriker "I thought you had more sense than that" was too ambiguous to constitute a serious threat).) Furthermore, if the violent conduct by the striker against a nonstriking employee was not strike related, the employer may not refuse reinstatement. (*See Mosher Steel,* 568 F.2d 436 (striker's violence against nonstriker was not strike related and some evidence of self-defense existed).)

Not all violent actions by an employee, however, will preclude reinstatement. A distinction is drawn between situations where the employee engaged in spontaneous unlawful conduct to a minor degree, and where the employee participated in flagrant violent misconduct. Mere trivial rough incidents or moments of "animal exuberance" are far different from misconduct of such a violent and serious nature which renders the striker unfit for further service. (*Milk Wagon Drivers Local 753 v. Meadowmoor Dairies, Inc.*, 312 U.S. 287, 293 (1941); *Advance Industries Division—Overhead Door Corp. v. NLRB*, 540 F.2d 878, 882 (7th Cir. 1976); *Allied Industrial Workers, Local 289 v. NLRB*, 476 F.2d 868, 879 (D.C. Cir. 1973).)

Some physical acts of threat or abuse do not rise to the level of serious or egregious misconduct. (*See, e.g., NLRB v. W.C. McQuaide, Inc.*, 552 F.2d 519 (abusive language at nonstrikers of ambiguous nature); *NLRB v. Hartmann Luggage Co.*, 453 F.2d 178 (under the circumstances, striker's threats were hardly to be believed, regarded more as picket line rhetoric).) Some damage to property has also been adjudged to be minor, innocent acts of strike exuberance. (*See, e.g., Advance Industries Division — Overhead Door Corp.*, 540 F.2d 878 (one of two strikers threw rocks at supervisor and employee's car, company could not prove who threw the rocks); *NLRB v. Wallick*, 198 F.2d 477, 480 (3d Cir. 1952) (strikers outside plant taunted workers inside by placing planks to block doorways, breaking one or two windows, and shouting threats of violence).) Thus, minor acts of violence caused by the "heat of the strike" will not be sufficient grounds for an employer to deny the striker reinstatement. However, the Board has recently held that an employer may lawfully refuse reinstatement to strikers whose threats and misconduct reasonably tended to coerce

157

or intimidate nonstrikers. (*Clear Pine Mouldings,* 268 N.L.R.B. No. 173 (1984).)

§ 3-4. Conclusion.

As discussed, strikers are still employees for purposes of the Act. They still command Section 7 rights for their concerted protected activity. Strikers may lose these rights, however, by acts of serious and egregious misconduct. Several important factors must be determined. First, is the strike of economic or unfair labor practice status? Second, how egregious is the misconduct which caused the employer to deny reinstatement after termination? Last, if it is an unfair labor practice strike, do the employer's business interests supersede the employee's protected rights? Although every situation differs factually, resolution of these questions will enable the Board and the courts to properly decide the issue of striker reinstatement.

CHAPTER 4

BARGAINING ORDERS IN LIEU OF SELECTION BY ELECTION

After the Taft-Hartley amendments in 1947, which made elections the only codified method for certification, the use of authorization card checks to determine majority support declined sharply. Employers, however, were allowed to recognize and bargain with a union claiming to possess authorization cards from a majority of employees. This decision was not without risk. In *International Ladies' Garment Workers' Union v. NLRB,* 122 N.L.R.B 1289, 1292, *aff'd,* 366 U.S. 731 (1961), an employer violated Section 8(a)(2) and Section 8(b)(1)(A) of the Act by recognizing a union claiming majority support when the union did not have that support. Further, the employer's good faith belief that the union represented a majority in the unit was not a defense, especially where no attempt was made to verify the claim by checking cards against payroll records. (*Id.*) The Board found, and the Supreme Court affirmed, that the union's execution of the collective bargaining agreement was a direct deprivation of the nonconsenting employees' organizational and bargaining Section 7 rights and ordered the employer to withhold all recognition from the union. (366 U.S. at 737. *But see NLRB v. Majestic Weaving Co.,* 355 F.2d 854 (2d Cir. 1966).)

In exceptional circumstances, however, the employer's duty to bargain may arise absent the employer's reliance on authorization cards or a Board-certified election. In cases in which no less effective remedy is available, the Board can issue an order to bargain though the union has not demonstrated elective majority support and despite the lack of statutory mandate. The card check has continued to hold its prominence in unfair labor practice proceedings where it is found that a fair election is unlikely. It is a well established policy of the Board to rely on a card-supported union majority in issuing an order to bargain without an election. Thus, an employer may be required to engage in collective bargaining with a "representative" who does not have the elective support of a majority of employees.

Prior to 1971, an employer who in good faith doubted the union's claim of a card majority could refuse to bargain pending a Board-conducted election. (*NLRB v. Joy Silk Mills, Inc.,* 85 N.L.R.B. 1263 (1949).) The employer's refusal to bargain, however, had to be based in fact upon this good faith doubt, and not on a desire to buy time in which to undermine the union's majority status prior to an election. (*See Aaron Bros.,* 158 N.L.R.B. 1077 (1966); *Converters Graveire Serv., Inc.,* 164 N.L.R.B. 379 (1967); *Terrel Mach. Co.,* 173 N.L.R.B. 1408 (1969); *Orion Corp.,* 210 N.L.R.B. 633, *enforced,* 515 F.2d 81 (7th Cir. 1975). *But see* Welles, *The Obligation to Bargain on the Basis of a Card Majority,* 3 Ga. L. Rev. 349 (1969).) If the Board found that the employer engaged in unfair labor practices, *i.e.,* refused in bad faith to bargain and subsequently undermined the union's majority support prior to the election, it would rely on the only proof of actual employee choice: the authorization cards. The Board would issue a bargaining order despite the union's failure to win majority support in the election. (*See Bryant Chucking Grinder Co.,* 160 N.L.R.B. 1526 (1966).)

Determining the employer's state of mind when refusing to bargain was difficult, and the Board altered its position in 1971 in *Linden Lumber Div., Summer & Co.,* 190 N.L.R.B. 718 (1971). Regardless of his reasons, an employer could refuse to bargain when confronted with a card majority, provided he committed no unfair labor practices prior to an election. (*Id.*) The Board's new position was affirmed by the United States Supreme Court. (*Linden Lumber Div., Summer & Co. v. NLRB,* 419 U.S. 301 (1974).) The Court agreed with the Board that employers did not violate Section 8(a)(5) solely by refusing to accept anything short of an election as evidence of majority status. The court further agreed that an employer is under no duty to file a petition for an election. In contrast, the Court expressly stated that the union bears this burden. (*Id.* at 310. *But see Snow & Sons,* 134 N.L.R.B. 709, *enforced,* 308 F.2d 687 (9th Cir. 1962) (employer violates § 8(a)(5) by rejecting card majority after express agreement to abide by a showing of majority status by a means other than election).) And while recognizing that the union has the alternative of pressing unfair labor practice charges, the Court stated that a policy of encouraging secret ballot elections is most favored under the Act. (419 U.S. at 310.)

The most significant case in the area of remedial bargaining orders is *NLRB v. Gissel Packing Co.,* 395 U.S. 575 (1969), a consolidation of four appeals: *NLRB v. Gissel Packing Co.,* 398 F.2d 336 (4th Cir. 1968); *NLRB v. Heck's, Inc.,* 398 F.2d 366 (4th Cir. 1968); *General Steel Products, Inc. v. NLRB,* 398 F.2d 339 (4th Cir. 1968); and *NLRB v. Sinclair Co.,* 397 F.2d 157 (1st Cir. 1968). In *Gissel, Heck's* and *General Steel,* the Board found that the employers had engaged in restraint and coercion of employees in violation of Section 8(a)(1). In addition, the employers in *Gissel* and *Heck's* had wrongfully discharged employees for engaging in union activities, in violation of Section 8(a)(3). Because all three had rejected the card-based majority in bad faith, the Board found all three in violation of Section 8(a)(5). (395 U.S. at 584. Because these cases preceded *Linden Lumber,* employer's state of mind was an issue.) In all three cases, the Fourth Circuit found that authorization cards were so inherently unreliable that their use afforded an employer a presumption of good faith, and the court, therefore, refused to enforce the Board's collective bargaining orders. Though the court did sustain the Board's finding of Section 8(a)(1)

161

and (3) violations, it held that the Board's only available remedy was to conduct a secret ballot election. (*NLRB v. Gissel Packing Co.*, 398 F.2d 336 (4th Cir. 1968); *NLRB v. Heck's*, 398 F.2d 337 (4th Cir. 1968); *General Steel Prod., Inc. v. NLRB*, 398 F.2d 339 (4th Cir. 1968).) The facts in *Sinclair* were essentially the same: the union's card majority was rejected by the employer. The First Circuit, however, upheld the Board's finding of unfair labor practices in actions other than the refusal to bargain and affirmed the Board's bargaining order. (*NLRB v. Sinclair Co.*, 397 F.2d 157 (1st Cir. 1968).)

The Supreme Court, in considering these four cases, specifically approved the use of a bargaining order where the employer's practices have a tendency to undermine majority strength and held that, despite the superiority of the election process, cards may surpass that reliability when the unfair labor practices make the holding of a fair election impossible. (*NLRB v. Gissel Packing Co.*, 395 U.S. 575, 601-10 (1969).) Most importantly, the Court defined three categories of employer misconduct to be used in determining whether a bargaining order was justified. The first category represents those cases marked by "outrageous and pervasive" employer unfair labor practices, in which a bargaining order may be imposed "*without need of inquiry into majority status* on the basis of cards or otherwise." (*Id.* at 613.) The second category includes those cases where the unfair labor practices were "less pervasive" but would nonetheless impede the election process. (*Id.* at 614.) The cases before the Court in *Gissel* were of this type. The third category represents those minor unfair labor practices which do not render a fair election impossible, but may warrant setting aside the election without issuing a bargaining order. (*Id.* at 615.) In such cases, the Board will conduct a "re-run" election when conditions have stabilized. (*But see* Pollett, *NLRB Re-Run Elections: A Study*, 41

N.C.L. Rev. 109 (1963); Getman & Goldberg, *The Myth of Labor Law Expertise,* 39 U. Chi. L. Rev. 681, 691-94 (1972).)

In cases where the union possesses a card majority but either loses the subsequent election due to employer unfair labor practices or foregoes the election process by filing refusal to bargain charges, the Board is faced with determining the nature of the employer unfair labor practices. Such determination will dictate, under *Gissel,* whether a category II bargaining order or a category III re-run election is warranted. The subjectivity involved in classifying employer conduct has given rise to some unpredictability and much criticism. (*See* Discretionary Justice, A Preliminary Inquiry 59-60 (1969); 1 Davis, Administrative Law Treatise § 6.13 at 142-50 (Supp. 1965); Pesk, *The Atrophied Rule — Making Powers of the National Labor Relations Board,* 70 Yale L.J. 729 (1961).) Recognizing this problem, the second circuit in *NLRB v. General Stencils, Inc.,* 438 F.2d 894 (2d Cir. 1971), vacated the Board's issuance of a bargaining order. Confused over the Board's failure to issue bargaining orders in seemingly factually similar cases, the court remanded for a clarification of the grounds underlying the order. While recognizing the deference to be given the Board determination of the appropriate remedy in a given situation, the court stated that "the [Board] . . . has a correlative duty to explain its imposition of a remedy . . . on a basis reviewing courts can understand." (*Id.* at 904. *See also Phelps Dodge Corp. v. NLRB,* 313 U.S. 177, 197 (1941); *NLRB v. Jamaica Towing, Inc.,* 602 F.2d 1100, 1103-05 (2d Cir. 1979); *NLRB v. Armcor Indus., Inc.,* 535 F.2d 239, 245 (3d Cir. 1976); *NLRB v. Madison Courier, Inc.,* 472 F.2d 1307, 1323-26 (D.C. Cir. 1972).)

Though the available remedial action, a bargaining order, is the same whether the Board places the unfair labor practices into the first or second category, the major difference is the degree of inquiry into union employer support. The Court in *Gissel* specifically authorized the Board, in category I cases, to issue a bargaining order without consideration of card majority status. However, because the employer practices in *Gissel* were not of this type, this suggestion was pure dictum and, for twelve years subsequent to *Gissel,* the courts treated it as such. In *Loray Corp.,* 184 N.L.R.B. 557 (1970), the Board refused to issue a bargaining order although the unfair labor practices were found to be of a "pervasive" nature. The union had not attained a card majority, and the Board, while alluding to its authority under *Gissel,* instead issued a remedy similar to that in the earlier case of *H.W. Elson Bottling Co.,* 155 N.L.R.B. 714 (1965). The employer was ordered to provide facilities for a union meeting, to give the union access to bulletin boards, and to eventually host a re-run election. This type of remedial authority attempts to re-establish the *status quo ante. (See Seeler v. Trading Port, Inc.,* 517 F.2d 33, 38-39 (2d Cir. 1975); *GPD, Inc. v. NLRB,* 430 F.2d 963, 964 (6th Cir. 1970).)* In *Bandag, Inc.,* 225 N.L.R.B. 72 (1976), the Board similarly refused to issue a bargaining order, holding that, as outrageous as the unfair labor practices were, they were not those anticipated by the court in *Gissel. (Id.* at 73, n. 7, Murphy Chairman, concurring.)

Finally, in 1981, the Board took the step mandated by *Gissel* and issued a bargaining order in *United Dairy Farmers Cooperative Ass'n,* 107 L.R.R.M. 1577 (1981), a case in which the union had never attained majority status. Immediately after organizing, activity was initiated among the employees. The employer embarked upon a series of unfair labor practices. The employer's president made a series of plant closure threats and its Board of Directors discharged a union-activist driver because of a trucking accident, although such action was unprecedented in accident occurrences at the company. In addition, several weeks prior to the election, the employer distributed an unprecedented cash bonus and, subsequent to the election, supervisors interrogated employees as to how they had voted. (*Id.* at 1578. *See also NLRB v. Exchange Parts Co.,* 375 U.S. 405 (1961); *Sugardale Foods, Inc.,* 221 N.L.R.B. 206 (1976) (examples of when benefits may constitute a violation of § 8(a)(1)). *But cf. Russell Stover Candies, Inc.,* 221 N.L.R.B. 441 (1975); *Ingersoll-Rand Co.,* 219 N.L.R.B. 77 (1975).)

When first considering *United Dairy* in 1979, the Board, though finding that the employer had engaged in "outrageous and pervasive" unfair labor practices, ordered remedies akin to those in *Elson Bottling Co.* Two Board members acknowledged the Board's authority to issue a bargaining order, despite the lack of majority support, but declined to do so because of the risk of imposing a union on nonconsenting employees. (*United Dairy Farmers Coop. Ass'n,* 242 N.L.R.B. 1026, 1028 (1979).) The two dissenting members, however, urged issuance of a bargaining order, arguing that such a risk exists whenever a bargaining order issues after a union has lost an election. (*Id.* at 1069.)

On appeal, the court of appeals reiterated the Board's authority, as stated in *Gissel,* to issue a non-majority bargaining order and remanded the case to the Board to determine whether the facts warranted such an order. (*United Dairy v. NLRB,* 633 F.2d 1054 (3d Cir. 1980).) By the time of remand, the composition of the Board had changed, and the majority, under the authority of *Gissel,* issued an order to bargain. What set *United Dairy* apart was the "gravity, extent, timing, and constant repetition" of the violations. (*United Dairy Farmer's Coop. Ass'n,* 107 L.R.R.M. 1577, 1578 (1981).) The Board, *citing Entwistle Manufacturing Co.,* 120 F.2d 432 (4th Cir. 1941), emphasized that the discharge of an employee because of union activity is a serious unfair labor practice which "goes to the very heart of the Act." The

165

effect of such discharges is the unmistakable message to the remaining employees that union support equals loss of livelihood. The Board found equally serious the employer's attempt to convert its employees to independent contractors, which would place them outside the scope of the Act. (*See* National Labor Relations Act § 2(3), 29 U.S.C. § 152(3) (1976); H.R. Rep. No. 245, 80th Cong., 1st Sess. 18 (1947), *reprinted in* Legislative History of the Labor Management Relations Act, 1947, at 292 (1948).) Moreover, in response to the issue of imposing a non-majority union on the employees, the Board noted that the union lost the election by a margin of only 12-14. (107 L.R.R.M. at 1580.)

A Board-issued bargaining order is effective as of either the date the union is found to have first attained majority support, or the date the employer first begins its unfair labor practices, whichever is later. (*Beasley Energy, Inc.,* 228 N.L.R.B. 93 (1977). *But see John Cuneo, Inc. v. NLRB,* 103 S. Ct. 831, 833 (1983) (Rehnquist, J. dissenting).) The effect is that any unilateral changes made by the employer subsequent to that date are in violation of Section 8(a)(5): changes made in the face of, and independent of, a collective bargaining agreement. Finding that the employer in *United Dairy* committed its first unfair labor practice on November 21, 1973, the bargaining order was deemed effective as of that date. (107 L.R.R.M. 1577, 1580 (1981).)

While *United Dairy* represents the Board's first instance of authority under *Gissel* category I, it was not the first instance of the Board imposing a non-majority union upon a work unit. In *Local 57, International Ladies' Garment Workers Union v. NLRB (Garwin Corp.),* 374 F.2d 295 (D.C. Cir. 1967), the Board found that the employer, in order to avoid the union and an effective collective bargaining agreement, closed its plant in New York and resumed substantially the same operations in Florida. (*Cf. NLRB v. Preston Feed Corp.,* 309 F.2d 346 (4th Cir. 1962).) The

Board, relying on the precedent in "partial closing" cases, *Textile Workers Union v. Darlington Mfg. Co.,* 38 U.S. 263 (1965), issued a bargaining order to the employer at his Florida location. The order was reversed on appeal because it denied the Florida employees their right to choose their own bargaining representative, and viewed the order as punitive rather than remedial. Unlike the scope of inquiry in partial closing cases, however, the court was unconcerned with the possible deterring effect on the Florida employees.

Like *Garwin,* the major criticism of *Gissel* category I bargaining orders was the risk of imposing a union on nonconsenting employees. (*See* Golub, *The Propriety of Issuing Gissel Bargaining Orders Where the Union Has Never Attained a Majority,* 29 Lab. L.J. 631 (1978); Comment, *Remedial Collective Bargaining Orders: Compelling Employer Recognition Where the Union Has Never Attained a Majority,* 15 J. Mar. L. Rev. 649 (1982).) Moreover, because Board review "promises to consume much time," *Linden Lumber Div., Summer & Co. v. NLRB,* 419 U.S. 301, 306 (1974), the high probability of employee turnover increases the likelihood that the union lacks support from the remaining employees. In *United Dairy,* for example, the bargaining order came almost eight years after the unfair labor practices and unsuccessful union election.

It was questionable furthermore whether *United Dairy* would act as effective precedent, because the Board so limited its holding to the particular facts of the case. The Board repeatedly stressed the 12-14 margin by which the union lost the election and avoided the *Garwin* "risk of imposing a minority" union argument with these election results. (*United Dairy Farmers Coop. Ass'n,* 107 L.R.R.M. 1577, 1580 (1981).) Thus, *United Dairy* fell short of being a true *Gissel* category I order, such orders being authorized

167

"without need of inquiry into majority status." (*NLRB v. Gissel Packing Co.,* 395 U.S. 575, 613 (1969).) And when enumerating the many employer unfair labor practices which warranted the bargaining order, the Board qualified its holding by finding that "it is rare indeed to encounter misconduct more grave than that which has occurred here." (*Id.*)

Apparently seeking to dispel any notions that *United Dairy's* holding was unique to its particular facts, the Board again issued a non-majority bargaining order in *Conair Corp.,* 110 L.R.R.M. 1161 (1982). Finding the employer's acts of interrogation, threatening discharge, and terminating benefits were both "outrageous" and "pervasive" under the test set out in *Gissel,* and that the acts possessed the "gravity, extent, timing, and constant repetition" to warrant a non-majority bargaining order under *United Dairy,* the Board issued the order retroactive to the date of the employer's first unfair labor practice. (*Id.* at 1165-67.) Though the Board pointed out that the risk of contravening the wishes of the employee majority is lessened by the card support of 46 percent, it also stated that it would not "necessarily withhold a bargaining order in the absence of a close election vote, a high majority percentage card showing or any other affirmative showing of a reasonable basis for projecting a union's majority support." (*Id.* at 1167.) Furthermore, the Board expressly rejected the dissent's view that a non-majority bargaining order is barred by the majority principle embodied in the Act: "[o]ur dissenting colleagues attempt to cloak their tolerance of Respondent's (employer's) actions in a defense by majoritarian principle. We reject that masquerade. It is they, not we, who accept and perpetrate Respondent's denial to employees of their right to determine for themselves whether or not to be represented." (*Id.* at 1166.) However, the Court of Appeals for the District of Columbia agreed with the Board dissenters that nonmajority bargaining orders are not within the NLRB's remedial powers, and accordingly, that court denied the bargaining order portion of the Board's remedy. (*Conair Corp. v. NLRB*, 114 LRRM 3169, 3185-90 (1983).)

Conversely, the Board declined to issue a non-majority bargaining order in *United Supermarkets, Inc.*, 110 L.R.R.M. 1173 (1982), decided the same day as *Conair Corp.* In *United Supermarkets,* the Board found the employers conduct, while extensive and serious, did not reach the level needed to justify a bargaining order as contemplated by *Gissel.* The Board, instead, set aside the election and ordered a second election to be held when conditions had stabilized. (*Id.* at 1176.)

The threshold test in cases warranting the issuance of a bargaining order, either pursuant to the *Gissel* I or II category, is the "but for" test. It must be shown that "but for" the employer's unfair labor practices, the union would have acquired a card majority; or, "but for" the employer's unfair labor practices, the union would have won the election. (*See, e.g., Conair Corp.,* 110 L.R.R.M. 1161, 1163 (1982).) Moreover, the *Gissel* court cautioned that the remedy of a bargaining order was to be used sparingly, in those situations where it is found "that the possibility of erasing the effects of past practices and of insuring a fair election (or a fair re-run) by the use of traditional remedies, though present, is slight and that employee sentiment once expressed through cards would, on balance, be better protected by a bargaining order." (*NLRB v. Gissel Packing Co.,* 395 U.S. 575, 614-15 (1969).) Thus, *Gissel* does not require that no other remedy would suffice, only that the best remedy is a bargaining order. (*Amalgamated Clothing Workers v. NLRB,* 527 F.2d 803, 807 (D.C. Cir. 1975), *cert. denied,* 426 U.S. 907 (1976). *See also John Cuneo, Inc. v. NLRB,* 681 F.2d 11, 24 (D.C. Cir. 1982).)

CHAPTER 5

STATUTORY PROTECTION FOR CONCERTED ACTIVITY IN THE ABSENCE OF A LABOR ORGANIZATION

While the scope of the National Labor Relations Act generally pertains to matters of union organizing and collective bargaining, Section 7 protects employees engaged in collective action without a formal labor organization. Employees have the right "to engage in ... concerted activities for the purpose of collective bargaining *or for other mutual aid or protection.*" (29 U.S.C. § 157 (emphasis added).) Thus, even in the absence of an organizing campaign or a union contract, employers may not "interfere with, restrain, or coerce employees" in the exercise of their rights to engage in concerted activities. (29 U.S.C. § 158(a)(1).)

Generally, the entitlement to Section 7 rights in a non-union setting is not significantly different from a situation where a union is present. In the absence of a union, however, establishing that the employees' acts were concerted raises some notably different issues. For example, without formal union activity or involvement, it is less reasonable, as a matter of law or fact, to make a presumption that an employee has acted in concert with his co-workers.

The National Labor Relations Board has fashioned liberal rules in availing Section 7 rights to workers in the non-union setting, particularly in recent years. Specifically, the Board has recognized that certain activities are concerted although they are unrelated to the presence of a formal labor organization. In 1975, the Board held that an employee *acting alone* could engage in "concerted" activity if his actions reasonably furthered the interests of his co-workers. (*Alleluia Cushion Co.,* 221 N.L.R.B. 999 (1975).) Recently, however, the Board overruled *Alleluia Cushion Co.* and announced an objective test under which an employee's activity will be considered "concerted" only if he engaged in that activity with or on authority of other employees rather than on his own behalf. (*Meyers Industries, Inc.,* 268 N.L.R.B. No. 73 (1984).) The courts of appeal have not consistently followed the Board, but have frequently applied a stricter test for finding concerted activity in the non-union setting. Further, in balancing the employer's right of control and maintenance of loyalty against the employees' Section 7 rights, the courts of appeals have granted greater deference to employer concerns than the Board has granted. To understand these differences, recent decisions of the Board and the courts in the non-union setting must be reviewed. The policies regarding concerted activity evolve not only from the "non-union" cases, but also from cases where the presence of a union or collective bargaining agreement is unrelated to the issue of concerted activity.

In *Washington Aluminum v. NLRB,* the United States Supreme Court endorsed the National Labor Relations Board's long-standing policy that Section 7 rights are guaranteed to unrepresented workers. (370 U.S. 9 (1962).) With support from the courts, the Board declared "employees shall have the right to engage in concerted activities for their mutual aid or protection even though no union may actively be involved, or collective bargaining be contemplated." (*NLRB v. Phoenix Mutual Life Ins. Co.,* 167 F.2d 953, 956 (7th Cir. 1948), *cert. denied,* 335 U.S. 845 (1948).) An employer who interferes with or restrains employees in

171

the exercise of their rights not only violates Section 8(a)(1), but Section 8(a)(3) may be violated as well where employees are discriminated against. (*Kaiser Engineers v. NLRB*, 538 F.2d 1379 (9th Cir. 1976); *Kennametal, Inc. v. NLRB*, 182 F.2d 817 (3d Cir. 1950).) The term labor organization as applied to Section 8(a)(3) is defined in broad language, and "it is perfectly clear that employees who informally join together to present their grievances fall well within the statutory definition." (*Kennametal, Inc.*, 182 F.2d at 818.)

In the non-union setting, the main issue is not the language of Section 8(a)(1) or (3), but the meaning of the words "concerted activity" for "mutual aid or protection" found in Section 7. In any factual context, four requirements are generally recognized as necessary in order to establish protected concerted activity:

(1) There must be a work-related complaint or grievance;

(2) The concerted activity must further some group interest;

(3) A specific remedy or result must be sought through such activity; and

(4) The activity should not be unlawful or otherwise improper.

(*Shelley v. Anderson Furniture Mfg. Co. v. NLRB*, 497 F.2d 1200 (9th Cir. 1974), citing 18B Business Organizations, *Labor Law*, Kheel, § 10.02(3), at 10-21 (1973).) While the courts of appeals have applied these tests somewhat strictly, the Board has until recently been more liberal in its application. (*Compare e.g., NLRB v. Buddies Supermarket, Inc.*, 481 F.2d 714 (5th Cir. 1973) *with Bighorn Beverage Co.*, 263 N.L.R.B. 753 (1978). Note the difference in the tests which are used to evaluate whether or not the employees were acting to further a group interest.)

172

§ 5-1. Work-Related Complaint or Grievance.

Concerted activity for mutual aid or protection must pertain to a *work-related* complaint or grievance. Typical subjects which relate to wages, hours, and working conditions clearly fall within this category. Thus, where unorganized employees walked out due to insufficient heat in their work areas, the Supreme Court held their activity was protected. (*NLRB v. Washington Aluminum Co.,* 370 U.S. 9 (1962).)

Difficulty in establishing that the employee conduct is work-related occurs when the employee is chiefly concerned with a management matter which does not affect employee wages, hours, terms, and conditions of employment. In *G & W Electric Specialty Co. v. NLRB,* the Seventh Circuit Court of Appeals found that employee activity involving a credit union was unprotected because it was employee controlled and the activity related to the employees' status as depositors-investors. (360 F.2d 873 at 876 (1966).) The court noted that Section 7 does not encompass the total range of possible mutual interests, but only those interests which bear significantly upon working conditions or the material aspects of the employment relationships. (*Id.* at 877.) In contrast, the same court of appeals found that where an employer increased the price of gasoline which was sold to employees at special discounted rates, employee protests were protected activity. (*Sullair P.T.O., Inc. v. NLRB,* 641 F.2d 500 (7th Cir. 1981) (reversing the NLRB's finding on other grounds).)

While hiring and firing supervisors is considered typically to be an exclusive management function, employee protests regarding supervisors have sometimes been held protected concerted activity, even in the absence of a union. And concerted activity related to the selection or discharge of supervisors is protected if it has a direct impact upon employee performances. (*Plastilite Corp.,* 153 N.L.R.B. 180, *enforced in relevant part,* 375 F.2d 343

173

(1965); *NLRB v. Guernsey-Muskingum Electric Co-op., Inc.,* 285 F.2d 8 (6th Cir. 1960). *But see NLRB v. Dobbs House,* 325 F.2d 531 (5th Cir. 1963).) In *NLRB v. Phoenix Mutual Life Ins. Co.,* 167 F.2d 933 (7th Cir.), *cert. denied,* 335 U.S. 845 (1948), the court of appeals held that sales employees had a legitimate interest in expressing views about the hiring of a cashier who would have impact upon their work. The court reasoned that while the employees had no authority to appoint or recommend anyone for employment, the capability of the person to fill the position did bear a reasonable relationship to conditions of employment. (*Id.* at 956.) In *Leslie Metal Arts Co.,* the National Labor Relations Board recognized the right to engage in concerted activity to protest management's failure to take disciplinary measures against an employee who had pulled a chair from under another employee at break time. (208 N.L.R.B. 323 (1974).) The Board held that a walkout was proper because "the quality of supervision and the manner in which it is exercised are directly related to working conditions. . . ." (*Id.* at 326.)

In *Kaiser Engineers v. NLRB,* 538 F.2d 1379 (9th Cir. 1976), professional employees were disciplined for writing their Congressmen regarding the easing of restrictions on the importation of engineers. The court held that the employees had engaged in concerted activity by expressing legitimate concerns which might have affected their "job security." (*Id.* at 1385.) The employees' actions were found to be protected even though the action sought was "beyond the strict confines of the employment relationship." (*Id.*) The activity involved no request for action on the part of the employer, and it did not concern a matter over which the employer had direct control.

The United States Supreme Court explicitly rejected the view that employees' concerted activity loses Section 7 protection if they seek to improve working conditions "through

174

channels outside the immediate employee-employer relationship." (*Eastex, Inc. v. NLRB*, 437 U.S. 556, 565 (1978).) In *Eastex, Inc.* union employees sought to distribute a union newsletter on the employer's property during non-working hours and in non-working areas of the company's property. The letter contained 4 sections. Sections 1 and 4 advocated union support and solidarity. Section 2 encouraged employees to write letters of protest to legislators opposing incorporation of a right-to-work statute into the state constitution. Section 3 criticized a recent Presidential veto of an increase in the federal minimum wage and urged employees to register to vote in order to elect persons into office who would represent their best interests.

The employer objected to distribution of the newsletter based on the contents of Sections 2 and 3. The union filed an unfair practice charge with the Board contending all sections of the newsletter were protected by Section 7 and the employer's refusal to allow distribution violated Section 8(a)(1). The Administrative Law Judge held all sections of the letter were protected by Section 7, even though parts 2 and 3 did not directly relate to the employer and the union. The Board affirmed the Administrative Law Judge and adopted his recommended order. The court of appeals enforced the order, and the Supreme Court affirmed.

The employer argued Section 7 protects only employees' concerted activities which are directed at conditions their employer has authority or power to change or control. The employer further contended that the object of the activities in Sections 2 and 3 was not mutual aid or protection because they did not involve a "specific dispute" between the employees and employer or concern the company's relationship with the union. (*Id.* at 563.) The object of the activities was alleged to be political, and therefore, outside the scope of Section 7 protection. (*Ford Motor Co.*, 221

175

N.L.R.B. 663 (1975). (Distribution on employer's property of a "purely political tract" held unprotected).) The employer's final contention was that distribution of the newsletter in non-working areas during non-working hours intruded on company property rights. (*See NLRB v. Babcock & Wilcox Co.,* 351 U.S. 105 (1956). Employer could prevent non-employees from distribution of union literature on employer's property if other effective means of distribution were available).)

The Supreme Court rejected the contentions of the employer. Section 2 of the newsletter was protected because "it bears such a relation to employees' interests as to come within the guarantee of the mutual aid or protection clause." (*Eastex,* 437 U.S. at 569.) The Supreme Court affirmed the Board's conclusion that union security is "central to the union concept of strength through solidarity." (*Id.* at 569, *citing* 215 N.L.R.B. 271, 274 (1974).) Section 3 was also found protected because "the union's call ... for these employees to back persons who support an increase in the minimum wage, and to oppose those who oppose it, fairly is characterized as concerted activity for the 'mutual aid or protection' of petitioner's employees and of employees generally." (*Eastex,* 437 U.S. at 570.) The object of the activities in Sections 2 and 3 was not purely political.

In *Eastex,* the Supreme Court relied on *Republic Aviation Corp. v. NLRB,* 324 U.S. 793 (1945) in ruling that the employer's reliance on violation of property rights was misplaced. In *Republic Aviation,* the employees were already rightfully on the employer's property in a work capacity. Therefore, the employer's management rather than property interests were involved. The employer could not prohibit distribution of union literature in non-working areas during non-working time without a special showing that discipline or production would be disrupted.

As in *Republic Aviation,* the employees in *Eastex* were already rightfully on the employer's property. Management interests were involved, but the employer failed to show how distribution would interfere with company discipline or production. The employer had no substantial countervailing interest which outweighed the protected concerted activity of the employees, even though all the sections of the newsletter did not deal with purely organizational matters.

Eastex approves an extension of Section 7 protection of concerted activity beyond organizational issues and efforts. The extension is without boundaries and is left to a case by case determination. "It is neither necessary nor appropriate, however, for us to attempt to delineate precisely the boundaries of the "mutual aid or protection" clause. That task is for the Board to perform in the first instance as it considers a wide variety of cases that come before it." (*Eastex,* 437 U.S. at 568.)

§ 5-2. The Furtherance of a Group Interest.

While the furtherance of a group interest is often undisputed in the typical union-organizing or collective bargaining case, in a non-union situation this element has caused some difficulty and controversy among the courts and the Board. The most important unsettled issue is whether employees are engaged in concerted activity when they act alone in furtherance of interests beneficial to other employees. In the hallmark decision, *Alleluia Cushion Co.,* 221 N.L.R.B. 999 (1975), an employee filed a complaint under the state's safety and health law. The employee received no outward manifestation of his co-workers' support, and there was no evidence that he purported to represent other employees. The Board found that minimum safety and health conditions were a matter of public inter-

177

est, and as such, it would be unreasonable to conclude that his fellow employees did not support his complaints regarding safety violations. (221 N.L.R.B. at 1000.) "(T)he consent and concert emanates from the mere assertion of such statutory rights." (*Id.*)

In a later decision, the Board held that concerted activity existed where an employee, acting alone, was discharged for inquiring at his employer's bank as to whether there were enough funds to cover payroll checks. (*Air Surrey Corp.,* 229 N.L.R.B. 1064 (1977).) In reaching its decision, the Board noted that *Alleluia* was based upon "the premise that an individual's actions may be considered to be concerted in nature if they relate to conditions of employment that are matters of mutual concern to all the affected employees." (*Id.* at 1064.)

Alleluia opened the door for charges arising from retaliatory actions against employees who, as individuals, complained to government agencies. A wide variety of employee actions have been held to be protected concerted activity under the *Alleluia* doctrine. (*See, e.g., Apollo Tire Co.,* 236 N.L.R.B. 1627 (1978) (an overtime complaint with the Wage-Hour Division of the United States Department of Labor); *Self Cycle & Marine Distributors,* 237 N.L.R.B. 75 (1978) (filing an unemployment compensation claim with a state agency); *King Soopers, Inc.,* 222 N.L.R.B. 1011 (1976) (filing charges with a state civil rights agency); *Ambulance Service of New Bedford, Inc.,* 229 N.L.R.B. 106 (1977) (filing a criminal charge against an employer for issuing bad payroll checks); *Massachusetts Women's Hospital, Inc.,* 227 N.L.R.B. 1289 (1977) (filing an affidavit in support of another employee at the state civil rights office); *Kiechler Mfg. Co.,* 238 N.L.R.B. 398 (1978) (complaint alleging an O.S.H.A. violation); and *Brooklyn Nursing Home, Inc.,* 223 N.L.R.B. 267 (1976) (complaint to state labor agency to collect wages).)

178

In *Diagnostic Center Hospital Corp.*, 228 N.L.R.B. 1215 (1977), the Board followed *Alleluia* and found concerted activity where an employee wrote a letter to the corporate chairman of the board complaining about wages and other matters. The employee used the word "we," but there was no evidence that she was designated by other employees to act on their behalf nor that she informed any employee about the letter. The Board said there is concerted activity if "fellow employees share the employee's concerns and interest in the common complaint." (*Id.* at 1217.)

In *Krispy Kreme Doughnut Corp.*, 245 N.L.R.B. 1053 (1979), the NLRB found that an employer violated Section 8(a)(1) when it discharged an employee for refusing to refrain from filing a workmen's compensation claim. The Board reasoned that workmen's compensation benefits "arise out of the employment relationship and are of common interest to other employees." (*Id.*) However, the Court of Appeals for the Fourth Circuit denied enforcement of the Board's order. (*Krispy Kreme Doughnut Corp. v. NLRB*, 635 F.2d 304 (4th Cir. 1980).) Concluding that the employee's refusal to forego his claim was not protected concerted activity, the court reasoned that there was no evidence that the employee in question contemplated group action, nor that he acted on behalf of other employees. The court also rejected the Board's contention that such individual employee action is "concerted" when it arises from the employment relationship and is of common interest to other employees who, it may be presumed, would have joined in the individual's activities had they known of them. (*Id.* at 308-10.)

Along with complaints to government agencies, employees have engaged in activities on the job pursuant to rights established by statutes. In *Batchelor Electric Co.*, 254 N.L.R.B. No. 156 (1981), the Board held that an employer violated the Act when it discharged an employee

who took a one-day absence to protest the company's failure
to pay prevailing rates required under the Davis-Bacon Act.
In another case, a woman, acting alone, refused to accept a
new job assignment until she was paid the same rate as the
men, as she claimed was her right under federal laws.
(*Dawson Cabinet Co.,* 228 N.L.R.B. 290 (1977).) The Board
found her refusal was protected concerted activity, but the
court of appeals reversed, holding that there was insufficient evidence to establish concerted activity. (*NLRB v.
Dawson Cabinet Co.,* 566 F.2d 1079 (8th Cir. 1977).) In
another decision, an unrepresented employee confronted his
employer with safety violations, but his actions were held to
protected activity. (*P. & L. Cedar Products Co.,* 224
N.L.R.B. 244 (1976).)

In 1984, the newly appointed Board majority abandoned
Alleluia Cushion in favor of an "objective" standard for
determining whether an employee's activity is concerted
within the meaning of the Act. (*Meyers Industries, Inc.,* 268
N.L.R.B. No. 73 (1984).) Under the Board's new test, the
employee's activity will be concerted if it was engaged in
with or on behalf of other employees, the employer knew of
the concerted nature of the employee's activity, the activity
was protected by the statute, and the employer's adverse
employment action was motivated by the employee's protected concerted activity. Unlike previous Board tests in
Section 8(a)(1) cases, this test engrafts a motive requirement for violations, and accordingly, it is unclear whether
the courts of appeals will accept so radical a departure from
traditional statutory analysis. *Meyers Industries* is more
than a simple overruling of *Alleluia Cushion*; it is a strong
repudiation of the long-held tenant that Section 8(a)(1) ordinarily may be violated by an employer without a showing
of unlawful motive.

Alleluia was the offspring of an earlier case, *Interboro
Contractors, Inc.,* 157 N.L.R.B. 1295 (1966), *enforced,* 388

F.2d 495 (2d Cir. 1967), which held that employees, acting alone, are engaged in a concerted activity when they take action to enforce their rights under a collective bargaining agreement. *Interboro* was rejected by some courts of appeals, and this limited the increased application of the *Alleluia* doctrine. In *NLRB v. Buddies Supermarket, Inc.,* the Court of Appeals for the Third Circuit found no concerted activity where a non-union employee tried to obtain an adjustment in the method of pay. (481 F.2d 714 (5th Cir. 1973).) Even though there were other employees similarly situated, the court specifically rejected *Interboro,* holding that the employee, at the minimum, must show an object of initiating, inducing, or preparing for group action. (*Id.* at 718, *citing Mushroom Transportation Co. v. NLRB,* 330 F.2d 683 (3d Cir. 1964).) The court also noted that the Court of Appeals for the Fifth Circuit questioned the *Interboro* approach to concerted activities. (*Buddies Supermarket,* 481 F.2d at 719, *citing NLRB v. Northern Metal Co.,* 440 F.2d 881 (3d Cir. 1971).) In 1984, the United States Supreme Court approved the NLRB's use of the *Interboro* doctrine in *NLRB v. City Disposal Systems, Inc.,* 115 LRRM 3193 (1984).

Participation in the grievance process is a recent example of concerted activity which has been found in the non-union setting. In *Carson, Pirie, Scott & Co.,* an employee was discharged allegedly for using the company's non-union, unilaterally established grievance procedure. (93 L.R.R.M. 1253 (1976) (N.L.R.B. Advice Memoranda).) But the Board declined to apply *Alleluia* because the grievance was pursued on "strictly a personal basis" unrelated to concerted activity. (*Id.*) In *Columbia University,* 236 N.L.R.B. 793 (1978), the Board held that an attempt by non-union employees to establish a grievance committee was concerted activity. The Board found protected activity in *Columbia* where one employee intervened to assist another

181

employee who was being disciplined. (*Id.* at 795.) The Board specifically declined to say whether the principles of *NLRB v. J. Weingarten, Inc.,* 420 U.S. 251 (1975) applied. (*Columbia,* 236 N.L.R.B. at 796.) In 1978, however, the Board indicated that the Section 7 rights as applied in *Weingarten* do apply in the absence of union representation. (*Glomac Plastics, Inc.,* 234 N.L.R.B. 1309, 1311 (1978).) The Board noted that *Weingarten* interpreted Section 7 to give employees "some measure of protection against unjust employer practices, especially those that threaten job security." (*Id.*) The Board pointed out that these concerns are "more compelling" in the absence of union representation. (*See also Du Pont Co. v. NLRB,* 115 LRRM 2153 (1983). *Compare, E.I. du Pont de Nemours v. NLRB,* 113 LRRM 2931 (1983).)

§ 5-3. Requirement to Seek a Specific Remedy.

Historically, to establish concerted activity, there must be an indication that a specific remedy or result was sought through the activity. When an employee engages in an activity such as a work stoppage or filing a complaint with a government agency, his or her intent to seek a specific remedy is stated or inferred. However, mere conversation does not, according to at least one court of appeals, establish concerted activity. If the activity consists of mere talk, it can only be considered protected if it "is looking toward group action." (*Mushroom Transportation v. NLRB,* 330 F.2d 683, 686 (3d Cir. 1964).) The Fifth Circuit Court of Appeals also held that "individual griping or complaining is not concerted activity." (*NLRB v. Buddies Supermarket,* 481 F.2d 714, 717 (5th Cir. 1973).) To find concerted activity, there must be evidence that the purpose of conversations was to arouse concerted activities. (*Id.* at 720. *But see* Myers Industries, Inc., 268 N.L.R.B. No. 73 (1984).)

§ 5-4. Activities Which Are Unlawful or Otherwise Improper.

Generally, in the non-union setting, employees must conform to the same standards of conduct as do employees acting in conjunction with a union. Violence, intimidation, slowdowns, and other indefensible or illegal activity may cause the non-union and non-organizing workers to lose protected status. Although the Supreme Court upheld the applicability of concerted rights to non-union employees, it simultaneously held that Section 7 does not protect concerted activity that is "unlawful, violent, in breach of contract, or disloyal to the employer." (*NLRB v. Washington Aluminum Co.,* 370 U.S. 9 (1962).) The Court did find that the spontaneous walk-out in that case was protected activity. In the *First National Bank of Omaha,* 171 N.L.R.B. 1145 (1968), *enforced,* 413 F.2d 921 (8th Cir. 1970), the Board found protected a previously unannounced concerted refusal to work overtime by a group of unrepresented employees. The Board subsequently held that while intermittent refusals to work overtime were presumptively protected activity, a pattern or plans of intermittent action inconsistent with "a genuine strike or genuine performance" could cause employees to lose their protected status. (*Polytech, Inc.,* 195 N.L.R.B. 695 (1972).)

Improper concerted activity has no definite scope, but generally employers have the right to expect a certain standard of conduct from their employees, such as loyalty and compliance with reasonable work rules. However, when employees held a lunch-time meeting to discuss safety measures which ran fifteen minutes over into the work period, the Board found that the employees had engaged in protected activity even though they violated work rules. (*Empire Steel Manufacturing Co.,* 234 N.L.R.B. 530 (1978).) The Board noted that the infraction of the rule did not cause any significant loss in production.

In the non-union settings, employees may also lose their protected status when their concerted activity is disloyal, disparaging, or abusive. Thus, an employee lost his protected status during concerted activity when he repeatedly used vulgar language in addressing his superiors about his complaint. (*Sullair P.T.O., Inc., v. NLRB*, 641 F.2d 500 (7th Cir. 1981).) Similarly, an employee who wrote his employer's clients to protest a dress code lost his protected status because he wrote in a tone which was "sarcastic" and "denigrating." (*American Arbitration Ass'n*, 233 N.L.R.B. 12 (1977).)

Employees may lose their protected status by disregarding reasonable rules pertaining to the employer's need to preserve confidentiality with respect to business matters. For example, an employee was denied the protection of Section 7 when he revealed confidential information to his employer's customers. (*NLRB v. Knuth Bros.*, 537 F.2d 950 (3d Cir. 1976).) But a nurse's statement in a television news broadcast, protesting wages and staffing conditions at a hospital, was held to be protected even though the employer considered the activity to be disparaging. (*Community Hospital of Roanoke Valley, Inc.*, 220 N.L.R.B. 217 (1975), *enforced*, 538 F.2d 607 (4th Cir. 1976).) And breach of confidentiality did not justify the discharge of an employee who violated company policy by discussing her wages with fellow employees. (*Jeanette Corp.*, 217 N.L.R.B. 122 (1975), *enforced*, 532 F.2d 916 (3d Cir. 1976).) The Board noted that maintaining unqualified rules or policies prohibiting employees from discussing wage rates with other employees violates Section 8(a)(1) because the rule impedes employees' rights to engage in protected concerted activity. (*Id.*)

§ 5-5. Conclusion.

Under the plain language of Section 7, all employees have

the right to engage in concerted activity for mutual aid or protection. The right is unqualified and it extends to employees in non-union situations. If the *Alleluia* doctrine is adopted by the United States Supreme Court or if its acceptance broadens in the courts of appeal, employees will continue to enjoy the protection of the statute when they engage in concerted action. With the declining rate of union membership in the American work force, the right to engage in "other" concerted activity may rise in importance because employees likely will turn to less formal modes of concerted activity. Further, employees will increasingly rely upon other employment laws as means of protected concerted activity. In sum, Section 7 rights will become increasingly significant to non-union employees in the coming years. The newly appointed Labor Board majority has overruled *Alleluia Cushion* and adopted an "objective" standard for finding concerted activity which severely narrows the instances in which individual employees may be found to have engaged in concerted acts. (*Meyers Industries, Inc.,* 268 N.L.R.B. No. 73 (1984).) Although several courts of appeals questioned the *Alleluia* doctrine, it is too early to predict judicial reaction to the Board's new *Meyers* test.

CHAPTER 6

EMPLOYEE RIGHT TO REPRESENTATION
IN A PREDISCIPLINARY
INTERVIEW

In *NLRB v. J. Weingarten, Inc.*, the Supreme Court held that an employee may refuse to accede to an investigatory interview without union representation where the employee reasonably fears that the interview might result in disciplinary action. (420 U.S. 251 (1975).) The Court held that an employee's refusal to participate is "concerted activity" within Section 7 of the National Labor Relations Act. The Court stated:

> The action of an employee in seeking to have the assistance of his union representative at a confrontation with his employer clearly falls within the literal wording of Section 7 that "(e)mployees shall have the right ... to engage in ... concerted activities for the purpose of ... mutual aid or protection." *Mobil Oil Corp. v. NLRB*, 482 F.2d 842, 847 (CA7 (1973). This is true even though the employee alone may have an immediate stake in the outcome.... The union representative whose participation he seeks is, however, safeguarding not only the particular employee's interests but also the interest of the entire bargaining unit by exercising vigilance to make certain that the employer does not initiate or continue a practice of imposing punishment unjustly. (*Id.* at 260-61.)

In addition to the literal construction of Section 7 rights, the Court recognized the inherent "inequality of bargaining power" between a lone employee and management at an interview at which the employee reasonably fears discipline. The Court noted that eliminating inequality in the employee/employer relationship goes to the heart and design of the Act, and thus, the presence of a union representative at an investigatory interview "is within the protective ambit of the section." (*Id.* at 262.)

Finally, the Court recognized the assistance that a union representative could lend to both the employee and employer in an investigatory interview. The union representative can best serve the fearful and inarticulate employee, relate the facts of the incident being investigated and assist the employer by "eliciting favorable facts, and save the employer production time by getting to the bottom of the incident." (*Id.* at 262-64.)

The Supreme Court was careful to qualify the employee's right to union representation based on four considerations. First, the right arises only when the employee requests union representation. Second, the employee's right to request representation is limited to situations where the employee reasonably believes or fears that the investigation will result in disciplinary action. Third, the exercise of the right must not interfere with legitimate employer prerogatives. The Court instructed that if an employee refuses to participate in an investigatory interview, the employer may still exercise the prerogative of continuing the investigation without the cooperation of the employee under investigation. Finally, the employer is under no duty to bargain with the union representative at the investigatory interview. The union representative is present to assist the employee. The Court distinguished the investigatory interview from a disciplinary interview, wherein the employer has an affirmative duty to meet with the union representative. (*Id.* at 256-60.)

From this framework, the courts and the Board have attempted to clarify the issues which have arisen since the Supreme Court's decision. As is often the case, the courts and the Board have disagreed on the proper application of *Weingarten* rights in the daily context of labor-management relations.

The Supreme Court in *Weingarten* clearly limited the union representative requirement "to where the employee

187

reasonably believes the investigation will result in disciplinary action." (*Id.* at 257.) The Court cited the Board's decision in *Quality Mfg. Co.,* where the Board held that "run-of-the-mill shop-floor conversations" will not trigger an employee's right to union representation. (195 N.L.R.B. 197, 199 (1972).) Beyond that statement, the courts and the Board were left to determine what constitutes an investigatory interview.

Whether an investigatory interview may result in disciplinary action against the employee is an objective inquiry based upon an evaluation of all the circumstances, and not the subjective reaction of the employee. In *Alfred M. Lewis, Inc.,* the Board held that a discussion of production quotas permitted the employee to invoke *Weingarten* rights since these discussions were a preliminary stage to imposing discipline. (229 N.L.R.B. 757 (1977).) At a meeting where the employee was told to accept his job responsibilities, be demoted, or quit, the Board held that the employee was entitled to union representation. (*Newton Sheet Metal, Inc.,* 238 N.L.R.B. 970 (1978).)

The Board in *Prudential Ins. Co. of America,* found a Section 8(a)(1) violation where an employee was denied a union representative at a meeting in which the employer audited the insurance agent's books. (251 N.L.R.B. 1591 (1980).) The Board held that there is no management right to information from an employee without a union representative, "where an investigatory interview with disciplinary overtones is concerned." (*Id.* at 1592.) At a meeting intended to announce already determined discipline, the employee's *Weingarten* rights were violated when the employer sought additional information indicating that the investigation was continuing. (*Louisiana Council No. 17, AFSCME, AFL-CIO,* 250 N.L.R.B. 880 (1980).)

In a different context, the Board held that there was no right to union representation at a meeting with the supervisor where the purpose of the meeting was to discuss the employee's job assignments and there was no reasonable fear of discipline. (*United Telephone Co. of Florida,* 251 N.L.R.B. 510 (1980); *Yellow Freight Systems, Inc.,* 247 N.L.R.B. 177 (1980).) At a meeting to communicate company policies, the Board held that the employer should have the right to do so without a union representative present. However, the Board cautioned that if the employer sought any information from the employee which the employee reasonably believes may result in discipline, *Weingarten* rights may arise. (*L.E. Solomon, Inc.,* 253 N.L.R.B. 499 (1980).) Where an employee was told that an interview would not result in discipline, the employee is not entitled to union representation. (*Stewart-Warner Corp.,* 253 N.L.R.B. 136 (1980).) Finally, the Board held that an employee is not entitled to have a union representative present at a physical examination conducted by the employer's physicians. (*U.S. Postal Service,* 252 N.L.R.B. 61 (1980).)

In *Lennox Industries, Inc. v. NLRB,* the court of appeals enforced the Board order that the employer had violated Section 8(a)(1) where the employee reasonably believed that the interview could lead to discipline in spite of the employer's assurance that a union representative would be provided if the employer believed it was necessary. (637 F.2d 340 (5th Cir. 1981).) However, where the employer assured the employee that the meeting would not result in discipline, the employer was entitled to discharge the employee for leaving the meeting without permission to find a union representative. (*Spartan Stores, Inc. v. NLRB,* 628 F.2d 953 (6th Cir. 1980).)

If an interview is investigatory and the employee has a reasonable fear of disciplinary action being taken as a result of that interview, a union representative may attend the meeting upon request of the employee. But the law is unclear in situations where the employer calls an employee into his office to announce the imposition of discipline.

In 1977, the Board ruled in *Certified Grocers of California, Ltd.,* that an employee has the right to union representation under *Weingarten* at an interview whose sole purpose is to announce a disciplinary decision made prior to the interview. (227 N.L.R.B. 1211 (1977).) But in *NLRB v. Certified Grocers of California, Ltd.,* the court of appeals denied enforcement of the Board order holding as they did in *Alfred M. Lewis, Inc. v. NLRB,* 587 F.2d 403 (9th Cir. 1978), that the Supreme Court in *Weingarten* did not intend to expand the right of representation to interviews announcing pre-determined discipline. (587 F.2d 449 (9th Cir. 1978).)

The Board overruled its decision in *Certified Grocers* in *Baton Rouge Water Works Co.,* 246 N.L.R.B. 995 (1979). In *Baton Rouge,* the Board found no Section 8(a)(1) violation where the employer called a meeting notifiying the employee that she was discharged. The Board held that *Weingarten* rights were not available in a situation where the employer reached a final and binding decision to discipline the employee prior to the interview, and the purpose of the interview is to inform the employee of the discipline. (*See also Houston Coca-Cola Bottling Co.,* 251 N.L.R.B. 860 (1980); *Southwestern Bell Telephone Co.,* 251 N.L.R.B. 625 (1980); *Airco Alloys,* 249 N.L.R.B. 524 (1980); *Texaco, Inc.,* 247 N.L.R.B. 688 (1980).)

Recent decisions by the Board have been careful to point out that the decision in *Baton Rouge* is not unconditional. If at a disciplinary interview, the employer engages the employee in an interrogation, going beyond informing the employee of a pre-determined discipline, then the full scope of *Weingarten* rights attach. (*L.E. Solomon, Inc.,* 253 N.L.R.B. 499 (1980); *Louisiana Council No. 17, AFSCME, AFL-CIO,* 250 N.L.R.B. 880 (1980).) However, when an

190

employee initiates a conversation with the employer to discuss previously determined discipline, the Board held in *Pacific Telephone & Telegraph Co.,* that this will not convert the conversation into one where *Weingarten* rights apply. (246 N.L.R.B. 1007 (1979).)

In *Kraft Foods, Inc.,* 251 N.L.R.B. 598 (1980) and *Ohio Masonic Home,* 251 N.L.R.B. 606 (1980), the Board outlined the shifting burden of proof in a situation where discipline followed an illegal interview. The General Counsel first must show that the employer conducted an interview in violation of an employee's Section 8(a)(1) rights. The burden of proof then shifts to the employer to prove that the decision to discipline was not based on any information elicited at the unlawful interview. Where an employer interviewed three postal workers, all implicating a fourth employee, and the employer subsequently interviewed and investigated the fourth employee about the theft, and then discharged the employee, the Board held that the employer's decision to discipline and discharge the employee was not based on the unlawful interview, but was based on the three prior implicating interviews. (*U.S. Postal Service,* 254 N.L.R.B. 703 (1981).)

The question of whether an employee has the right to consult with the union representative on company time before the investigatory interview has spawned frequent disagreements between the courts and the Board. In *Climax Molybdenum Co.,* the Board held that an employee has a right to consult with the union representative on company time prior to the interview. (227 N.L.R.B. 1189 (1977).) The Board found supporting language in the Supreme Court's opinion in *Weingarten* to the effect that a knowledgeable representative would assist both the employee and employer. The Board stated that "the right to representation clearly embraces the right to prior consultation." (*Id.* at 1190.) However, in *Climax Molybdenum*

Co. v. NLRB, the Tenth Circuit Court of Appeals denied enforcement of the Board's order. The court interpreted *Weingarten* to require that the employer set the time for the investigatory interview far enough in advance so as to allow the employee and the union representative adequate time to consult on their own time. (584 F.2d 360 (10th Cir. 1978).) The Board, however, adhered to its view in *Colgate-Palmolive Co.,* 257 N.L.R.B. No. 28 (1981).

The question of whether an employee's *Weingarten* rights can be waived arises in two contexts: first, whether an individual employee can waive his rights, and second, whether the employee's collective bargaining representative can waive the employee's rights.

The Sixth Circuit Court of Appeals held in *Super Valu Xenia v. NLRB,* that an employee waived his right to union representation when he agreed to proceed with the interview without the benefit of union representation. (627 F.2d 13 (6th Cir. 1980).) However, the Board has found that signed statements by employees that the employer "may interview them . . . on matters relating to company business" did not constitute a waiver of the employee's *Weingarten* rights. (*Montgomery Ward & Co.,* 254 N.L.R.B. 826 (1981).) There, the Board held that a waiver of *Weingarten* rights must be specific and unequivocal. And in *U.S. Postal Service,* the Board held that a postal worker who was being investigated for theft did not waive his rights to union representation at an investigatory interview even though he had executed a waiver of his *Miranda* rights. (254 N.L.R.B. 703 (1981).)

The leading Board case on the right of a union to waive an employee's *Weingarten* rights is *Prudential Insurance Co. of America,* 251 N.L.R.B. 1591 (1980). (*See also New York Telephone Co.,* 219 N.L.R.B. 679 (1975).) In *Prudential,* the union and the company negotiated a collective bargaining agreement which included a clause allowing the

192

employer to interview any employee "with respect to any phase of his work without the grievance committee being present." The Board found that the company's reliance on this clause to deny an employee the right to a union representative at an investigatory interview was misplaced. First, the clause was inserted into the collective bargaining agreement 19 years before the *Weingarten* decision, and subsequently, the union had tried unsuccessfully to remove the clause arguing it was unlawful and unenforceable. The Board held that this was a clear indication that the union did not waive the employee's rights. Second, the Board stated that the clause specifically referred to a "grievance committee" and not to a *Weingarten* representative. Finally, the Board held that there was no "clear and unequivocal" waiver of the employee's *Weingarten* rights which is necessary before there can be a contractual waiver of statutory rights.

The Board later reaffirmed its position in another case involving the same employer on essentially the same grounds. (*Prudential Insurance Co. of America*, 254 N.L.R.B. 247 (1981).) On appeal, the Fifth Circuit Court of Appeals denied enforcement of the Board's order holding that by leaving the clause in the collective bargaining agreement after the *Weingarten* decision, the union had executed a waiver of the employee's rights to union representation at an investigatory interview. (*Prudential Insurance Co. of America v. NLRB*, 661 F.2d 398 (5th Cir. 1981).)

In *U.S. Postal Service*, the collective bargaining contract contained a clause that allowed private interviews without union representation concerning "minor offenses." A postal worker who worked overtime without permission, a clear violation of postal service policy, was called to his supervisor's office for an interview. The employee's request for a union representative was denied. The employer argued

193

that this was a "minor offense" as to which the union had waived the right to representation. The Board held that since there was no definition of "minor offenses," working overtime without management permission was not a minor offense. The Board also held that because the employer reasonably believed that the interview could result in discipline, the denial of the employee's right to representation violated Section 8(a)(1). (256 N.L.R.B. 78 (1981).)

It is clear that in order to invoke one's *Weingarten* rights, the employee must make a request for union representation; it is not an automatic right. (*Kohl's Food Co.,* 249 N.L.R.B. 75 (1980).) An employer did not violate an employee's *Weingarten* rights when it conducted an investigatory interview that resulted in the employee's discharge since the employee failed to request a union representative. (*First National Supermarkets, Inc.,* 247 N.L.R.B. 1136 (1980).) In *NLRB v. Columbia University,* the Second Circuit Court of Appeals held that although a discharged employee did not specifically request a union representative at the time of the interview, failure to do so would not necessarily negate the employee's *Weingarten* rights if the employee had not been given an adequate opportunity to make the request. (541 F.2d 922 (2d Cir. 1976).)

The Sixth Circuit Court of Appeals in *Spartan Stores, Inc. v. NLRB,* held that an employee did not properly make a request for union representation when he sought out his union representative contrary to his supervisor's orders and an established company rule that only supervisors are permitted to procure union representatives in order to avoid disruption on the plant floor. (628 F.2d 953 (6th Cir. 1980).) The court held that the employee's improper request was just cause for his discharge.

The employee's request for union representation must be made before the interview is concluded. (*Greyhound Lines, Inc.,* 239 N.L.R.B. 849 (1978).) This is significant because

194

often the employee is initially unaware that the purpose of the interview may be investigatory. The Board has held that the request must be made to the management official who has the knowledge of the purpose of the meeting, and is thus in the best position to determine whether the employee's request is justified by the circumstances of the pending interviews. (*Appalachian Power Co.*, 253 N.L.R.B. 931 (1980).)

In *Sun Oil Co.*, (257 N.L.R.B. No. 48 (1981)), the Board held that an employer did not violate Section 8(a)(1) when it refused to conduct an interview in the presence of a union representative. The Board found that this option exercised by the employer was consistent with the employer's *Weingarten* right as long as no investigatory interview had taken place. Once the employer begins the interview in derogation of the employee's request for representation, the employer has violated Section 8(a)(1).

In some instances, the union representative is not available when the employee makes the request for a union representative. In this situation, the Board has held that the investigatory interview must be postponed until the employee's request for a union representative can be fulfilled. (*Super Value Xenia,* 236 N.L.R.B. 1581 (1978).) Consistent with this interpretation of *Weingarten,* the Board does not require that the interview be postponed if an employee's particular union representative is unavailable and another union representative is available (*Coca-Cola Bottling Co.,* 227 N.L.R.B. 1276 (1977).) In *Newport News Shipbuilding & Dry Dock Co.,* (254 N.L.R.B. 375 (1981)), the Board agreed with the Administrative Law Judge that the employer need not provide the best representative possible. The Board observed that there was no violation of the employee's *Weingarten* rights when the employer provided the employee with a union representative other than the one requested, since the nearest representative was 60 miles away and had no relationship to the employer. (*See also Pacific Gas & Electric Co.*, 253 N.L.R.B. 1143 (1981).)

In one case, the Board held that where there was no officially designated shop steward available, the employee was entitled to have a co-worker present at the interview. (*Illinois Bell Telephone Co.*, 251 N.L.R.B. 932 (1980).) The Sixth Circuit Court of Appeals went a step further in *NLRB v. Columbia University*, holding that the representative did not even have to be a member of the union as long as the employee was represented at the investigatory interview. (541 F.2d 922 (2d Cir. 1976).)

The Supreme Court in *Weingarten* clearly stated that the employer is not under a duty to bargain with the union representative at an investigatory interview. The Supreme Court emphasized that the function of the union representative is not that of an adversary at the interview, but is to assist both the employee and the employer in resolving the incident that gave rise to the interview. (420 U.S. at 256-60.) Relying on *Weingarten*, the Board has further clarified the union representative's limited role by finding Section 8(a)(1) violations where the employer has insisted that the union representative remain silent throughout the interview or until the employee has confessed under questioning by the employer. (*Southwestern Bell Telephone Co.*, 251 N.L.R.B. 612 (1980); *Texaco, Inc.*, 251 N.L.R.B. 633 (1980); *Illinois Bell Telephone Co.*, 251 N.L.R.B. 932 (1980).)

The Board has consistently found Section 8(a)(1) violations where an employer has disciplined an employee for requesting union representation at an investigatory interview. (*Southwestern Bell Telephone Co.*, 227 N.L.R.B. 1223 (1977); *Illinois Bell Telephone Co.*, 221 N.L.R.B. 989 (1975).) Yet, the Sixth Circuit Court of Appeals upheld an employee's discharge and found that there was no Section 8(a)(1) violation when the employee left the interview to get

196

his steward in contravention of company policy and his supervisor's orders. (*NLRB v. Spartan Stores, Inc.*, 628 F.2d 953 (6th Cir. 1980).) On the related question of whether union representatives can be disciplined for asserting their right to represent an employee at an investigatory interview, the Board has held that such action is a Section 8(a)(1) violation. (*Columbus Foundries, Inc.*, 229 N.L.R.B. 34 (1977); *Georgia Power Co.*, 238 N.L.R.B. 572 (1978).)

A frequently litigated question is whether *Weingarten* rights exist where there is no union certified as the employee's exclusive bargaining representative. In *Glomac Plastics, Inc.*, the Board recognized the employee's *Weingarten* rights where the Board certified the union, but the employer refused to recognize the union. (234 N.L.R.B. 1309 (1978). *See also Brown & Connolly, Inc.*, 237 N.L.R.B. 271 (1978); *Anchortank, Inc.*, 239 N.L.R.B. 430 (1978).) In *Newton Steel Metal, Inc.*, the Board stated that there was no need to establish statutory representative status before employees can enjoy the benefits of *Weingarten* rights. (238 N.L.R.B. 970 (1978). *See also Crown Zellerbach, Inc.*, 239 N.L.R.B. 1124 (1978); *PPG Industries, Inc.*, 251 N.L.R.B. 1146 (1980).)

In *Good Samaritan Nursing Home, Inc.*, the Board stated that a union representative may be a fellow employee or the representative of a union that has not been certified. (250 N.L.R.B. 207 (1980).) The Board has distinguished these cases on whether or not an election has been held. In *Anchortank, Inc. v. NLRB*, the Fifth Circuit Court of Appeals held that during the hiatus where the employer challenged the union election victory, the employees have the right to union representation at investigatory interviews. The court, in enforcing the Board, held that before a representation election, there is no right to union representation because there is no concerted activity. An employee's activity at the pre-election stage does not have

197

the requisite effect on his fellow employees to be concerted activity. (618 F.2d 1153 (5th Cir. 1980).)

In fashioning a proper remedy for violating an employee's *Weingarten* rights, the Board has two options available. The Board may issue a traditional cease and desist order or order reinstatement of the employee and back pay. In *Kraft Foods, Inc.,* the Board set forth the analysis upon which the Board determines what the proper remedy is for *Weingarten* violations. (251 N.L.R.B. 598 (1980).) First, the General Counsel must make a *prima facie* showing that the employer conducted an illegal interview and subsequently, the employee was disciplined for the conduct that was the subject of the unlawful interview. If the General Counsel sustains his burden, the employee is entitled to a make-whole remedy. The burden then shifts to the employer to show that its decision to discipline the employee was not based on information obtained at the unlawful interview. If the employer does not meet its burden, the Board will issue a cease and desist order to remedy the Section 8(a)(1) violation. *(Id.)*

In *Coyne Cylinder Co.,* an employee was caught smoking marijuana and was discharged. Prior to the employee's discharge, the employer interviewed the employee and violated his rights by denying him the right to union representation. The Board agreed with the Administrative Law Judge that the employee's rights were violated, but did not order back pay and reinstatement because the decision to fire the employee was made before the interview. (251 N.L.R.B. 1503 (1980). *See also Colgate-Palmolive Co.,* 257 N.L.R.B. No. 28 (1981); *Ball Corp.,* 257 N.L.R.B. No. 126 (1981).)

In *Montgomery Ward & Co.,* the Board held that affirmative relief was warranted where the employee was discharged as a result of information obtained at an illegal interview. Overruling the Administrative Law Judge, the

Board noted that even though the information obtained was a direct admission of guilt on the part of the employee, the employee was still entitled to back pay and reinstatement. (254 N.L.R.B. 826 (1981). *See also Kahn's & Co.,* 253 N.L.R.B. 25 (1980); *Southern Bell Telephone & Telegraph,* 251 N.L.R.B. 1194 (1980); *Ohio Masonic Home,* 251 N.L.R.B. 606 (1980).) And where the employer obtained an employee's resignation through the denial of an employee's right to union representation, the Board ordered back pay and reinstatement, and additionally ordered that the employee's records be expunged of any disciplinary notices. (*Penn-Dixie Steel Corp.,* 253 N.L.R.B. 91 (1980).)

What appeared to be a neat delineation of an employee's rights by the Supreme Court in *Weingarten* has evolved over the years into anything but a clear and concise statement of the law. The contraction and expansion of the rights of employees by the courts and the Board have contributed to a body of law that requires a careful analysis of the factual situation before one's rights can be described with any accuracy. This analysis begins with a description of the interview. Is it disciplinary, investigatory, or run-of-the-mill shop talk? Even after this crucial, initial determination is made, the full scope of rights available to employees will vary depending on the particular facts of the case.

CHAPTER 7

FAIR REPRESENTATION

The duty of fair representation requires bargaining representatives to act "fairly" toward all employees whom they represent. The doctrine of fair representation has no explicit statutory origin, but was developed by the courts which interpreted the duty as a mandate of Congress. The courts reasoned that Congress would not grant the exclusive power of representation without requiring an agent to represent the employees fairly. The doctrine was later adopted by the National Labor Relations Board in representation proceedings and was subsequently applied in unfair labor practice cases.

The scope of the duty is often imprecise, and actions arising under the fair representation theory range widely from allegations of individual discrimination to charges of adverse treatment of an entire class of employees.

Typically, actions asserting breach of the duty of fair representation arise against the union, but employers may also be subject to court and Board actions under the doctrine. While many issues pertaining to this doctrine are unsettled, this chapter will present the established principles and review recent trends in the development of the doctrine.

§ 7-1. Origin and Historical Development.

The doctrine of fair representation was first articulated in cases arising under the Railway Labor Act which, like the National Labor Relations Act, authorizes the selection of a labor organization to represent all employees of a bargaining unit. In announcing the doctrine, the Supreme Court, in *Steele v. Louisville & Nashville R.R.*, 323 U.S. 192 (1944), held that in granting authority to bargaining representatives, the statute imposed "the duty to exercise fairly the power conferred upon it in behalf of all those for whom it acts, without hostile discrimination against them." (*Id.* at 202-03.) Although the *Steele* case involved racial discrimination, the Court held that the statute proscribed all "hostile" and "invidious" discrimination and imposed the duty to act "fairly, impartially, and in good faith." (*Id.* at 204.) Less than a decade later, the Supreme Court announced that the duty to act "fairly and impartially" was also imposed upon bargaining representatives under the Labor Management Relations Act. (*Ford Motor Co. v. Huffman,* 345 U.S. 330 (1953).)

From the inception of the doctrine, the courts have held that fair representation rights are enforceable in the courts through damages and appropriate injunctive relief against the union and the employer. (*Steele,* 323 U.S. at 207).) However, the courts have not agreed as to whether, and to what degree, Labor Board machinery may be employed to enforce fair representation rights. While the Board invoked the doctrine early in the representation proceedings. (*Hughes Tool Co.*, 104 N.L.R.B. 318 (1953)), it was not until its *Miranda Fuel* decision in 1962 that the Board found that a breach of duty of fair representation could be an unfair labor practice under the Act. (140 N.L.R.B. 181 (1962).) In recent years the doctrine has been broadened significantly, due primarily to two leading Supreme Court decisions, *Vaca v. Sipes*, 386 U.S. 171 (1967), and *Hines v. Anchor Motor Freight, Inc.*, 424 U.S. 554 (1976). In *Vaca*, the definition of breach of the duty was broadened beyond hostility to include conduct toward a member which is "arbitrary, discriminatory, or in bad faith." (386 U.S. at 190.) Further, the *Vaca* court held that a union may not ignore a meritorious grievance or process in a perfunctory fashion. (*Id.*) Some recent cases have extended this standard to the point of finding a breach where a union has been negligent in processing a grievance. (*See, e.g., Ruzicka v. General Motors Corp.*, 523 F.2d 306 (6th Cir. 1975).) In the *Hines* decision, the Supreme Court further opened the gate for fair representation actions by holding that, where a union's malfeasance renders the grievance process or machinery ineffective, the employee may resort to the courts to enforce contractual rights notwithstanding an arbitration and finality clause in the collective bargaining agreement. (424 U.S. at 566.)

§ 7-2. General Nature of the Duty.

The union must comply with the duty of fair representation in all matters relating to wages, hours, terms, and conditions of employment. The obligation of fair representation applies when a union is negotiating or administering a collective bargaining agreement and may be breached with regard to one employee or any large number.

Steele and other early cases confronted breach of the duty in the form of racial discrimination, but the duty has always been characterized in general, malleable terms. (*See, e.g.,* *Vaca v. Sipes,* 386 U.S. 171 (1967).) The duty is affirmative, requiring that employees be treated "fairly" and "in good faith." Nevertheless, much emphasis is placed on avoiding "hostile" and "invidious" discrimination (*Id.* at 177), and different treatment of employees is clearly prohibited where bad faith or malice is a motivating factor in the representative's actions. (*Hines,* 424 U.S. at 564.) In some recent decisions, "bad faith" has been interpreted to include a lack of diligence or even carelessness in representing an employee's interest. (*See* subsection *Negligent Representation, infra.*)

The duty clearly does not proscribe discriminatory action simply because it adversely affects particular employees. For instance, when negotiating a collective bargaining agreement, a union may exercise its discretion to draw reasonable distinctions among groups of employees. (*Ford Motor Co. v. Huffman,* 345 U.S. 330, 337-38 (1953).) Further, in the administration of a contract, a union may exercise its judgment in a manner which has unfavorable impact on particular employees. Thus, a union is not required to take every grievance to arbitration. (*Vaca,* 386 U.S. at 191.) In *Huffman,* the Supreme Court noted that "[a] wide range of reasonableness must be allowed a statutory bargaining representative in serving the unit it represents, subject always to complete good faith and honesty of purpose in the exercise of its discretion." (345 U.S. at 338.) Thus, it is not unreasonable in negotiating wages to consider factors of seniority (*Id.* at 338-43), or to give veterans' credit in job seniority for time spent in military service. (*Goodin v. Clinchfield R.R.,* 229 F.2d 578 (6th Cir. 1956).) Where two groups of employees are merged, a union may adjust their seniority rights or dovetail the employees based on reasonable rationales, such as prior individual seniority. (*Humphrey v. Moore,* 375 U.S. 335 (1964).) Fair representation requires "fair," not equal or identical, treatment of employees.

§ 7-3. Specific Applications of the Duty.

While the courts have expanded the application of the duty of fair representation to include more situations, the doctrine has always been defined in the same terms, that is, "fairly, impartially, and in good faith" and "without hostile discrimination." (*Steele*, 323 U.S. at 204.) The courts have uniformly agreed that this standard applies to blatant types of discrimination such as race, union membership, or malicious personal discrimination. (*See R. Gorman, Basic Text on Labor Law*, at 707-10 (1976).) However, where the employee complains of arbitrary or perfunctory conduct, the courts have not charted a clear course. (*Id.* at 715-19.)

Race, Sex, and National Origin

In *Steele*, the United States Supreme Court declared that "discriminations based on race alone are obviously irrelevant and invidious." (323 U.S. at 203.) In the period preceding the Civil Rights Act of 1964, the courts consistently held that racial discrimination absolutely violated the fair representation duty inherent within the National Labor Relations Act and the Railroad Labor Act. (*See, e.g., Brotherhood of R.R. Trainmen v. Howard*, 343 U.S. 768 (1952).) The duty to avoid racial discrimination applies not only when negotiating contracts, but to processing grievances as well. In *Local 12, United Rubber Workers v. NLRB*, 368 F.2d 12 (5th Cir. 1966), for example, the Court of Appeals for the Fifth Circuit found that the union violated the Act by refusing to process grievances for black employees. Similarly, discriminations based on national origin, citizenship, and inability to speak English have also been held violative of the duty of fair representation. (*See, e.g., NLRB v. Longshoremen's Local 1581*, 489 F.2d 635 (5th Cir. 1974), *cert. denied*, 419 U.S. 1040 (1974) (citizenship); *Retana v. Apartment & Elevator Operators Local 14*, 453 F.2d 1018 (9th Cir. 1972) (language ability).) Recent decisions have declared that discrimination on the basis of sex also violates the duty under the Act. (*See, e.g., NLRB v. Local 106, Glass Bottle Blowers Ass'n*, 520 F.2d 693 (6th Cir. 1975).) Sex discrimination issues frequently arise where collective bargaining agreements encourage, permit, or tolerate sex discrimination. For example, if a union denies the right of women to bump less-senior male employees, a breach of the duty may be found. (*Petersen v. Rath Packing Co.*, 461 F.2d 312 (8th Cir. 1972).) Similarly, sex discrimination in union hiring hall practices, (*Pacific Maritime Ass'n*, 209 N.L.R.B. 519 (1974)), and in handling grievances also violates the duty of fair representation. (*Glass Bottle Blowers*, 520 F.2d at 696.)

§ 7-4. Union Membership.

Under Section 9(a) of the National Labor Relations Act, a union has a statutory duty to represent employees in the bargaining unit who are not union members as well as those who are members of the union. (*Wallace Corp. v. NLRB*, 323 U.S. 248 (1944).) However, a union does not have to include all categories of employees within its bargaining unit. (*Smith v. Local 25, Sheet Metal Workers*, 500 F.2d 741 (5th Cir. 1974).) It may exercise its discretion in advocating a unit of particular employees if it is based upon reasonable, non-hostile factors. All employees within the unit must be represented fairly without regard to union membership.

Discrimination based on activities or union politics is also considered to be irrelevant and invidious. (*Radio Officers' Union v. NLRB*, 347 U.S. 17 (1954).) Union discrimination against an employee based on union membership is

205

specifically prohibited by Section 8(b)(2) of the Act, and an employer is subject to a charge of unfair labor practice under Section 8(a)(3) if it cooperates with, or enters into agreements which effectuate, such discrimination. (*Id.* at 47.) In the *Red Ball Motor Freight, Inc.,* decision, a union unfair labor practice under Section 8(b)(1)(A) was found where a union placed employees who worked for rival organizations at the bottom of a seniority list for "purely political reasons." (157 N.L.R.B. 1237 (1966), *enf'd sub nom. Truck Drivers Local 568 v. NLRB,* 379 F.2d 137 (D.C. Cir. 1967).)

§ 7-5. Personal Discrimination or Animosity.

Personal discrimination or animosity, where individual employees are treated differently for malicious or irrelevant reasons, is also clearly proscribed under the doctrine of fair representation. The leading illustration is the *Miranda Fuel* case in which the Board first declared that the breach of fair representation was an unfair labor practice. (140 N.L.R.B. 181 (1962), *enforcement denied,* 326 F.2d 172 (2d Cir. 1963).) In that case, union officials, for hostile and invidious reasons, caused an employee to lose his seniority. Personal hostility is plainly prohibited by the basic rule in *Vaca* which states that a union has a duty "to serve the interest of all members without hostility or discrimination toward any, to exercise its discretion with complete good faith and honesty, and to avoid arbitrary conduct." (*Vaca,* 386 U.S. at 177.)

The duty of fair representation is not necessarily breached when a union exchanges an employee's meritorious grievance for a bargaining demand or another grievance. (*Buchholtz v. Swift & Co.,* 609 F.2d 317 (8th Cir. 1979), *cert. denied,* 444 U.S. 1018 (1980); *Union News Co. v. Hildreth,* 295 F.2d 658 (6th Cir. 1961), *cert. denied,* 375

U.S. 826 (1963).) Although the courts have decided these cases with mixed results, the duty is certainly breached if the victim of the swap is sacrificed because of union activities or personal animosity. (*Simberlund v. Long Island R.R.*, 421 F.2d 1219 (2d Cir. (1970). *Cf. Local 13, Longshoremen's & W. Union v. Pacific Maritime Ass'n*, 441 F.2d 1061 (9th Cir. 1971), *cert. denied*, 404 U.S. 1016 (1971).)

§ 7-6. Arbitrary or Perfunctory Representation.

Acting without hostility, malice, or animosity, a union may fail to diligently carry out its duty of representation. The *Vaca* decision made it abundantly clear that "arbitrary" and "perfunctory" representation is banned under the fair representation doctrine. (386 U.S. at 194.) Noting that unions should have latitude to decide whether to process grievances, the Court emphasized that unions must make decisions regarding the merits of particular grievances in "good faith and in a non-arbitrary manner." (*Id.*) In *Holodnak v. Avco Corp.*, a federal district court held that the duty of fair representation was breached by a union which acted in a "perfunctory" manner, having failed to zealously defend an employee in an arbitration proceeding. (381 F. Supp. 191 (D. Conn. 1974), *modified*, 514 F.2d 285 (2d Cir. 1975).) Specifically, the union's attorney neglected to challenge a company rule which was obviously overly broad. In another decision, *Figueroa de Arroyo v. Sindicato de Trabajadores Packinghouse*, 425 F.2d 281 (1st Cir. 1970), *cert. denied*, 400 U.S. 877, the court found a breach of the duty due to the "perfunctory attention" given to grievance processing. There, without any real justification, the union failed to investigate the grievant's claims.

In 1975, the Labor Board endorsed a standard of fair representation which imposes a duty to refrain from arbitrary action. (*General Truck Drivers' Local 315*, 217 N.L.R.B. 616 (1975).) The Board held that at every stage of representation, from bargaining to grievance processing, "there at least . . . be a reason for action taken." (*Id.* at 618.) Even with good faith and complete lack of hostile motive, the union must avoid arbitrary and perfunctory conduct.

"Perfunctory" representation, as distinguished from "arbitrary" conduct, means "without concern or solicitude; indifferent." (*Ethier v. United States Postal Service*, 590 F.2d 733, 736 (8th Cir. 1979), *cert. denied*, 444 U.S. 826.) In one decision, however, the Labor Board upheld a finding of unfair representation merely because the union unreasonably failed to consider the validity of a dischargee's grievance. (*Service Employees International Union, Local No. 579, AFL-CIO*, 229 N.L.R.B. 692, 695 (1977).) In its decision, the Board characterized the duty of fair representation as analogous to that of a legislator to a constituent. (*Id.* at 692, n. 2.)

§ 7-7. Negligent Representation.

Frequently, the duty to avoid arbitrary and perfunctory conduct is characterized in terms which approach a negligence standard. In *Foust v. I.B.E.W.*, 572 F.2d 710 (10th Cir. 1978), *rev'd in part*, 442 U.S. 42 (1979), for example, the test was whether acts of the representatives were "reasonable or unreasonable under the circumstances." (572 F.2d at 714.) While the courts have not uniformly adopted a negligence standard for determining breach of the duty of fair representation, several courts have ostensibly applied a standard similar to traditional negligence. The Court of Appeals for the Sixth Circuit in *Ruzicka v. General Motors Corp.*, 523 F.2d 306 (6th Cir. 1975), for example, held that the union breached the duty by failing to file a required procedural notice which would have allowed an employee's claim to go to arbitration. In a federal district court decision, a union was held liable for simply performing poorly in preparing and arguing an employee's grievance, (*Thompson v. International Ass'n of Machinists & Lodge 1049*, 258 F. Supp. 235 (E.D. Va. 1966).) And in another case, the Court of Appeals for the Ninth Circuit held that a union breached its duty of fair representation by failing to notify an employee that it decided against taking her case to arbitration, thereby leading the employee to reject a settlement offer she otherwise would have accepted. (*Robesky v. Qantas Empire Airways, Ltd.*, 573 F.2d 1082 (9th Cir. 1978).)

A substantial number of courts have clearly rejected a negligence type of standard under the duty of fair representation. (*See, e.g., Ryan v. N.Y. Newspaper Printing Pressman's Union No. 2*, 590 F.2d 451 (2d Cir. 1979).) Further, the Labor Board has issued decisions which have rejected a traditional negligence concept in the duty. In *Local 18, Operating Engineers*, for instance, the Board held that "mere forgetfulness or inadvertent error is not the type of conduct" which constitutes a breach under the standard announced in *Miranda Fuel*. (144 N.L.R.B. 1365 (1963). *See also* summary of the Board's position in *Service Employees Int'l Union, Local 579*, 229 N.L.R.B. 692, 695 (1977).)

The distinction between "arbitrary," as defined under the duty of fair representation, and "negligence" is often murky indeed. The terminology has differed among the courts, and inconsistent application has produced varying results under similar fact patterns. A recent district court decision, *Kleban v. Hygrade Food Products Corp.*, reconciled some of the varying approaches used to resolve the question of negligent representation. (102 LRRM 2773 (E.D. Mich. 1979).) The court concluded that negligent representation established a claim under the duty only where the representative's action undermined the "integrity" of the arbitral process. (*Id.* at 2778.) "The courts must finally ensure that the system *does* work; negligence that prevents it from working well will be remedied," the *Kleban* court noted. *(Id.)* Perfunctory processing is an illustration of one kind of negligent processing which undermines the integrity of the system. In sum, while some courts have seemingly followed a traditional concept of negligence, the *Kleban* approach is more indicative of the general trend. Nevertheless "the mere fact that the union is inept, negligent, unwise, and insensitive, or ineffectual, will not, *standing alone,* establish a breach of the duty." (*NLRB General Counsel Memorandum,* 48 L.W. 2081 (July 31, 1979) (emphasis added).)

§ 7-8. NLRB Actions Under the Duty — Unfair Labor Practices.

The Labor Board has generally followed the courts, applying the duty of fair representation in representation proceedings and unfair labor practice cases. In *Miranda Fuel,* the Board held that Section 9(a) of the Act imposed upon exclusive bargaining representatives a duty of fair representation which was enforceable through the unfair labor practice provisions of the Act. (140 N.L.R.B. 181 (1962), *enforcement denied,* 326 F.2d 172 (2d Cir. 1963).) The Board held that under Section 7, employees had a right to be free from unfair, irrelevant, or invidious discrimination. (*Id.* at 185.) A majority of the Board concluded that the union had violated Section 8(b)(1)(A) and (2). (*Id.*) Although *Miranda Fuel* was reversed by the Court of Appeals for the Second Circuit in a split decision, the Board continued to find Section 8(b)(1)(A) and/or (2) violations in subsequent cases when the union engaged in invidious or arbitrary discrimination which deprived employees of their entitled representation. (*Truck Drivers & Helpers, Local 568, Teamsters v. NLRB (Red Ball Motor Freight),* 379 F.2d 137

(D.C. Cir. 1967).) For example, in *Barton Brands, Ltd. v. NLRB,* 529 F.2d 793 (7th Cir. 1976), the Board followed the Supreme Court's decision in *Radio Officers' Union v. NLRB,* 347 U.S. 17 (1954), which held that Section 8(b)(2) "applies where the union has induced the employer to discriminate on the basis of any invidious or arbitrary classification." (*Barton Brands,* 529 F.2d at 799.) In *Hughes Tool,* the Board declared that a breach of the fair representation duty also violated Section 8(b)(3). (147 N.L.R.B. 1573 (1964).) The Board reasoned that the duty to bargain in good faith was violated by "bad faith" bargaining. (*See also Local 12, United Rubber Workers v. NLRB (Goodyear Tire & Rubber Co.),* 150 N.L.R.B. 312 (1964).)

The Board has also found accompanying unfair labor practices against an employer if it assists in the breach of the duty of fair representation. While the employer is not the bargaining representative of employees, *Miranda Fuel* held that an employer violates Section 8(a)(1) by acceding to a union demand which is discriminatory. (140 N.L.R.B. at 190.) The Board further held that Section 8(a)(3) may be violated if such activity by the employer tends to discourage union membership. (*Id.*)

§ 7-9. Representation Cases.

The doctrine of fair representation has been applied in representation cases before the Board, albeit with some inconsistency. The inconsistency has notably occurred in the area of processing election petitions. In *Bekins Moving & Storage Co. of Florida, Inc.,* 211 N.L.R.B. 138 (1974), the Board declared that the statute and the Constitution prohibited the granting of certification to a union that practices discrimination on the basis of race, alienage, or national origin. But in a subsequent case the Board refused to apply the same prohibition to discrimination on the basis of sex. (*Bell & Howell Co.,* 213 N.L.R.B. 407 (1974).) In

211

1977, the Board overruled *Bekins* in its *Handy-Andy, Inc.,* decision, holding that the Board will no longer consider the issues of discrimination on the basis of race, alienage, or national origin in granting certification. (228 N.L.R.B. 447 (1977).) The Board stated that it does not "place its imprimatur on all of the organization's activities, lawful or otherwise." (*Id.* at 450.) The Board further noted that Congress has provided other machinery specifically designed to address the problems of racial and other discrimination. (*Id.* at 454.) The Board did indicate, however, that invidious discrimination could be considered in representation proceedings if the discriminatory practices interfered with employees' right to freely choose their bargaining representatives. The Board has followed *Handy-Andy* in subsequent decisions. (*Plumbers Local 393 (Hall-Way Contracting Co.),* 232 N.L.R.B. 644 (1977).) It should be noted that the Court of Appeals for the Eighth Circuit, in *NLRB v. Mansion House Center Mfg. Corp.,* has held that an employer can maintain a defense to a refusal to bargain charge if the union restricts membership on the basis of race. (473 F.2d 471 (8th Cir. 1973).)

The Board held in *Hughes Tool Co.,* 147 N.L.R.B. 1573 (1964), a racial discrimination case, that a union's certification could be revoked if the union failed in its duty to provide equal representation. Upon the same principle, the Board had earlier held that the contract bar could not protect from ouster a union which openly practiced racial discrimination. (*Pioneer Bus Co.,* 140 N.L.R.B. 54 (1962).)

§ 7-10. Jurisdiction and Related Issues.

§ 7-10(A). Statutory Jurisdiction Generally.

In 1955, the Supreme Court decided, *per curiam,* that federal or state courts could hear cases alleging breach of fair representation under Taft-Hartley, even if a contractual claim is alleged. (*Syres v. Oil Workers, Local 23*, 350 U.S. 892 (1955).) The Court further stated that the federal courts could hear contractual matters even in the absence of diversity of citizenship. Section 301 of Taft-Hartley (29 U.S.C. § 185), specifically grants federal jurisdiction to the parties of a collective bargaining agreement, allowing them to enforce contractual obligations. Further, in 1962, the Supreme Court extended Section 301 rights to individual employees. (*Smith v. Evening News Ass'n*, 371 U.S. 195 (1962).)

Fair representation suits often are not directly founded upon contractual grounds, but breaches of the duty of fair representation clearly are jurisdictional under 28 U.S.C. § 1337 which grants district courts "original jurisdiction of any civil action or proceeding arising under an Act of Congress regulating commerce. . . ." Some courts have held that, in the absence of a contractual claim, a fair representation action can only be based on Section 1337 because Section 301 of Taft-Hartley is specifically limited to " [s]uits for violation of contracts." (*Mumford v. Glover*, 503 F.2d 878 (5th Cir. 1974); *Smith v. Local 25, Sheet Metal Workers*, 500 F.2d 741 (5th Cir. 1974).) In *Nedd v. United Mine Workers*, for example, a union's pension trustees had not fairly represented retiree interests with the apparent motive of favoring the active employees. (556 F.2d 190 (3d Cir. 1977).) The Court of Appeals for the Third Circuit held that, unless a breach of contract was alleged, no jurisdiction existed under Section 301. (*Id.* at 198.) However, the court did find jurisdiction under Sections 1337 and 1331 of Title 28 of the United States Code which grants jurisdiction where there is a federal question and an amount in controversy exceeding $10,000. (*Id.* at 199.) In sum, Section 301 may be plead in fair representation actions involving a contractual breach, but Section 1337 should be plead where contractual grounds are absent or uncertain.

§ 7-10(B). The Doctrine of Preemption.

In *San Diego Building Trades Council v. Garman,* the United States Supreme Court held that state courts are preempted of jurisdiction in specified areas granted to the National Labor Relations Board by Congress in the National Labor Relations Act. (359 U.S. 236 (1959).) In an effort to effectuate a uniform national labor policy, the Labor Board was granted primary jurisdiction over matters such as those involving unfair labor practices. *(Id.)* Thus, the doctrine ostensibly denied jurisdiction to state and federal district courts over matters designated as within the Board's jurisdiction. As discussed, *supra,* the Board did not classify the breach of the duty of fair representation as an unfair labor practice until *Miranda Fuel* in 1962. (140 N.L.R.B. 181 (1962), *enforcement denied,* 326 F.2d 172 (2d Cir. 1963).) After the Board's assertion of jurisdiction over fair representation matters, some courts, relying on *Garman,* declared that they no longer had jurisdiction over cases arising under breach of the duty. (*See* R. Gorman, *Labor Law* 703.) However, in *Humphrey v. Moore,* the Supreme Court recognized that breaches of collective bargaining agreements, with or without collateral issues relating to unfair labor practices, are actionable in state or federal courts, "subject, of course, to the applicable federal law." (375 U.S. at 344.) Later in *Vaca v. Sipes,* the Supreme Court held that the Labor Board did not have an exclusive right to enforce the duty of fair representation. (386 U.S. at 184.) The Court reasoned that the doctrine was initially court-created and that Section 301 granted specific jurisdiction for contract actions which were inextricably intertwined with fair representation claims. The Court also indicated that the Board, including the General Counsel's Office, would not have the interest, resources, or the remedial machinery needed to handle all the fair representation type claims brought under Section 301. (*Id.* at 183.) The *Vaca* Court suggested that actions relating to discharge without cause or loss of seniority rights would be better handled in the courts. Thus, *Vaca* cleared the way for further fashioning of fair representation rights in the courts, notwithstanding the Board's concurrent handling of similar matters in unfair labor practice proceedings. The cases subsequent to *Vaca* have continued to hold that state and federal actions for breach of the duty of fair representation under Section 301 are generally not preempted by the Labor Board's jurisdiction. (*See, e.g., Kuhn v. Letter Carriers,* 528 F.2d 767 (8th Cir. 1976).)

§ 7-10(C). Exhaustion and Finality of Contractual Remedies.

Fair representation actions frequently involve issues relating to the administration of the contract, particularly the grievance machinery. Typically, collective bargaining agreements contain specified grievance procedures which restrict or bar parties from resorting to the courts for enforcement or damages. (*Republic Steel Corp. v. Maddox,* 379 U.S. 650 (1965).) Generally, the courts have held that such a grievance or remedy provision may properly bar litigation in the judicial system. In *Vaca,* the Court stated that before an employee may sue on a claim based upon breach of a collective bargaining agreement, "the employee must at least attempt to exhaust the exclusive grievance and arbitration procedures established by the collective bargaining agreement." (386 U.S. at 184.) However, the Court delineated circumstances under which an employee would not be limited to these internal remedial procedures. Specifically, "when the conduct of an employer amounts to repudiation of those contractual procedures," the employee may seek outside judicial enforcement without exhaustion

215

of the contract's remedial machinery. (*Id.* at 185.) Likewise, "if the union has the sole power under the contract to invoke the higher stage of the grievance procedure, and ... the employer-plaintiff has been prevented from exhausting remedies by the union's *wrongful* refusal to process the grievance," an employee may proceed to pursue his claim in the courts. (*Id.*) "Wrongful refusal to process a grievance" would include an arbitrary refusal or perfunctory handling of a grievance or even circumstances which would render arbitration futile. (*Smith v. Pittsburgh Gage & Supply Co.*, 464 F.2d 870 (3d Cir. 1972).)

The United States Supreme Court recently declined to impose a "universal exhaustion requirement." (*Clayton v. International Union, U.A.W.*, 451 U.S. 679, 689 (1981).) The Court specifically held that an employee need not exhaust internal procedures if any of three factors is present: (1) the existence of union hostility which would preclude any hope of a fair hearing; (2) internal union procedures which are inadequate either to reactivate the employee's grievance or to grant full relief sought under Section 301; or (3) the exhaustion of internal union procedures would unreasonably delay the employee's opportunity to obtain a judicial hearing on the merits of his claim. (*Id.* at 689.)

In 1976, the Supreme Court declared in *Hines v. Anchor Motor Freight, Inc.*, 424 U.S. 554 (1976), that a submission of a claim to the final stage of the contractual grievance process does not necessarily bar further redress in the courts. The Court held that an employer may be liable in a fair representation action even though the contract specified that arbitration was final and binding, if the union's breach of duty seriously undermined "the integrity of the arbitral process." (*Id.* at 556.) This rule applies even if the employer has acted in good faith, the Court indicated, because an employer cannot justifiably escape its contractual obligations due to the union's malfeasance or misfeasance. *(Id.)*

§ 7-11. Remedies in the Courts.

The courts disagree as to the nature of the substantive cause of action in cases alleging breach of the duty of fair representation. The Supreme Court has often characterized the action as a breach of "duty" thereby inferring an action in tort. *(See, e.g., Vaca,* 386 U.S. at 190.) On the other hand, most fair representation actions are partially based upon contract, *i.e.,* the collective bargaining agreement. The courts of appeals have split on this issue, and the Court of Appeals for the Eighth Circuit has summarized the varying approaches in *Butler v. Teamsters, Local 823,* 514 F.2d 442 (8th Cir. 1975). The determination of whether fair representation actions are in tort or contract is of critical importance because the statute of limitations under state law is generally longer for actions brought in contract. There is no single federal statute of limitations period, although there is a six-month period under the National Labor Relations Act for unfair labor practice charges. In *Del Costello v. Teamsters,* 103 S. Ct. 2281 (1983), the Supreme Court clarified this issue, holding that the six-month statute of limitations found in Section 10(b) of the National Labor Relations Act governed in employee suits for breach of the duty of fair representation in handling grievances or arbitrations under a collective bargaining agreement.

Jury Trials

Another area in which the courts of appeals differ is the availability of jury trials. The mixed nature of the doctrine, being both legal and equitable, has divided the courts in resolving the question of whether jury trials are appropriate. Some courts have held that a jury trial is appropriate

(*Minnis v. Automobile Workers,* 531 F.2d 850 (8th Cir. 1975)), and at least one court has allowed a jury trial for legal claims, but reserved the equitable aspects of fair representation for resolution by the court. (*Rowan v. Howard Sober, Inc.,* 384 F. Supp. 1121 (E.D. Mich. 1974).) Recent cases seem to favor the granting of jury trials in fair representation cases. (*See, e.g., Smith v. Hussmann Refrigerator Co.,* 619 F.2d 1229 (8th Cir. 1980); *Cox v. C.H. Masland & Sons, Inc.,* 607 F.2d 138 (5th Cir. 1979).)

§ 7-11(A). Damages and Injunctive Relief.

In actions alleging breach of contract, both the employer and the union may be liable. However, the union's liability is usually limited to an amount for the damages which result from its breach of the duty of fair representation, and often the amount is *di minimus.* (*Vaca,* 386 U.S. at 197. *See also Zosek v. O'Mara,* 397 U.S. 25 (1970).) In *Vaca,* (the Supreme Court held that liability in fair representation cases must be apportioned according to the fault of each party. (*Richardson v. Communications Workers of America,* 443 F.2d 974 (8th Cir. 1971), *cert. denied,* 414 U.S. 818 (1973).) In *Hines,* the Court indicated that an employer could possibly be liable for damages which were caused or increased as a result of the union's breach of the duty of fair representation. (424 U.S. at 566.)

Injunctive relief, such as ordering reinstatement, may be granted by a court to remedy a breach of the duty of fair representation. (*Steele v. Louisville & Nashville R.R.,* 323 U.S. 192 (1944); *Central of Ga. Ry. v. Jones,* 229 F.2d 648 (5th Cir. 1956), *cert. denied,* 362 U.S. 848 (1956).) In addition, compensatory damages for past economic losses may be awarded (*see, e.g., St. Clair v. Local No. 515 of Int'l Brotherhood of Teamsters,* 422 F.2d 128 (6th Cir. 1969)), and the Court of Appeals for the First Circuit has held that future economic damages may be awarded if injunctive relief is not available.

218

In 1979, the Supreme Court held that punitive damages may not be awarded under the Railway Labor Act. (*I.B.E. v. Foust,* 442 U.S. 42, 52 (1979).) It is possible that the Supreme Court would reach the same conclusion under Taft-Hartley since the doctrine of fair representation is based upon the same underlying principle in both statutes.

§ 7-11(B). Award of Attorney Fees.

Attorney fees in fair representation cases have been awarded in some cases based upon a theory that evolved in a Landrum-Griffin Act case, *Hall v. Cole,* 412 U.S. 1 (1972). There, the Supreme Court held that federal courts had the equitable power to assess attorney fees against a union if substantial benefits were conferred upon all union members as a result of the action. (*Id.* at 14. For application under the L.M.R.A., *see, e.g., Scott v. Teamsters, Local 377,* 548 F.2d 1244 (6th Cir. 1977).) In one decision, however, an award of attorney fees with pre-award interest was disallowed by the Court of Appeals for the First Circuit. (*Sanabria v. International Longshoremen's Ass'n, Local 1575,* 597 F.2d 312 (1st Cir. 1979).)

§ 7-12. Remedies Before the Board.

The Board, as noted in the section entitled *NLRB Actions Under the Duty, supra,* can in some circumstances deny or revoke representative certification based upon evidence of fair representation violations. Further, the Board may find unfair labor practices as a result of the breach of the duty. The Board may employ its full range of remedies to correct unfair labor practices against the union and the employer, including the issuance of remedial and bargaining orders. (*See, e.g., Miranda Fuel Co.,* 140 N.L.R.B. 181 (1962) and R. Gorman, *Labor Law* 726.) Employees terminated as a result of the breach of the duty of fair representation may be made "whole" according to the usual Board backpay and reinstatement standards. *(Id.)* Unfair labor practice charges must be filed within 6 months of the alleged violative practice. (29 U.S.C. § 160(b) (1947).)

§ 7-13. Comparison of Board and Court Causes of Action.

There are significant differences in the causes of action and remedies available in fair representation cases before the Board and those available through the courts. First, a breach of the duty is not determined according to the same elements and standards. For example, an unfair labor practice complaint has elements of proof which differ from those found in a Section 301 contract action. Similarly, remedies under a Board action may be limited to rectifying the unfair labor practice while remedies under a contract action may be more expansive under the doctrine of fair representation. Unlike the Board, some courts allow future damages and attorney fees. On the other hand, where plaintiff is seeking to correct an ongoing practice, the Board may be able to issue a comprehensive remedial order which a court of equity would not issue due to the traditional restrictions on mandatory injunctions.

Practical considerations, such as greater expense and delay in the judicial proceedings, should not be overlooked.

CHAPTER 8

SECONDARY PRESSURE AND CONSUMER BOYCOTTS

§ 8-1. Generally.

The distinction between primary and secondary union activities is critical yet sometimes elusive. In order to understand Section 8(b)(4)(B), it is essential to grasp that primary activity is the term applied to direct union pressure against a primary employer. The dispute between the union and primary employer may concern, for example, economic, recognitional and organizational, or unfair labor practice issues. Most types of primary pressures are protected by the NLRA. (See *NLRB v. International Union of Operating Engineers, Local 825,* 400 U.S. 297, 302-03, 91 S. Ct. 402 (1971).) On the other hand, secondary activities are those pressures applied to neutral parties doing business with the primary at arm's length, such as customers or suppliers, usually for the purpose of exerting indirect pressures on the primary employer.

Certain secondary activities are lawful under the NLRA. However, one type, the secondary boycott, may be illegal. As Judge Learned Hand commented,

> The gravamen of the secondary boycott is that its sanctions bear, not upon the employer who is alone a party to the dispute, but upon some third party who has no concern in it. Its aim is to compel him to stop business with the employer in the hope that this will induce the employer to give in to his employee's demands.

221

(*Local 501, IBEW v. NLRB*, 181 F.2d 34, 37 (2d Cir. 1950), *aff'd*, 341 U.S. 694, 71 S. Ct. 954 (1951).)

A primary boycott is one in which a union, usually with the collaboration of other similarly situated unions, applies economic pressures to discourage use, handling, or purchase of services or products of a primary employer with whom the union has a dispute. However, if the union extends its pressure to other persons to cease doing business with the primary employer because of the dispute, the union engages in a secondary boycott.

Section 8(b)(4)(B) is commonly referred to as the secondary boycott provision of the NLRA. Ironically, however, the section does not use the terms "boycott" or "secondary." Instead, the section makes it an unfair labor practice for a union to engage in certain specific activities directed at obtaining certain prohibited objectives. The section seeks to prevent needlessly embroiling a neutral secondary party in a primary labor dispute between a union and an employer.

The two types of prohibited activity include:

(i) Engaging in a strike or boycott or inducing others to do so (*i.e.,* an actual strike occurs); or

(ii) Threatening, coercing, or restraining others involved in commerce where its object is to exert pressure on a neutral secondary in furtherance of its dispute with a primary.

The inducement may take the form of a request to cease work or picketing. But to be prohibited and therefore illegal, the activity must also have "an object" designated in clause (B) of Section 8(b)(4). The three objects are:

1. Forcing or requiring the employer to cease handling or dealing in goods.

2. Forcing or requiring the employer to cease doing business with the other person.

3. Forcing or requiring the employer to recognize an uncertified union.

The combination of a proscribed means with one of the proscribed objectives establishes a prima facie case of a violation, unless one of the three exceptions, or provisions, applies. The provisions exempt certain activities from the prohibition. Sympathy strikes, primary picketing, and publicity other than picketing may not be violative if certain guidelines are followed.

§ 8-2. The Ally Doctrine.

Section 8(b)(4) is designed to protect only those employers who are truly neutral from proscribed secondary activity. Thus, a secondary who is not neutral, *i.e.,* who willingly becomes involved in the primary dispute, may not be protected. A secondary who knowingly does business *for* the primary employer, not *with* the primary employer, voluntarily becomes involved in the dispute if he takes struck work in cooperation with the primary employer. The NLRB and the courts have held that such employers may lose their neutral status and become "allies" of the primary employer. In that case union pressure directed against them will be considered primary activity. (*NLRB v. Business Machine & Office Appl. Mech. Conf. B., Local 459,* 228 F.2d 553 (2d Cir. 1955), *cert. denied,* 351 U.S. 962 (1956); *Douds v. Metropolitan Fed. of Architects, Engineers, Chemists & Technicians, Local 231,* 75 F. Supp. 672 (S.D.N.Y. 1948).)

The Ally Doctrine is basically applicable in two situations: (1) employers who perform struck work for the primary employer which they would not have received but for the strike; and (2) employers who become so identified with the primary employer due to common ownership, control, and integration of operations that their businesses are treated as a straight line operation or single business entity.

The first category can be further broken down by virtue of existing business relations between the primary and secondary employers prior to and after the beginning of the strike. Employers who are already dealing with the struck primary employer, but who receive a larger quantity of work due to the strike fall into the first sub-category.

The Ally Doctrine was first articulated in 1948 in *Douds v. Metropolitan Architects, Local 231 (Ebasco)*. In *Ebasco*, a corporation dealing in engineering services was struck. Ebasco had subcontracted work to Project Engineering Company for one year prior to the strike. Once the strike began, Ebasco greatly increased the percentage of work being subcontracted to Project Engineering, including some work started by Ebasco employees and in progress at the time it was sent to Project. Ebasco paid Project directly, and its supervisors oversaw the work. When Project refused the union's request to cease their subcontracting work with Ebasco, the union picketed Project. The district court held that Project was not "doing business" with Ebasco within the meaning of Section 8(b)(4)(A), which was later amended to be Section 8(b)(4)(B), and that the union had not committed an unfair labor practice. The court did not literally apply the section, reasoning that Congress had not meant to ban a union's traditional weapons, and held that Congress had enacted Section 8(b)(4) to outlaw secondary activity against a *neutral*. The court found that Project had "made itself a party to the contest." In applying the "but for" test, the court held that "the evidence is abundant that Project's employees did work, which, but for the strike of Ebasco's employees, would have been done by Ebasco." Project thus lost its neutral status and made itself an ally of the primary employer, Ebasco. The economic effect of Project's actions was the same, the court analogized, as the hiring of strikebeaters, so the union's pressure was not an illegal secondary boycott of a neutral. Rather, the union

224

was exercising a protected primary activity at a site close and "intimately and indeed inextricably united to it." (*Douds v. Metropolitan Architects, Local 231*, 75 F. Supp. 672, 677 (S.D.N.Y. 1948).)

In *Douds*, the court's holding was based upon the existing business relationship between Ebasco and Project and the transfer to the secondary employer of the work, which, "but for" the strike, would have been performed by Ebasco employees.

In a later case the court held that, "In determining the applicability of the Ally Doctrine, the relevant question is not whether the ally duplicates the work of the striking employees but whether diverting work to the ally helps the struck employers to evade the economic pressure exerted by the strike." (*Seeler v. Teamsters, Local 375*, 81 LRRM 2575, 2578 (W.D.N.Y. 1972).) A later court held that no violation existed in a hiring hall setting when, for purposes of forcing a maintenance firm to cease doing business with the employer, a union refused to refer workers to a petroleum refinery. The court found that the workers would be performing tasks of the same nature as the striking employees at the plant. (*OCAW, Local 1-128 (Petroleum Maintenance Co.)*, 223 N.L.R.B. 757 (1976).)

A second category of cases includes employers who have had no prior dealings with the primary employer regarding the struck work and who take farmed out work during the strike. Such a case is *Royal Typewriter, NLRB v. Business Machines Local 459, IUE*, 228 F.2d 553 (2d Cir. 1955), *cert. denied*, 351 U.S. 96 (1956), in which a Board finding of a Section 8(b)(4) violation was reversed by the District court. In *Royal*, typewriter repairmen employed by Royal went on strike. Royal informed their customers who had repair service contracts with Royal to have work completed by independent repairmen and send the bills to Royal, who would then pay the independent contractors directly. The union

225

picketed Royal's larger customers and a number of independent repair services. The court, citing *Douds,* applied the ally doctrine to work not directly farmed out by arrangement with the primary employer, but which the secondary employer knew was struck work. The court held that where an employer seeks to avoid the economic consequences of a strike by securing the services of independent contractors who are not neutral, the striking union has a legitimate interest in preventing those services from being performed. The court further held that "an employer is not within the protection of Section 8(b)(4)(A) when he knowingly does work which would otherwise be done by the striking employees of the primary employer and where this work is paid for by the primary employer pursuant to an arrangement devised and originated by him to enable him to meet his contractual obligations. The result must be the same whether or not the primary employer makes any direct arrangement with the employers providing the services." (*Id.,* 228 F.2d at 558-59.) The concurring opinion provided a list of factors to be analyzed in determining neutrality, and pointed out that the issue of neutrality must be resolved on a case-by-case application of these factors, and not by applying a *per se* rule. The 1959 amendments changed Section 8(b)(4)(A) to 8(b)(4)(B).

Generally, an employer is not protected by Section 8(b)(4)(B) when he knowingly does work that would be done by striking employees and where work is paid for by the primary employer. Based on the *Ebasco* doctrine, independent contractors were not neutral and were allies of the primary employer if the relation between the independent contractor and the primary employer was direct and ongoing, and the strike merely increased the amount of work given to the independent contractor. An independent contractor is not a neutral if he knowingly assists and helps a primary employer during a strike by lessening its economic impact and benefits from the employer's payment.

Recent cases have held that: (1) "a secondary employer will not be considered an ally when the impetus for the arrangement by which the secondary performs the work comes solely from the customer of the primary employer and the otherwise struck work is not performed in the primary's name or for his benefit." (*Blackhawk Engraving Co. v. NLRB*, 540 F.2d 1296, 1301 (7th Cir. 1976)); (2) the ally doctrine applied although the employer announced that he had decided to discontinue the struck portion of his business which had been subcontracted during the strike. (*Graphic Arts Union, Local 277*, 222 N.L.R.B. 280 (1976)); (3) that the struck employer has the customer contract for the ally's services does not prevent an ally relationship from existing where the struck employer "orchestrated" the arrangements and the ally knew he was doing struck work. (*Id.*, and also at 225 N.L.R.B. 1253 (1976), *aff'd*, 545 F.2d 1079 (7th Cir. 1976)); and (4) a contractor can become an ally of a primary employer by "unknowingly" performing struck work for him. An employer has the burden of determining whether he is an ally or is doing struck work. (*Teamsters Local 563*, 176 N.L.R.B. 386 (1969).)

Following the concurring opinion in *Royal*, courts weigh various factors in determining whether or not an ally relationship exists. Not every employer performing struck work forfeits the protection of Section 8(b)(4). The Board and courts generally agree that there must be an arrangement between the primary employer and the ally, but the holdings based upon interpretation and application of the factors vary. (*See Truck Drivers Local 413*, 140 N.L.R.B. 1474, 1483 (1963) and *Graphic Arts Union*, 225 N.L.R.B. 1253 (1963).) Employers who merely handle products of a struck employer or purchase such materials do not become allies based upon this business relationship. (*See Steel Fabricator Local 810*, 131 N.L.R.B. 59, 71 (1961), *enforced*, 229 F.2d 636 (2d Cir. 1962).) The courts have further held

227

that the amount of pressure to be exerted upon an ally depends upon the identifiability of the primary employer's struck work, and if an economic alliance exists, employees of the secondary employer may be induced to stop work altogether and not merely to quit work on products for the primary employer. (*Shopmen's Local 501*, 210 N.L.R.B. 856 (1958). *See General Metals*, 120 N.L.R.B. 1227 (1958).)

Generally the burden of proof of showing that an ally relationship exists falls upon the union, which must show that the employer being picketed was in fact performing struck work, either farmed out or subcontracted. The Board has also placed a burden upon the employer to prove, by clear and convincing evidence, that its actions were appropriate when the employer claimed he had discontinued permanently dealing in the struck goods and the union continued to picket. (*Graphic Arts, reversed sub nom. Kable Printing Co. v. NLRB*, 532 F.2d 757 (7th Cir. 1976). *See Supplemental Decision on remand*, 225 N.L.R.B. 1253 (1976).) An employer who has accepted struck work and is in an ally relationship may relinquish this position and regain his neutral position by giving notice to the union that he is no longer performing struck work and relinquishing the struck work. (*Laundry, Dry Cleaning & Dye House Workers Int'l Union, Local No. 259*, 164 N.L.R.B. 426 (1967).)

Another way in which a secondary employer may be allied to a primary employer is through a community of common interest, ownership, and control. If the secondary employer is so closely aligned with the struck employer that the two are treated as a single economic entity, the secondary employer will be considered an ally for purposes of Section 8(b)(4) even if there is no struck work involved. Where a single corporate entity does business at more than one location, employees on strike at one location may picket plants at other locations to enlist the aid of the employees there. This is considered by the courts as primary picketing despite the difference in the work location. (*Milwaukee Plywood Co. v. NLRB*, 285 F.2d 325 (7th Cir. 1961).) Where a business is essentially a single enterprise with integration between its branches, its employees have the right to picket geographically separated parts in support of a primary dispute with one branch without proving the direct relationship between the parts at a local level. (*Teamsters Local 560*, 248 N.L.R.B. 1212 (1980).) The Board weighs four factors in determining whether several businesses are integrated sufficiently to be treated as one entity: (1) interrelation of operations; (2) common management; (3) centralized control of labor relations; and (4) common ownership or financial control. (*Radio & Television Broadcast Technicians Local 1264 v. Broadcast Service*, 380 U.S. 255, 256 (1965).) On the other hand, where a separate legal entity is picketed which has a degree of common ownership or control with a struck employer, the court has usually found a violation. For example, when the union had a dispute with the *Miami Herald*, owned by Knight Newspapers, Inc., the union picketed and shut down the *Detroit Free Press*, another Knight-owned paper in Detroit. The Board held that picketing at the *Free Press* was illegal secondary activity under Section 8(b)(4) because although there was common ownership and *potential* common control, no *actual* common control existed and the papers were not allies for purposes of the statute. (*Miami Newpaper Printing Pressmen*, 138 N.L.R.B. 1346 (1962).) In other words, common ownership alone is not enough to create an ally situation. Common operation, degree of integration, and actual common control are scrutinized and weighed by the Board and courts when arriving at a decision as to whether an ally relationship exists.

229

§ 8-3. Primary Picketing.

As discussed above, a union which has a dispute with a primary employer generally has a right to picket that employer for the purpose of exerting economic and public pressures. Subsection (i) of Section 8(b)(4) makes it an unfair labor practice for unions to "engage in, or to induce or encourage an individual employed by any person ... to engage in, a strike or a refusal in the course of his employment to use, manufacture, process, transport, or otherwise handle or work on any goods ... or to perform any services." This section is primarily aimed at union pressure on secondary employers, but at times unions may exert the same pressures upon employees of secondary employers. Primary picketing may serve as an exception for conduct found within the normal prohibition of Section 8(b)(4). The key case in this area is *NLRB v. International Rice Milling Co.,* 341 U.S. 665, 71 S. Ct. 961 (1951). In *Rice Milling* the union was engaged in recognitional picketing at a rice mill. A truck belonging to a neutral, with whom the union had no dispute, attempted to make a pickup at the site. Picketers sought to convince the two employees in the truck to turn back. A vice-president of the primary employer confronted the two truck drivers on the street and convinced them to return to the mill with him; however, the picketers confronted the three within the truck by throwing rocks at the vehicle. The Supreme Court acknowledged that: (1) the union, through its conduct, had encouraged the drivers to leave the plant, thereby causing them to stop performing services and handling materials for their employer; and (2) that the union's objectives were to exert pressure on the primary employer to recognize the union and to cause the secondary, the customer, to cease doing business with the mill. The Court, however, found no Section 8(b)(4) violation. The Court's decision was based partially on the require-

230

ment of an inducement of a "concerted" refusal to work on the part of employees of secondary employers. This inducement of "concerted" activity was changed in 1959 by amendment. An explanation of the Landrum-Griffin bill provides, "As the present act forbids inducing 'employees' to engage in a strike or 'concerted' refusal to do their work, the courts have held that unions may induce employees one at a time to engage in secondary boycotts. By changing 'employees' to 'any individual' and omitting the word 'concerted,' the proposed revision . . . closes this loophole." (105 Cong. Rec. 14347 (1959).) The new proviso inserted provides that, "Nothing contained in clause (B) of this paragraph (4) shall be construed to make unlawful, where not otherwise unlawful, any primary strike or primary picketing." In explanation, the drafters said, "The purpose of this provision is to make it clear that the changes in Section 8(b)(4) do not overrule or qualify the present rules of law permitting picketing at the site of a primary labor dispute. This provision does not eliminate, restrict, or modify the limitations on picketing at the site of a primary labor dispute that are in existing law. (*See for example, NLRB v. Denver Building & Construction Trades Council,* (341 U.S. 675 (1951); *Brotherhood of Painters, Decorators & Paper Managers & Pittsburgh Plate Glass Co.,* (110 N.L.R.B. 455 (1954); *Moore Dry Dock Co.,* (81 N.L.R.B. 1108); *Washington Coca-Cola Bottling Works, Inc.,* (107 N.L.R.B. 299 (1953))." (H.R. Rep. No. 1147, 86th Cong., 1st Sess. 38 (1959).)

More importantly, the Court found the picketing was primary because the union was picketing a primary employer with whom the union had a primary dispute. Primary picketing is not proscribed, and some incidental impact is associated with primary picketing. This secondary incidental impact is predictable, and yet not proscribed by Section 8(b)(4). In summary, so long as the picketing is primary, secondary and incidental impact which derives therefrom is not prohibited. The Court looked upon the violence in *Rice Milling* as immaterial to the Section 8(b)(4) charge, since the employer's charge was not based thereon, and, according to the Court, the statute sought to proscribe the *object* of union encouragement rather than the *means* utilized by the union to effectuate it. (*Id.* at 672.) The Court emphasized that Congress did not seek to infringe upon or diminish traditional union rights, such as the right to strike, unless such limitations were specifically enumerated in the statute. The incident in *Rice Milling,* therefore, was not reached by any specific provision of Section 8(b)(4). (*Id.*)

Although a portion of *Rice Milling* was invalidated by the 1959 amendments, the portion relating to incidental impact arising from primary picketing is still valid law.

§ 8-4. Common Situs Picketing.

In ascertaining whether union activity is primary or secondary, one important consideration is its location. (*International Rice Milling Co.,* 341 U.S. 665, 671, 7 S. Ct. 961 (1951).) Picketing of an employer with whom the union has a dispute is generally considered primary, whereas picketing at the premises of a neutral employer is considered secondary. (*Id.* at 671.) A particular problem arises with picketing the work place of an employer when that work site is coincidental with the work place of one or more neutral employers. This situation is generally defined as a common situs. In order to determine when such picketing is violative or protected activity under the statute, the NLRB has developed a four-pronged test derived from the landmark case in the area. (*Sailor's Union of the Pacific (Moore Drydock)*, 92 N.L.R.B. 547 (1950).) In designing the test, the court balanced the dual legislative objectives of protecting rights of unions to bring pressure to bear on primary employers versus guarding neutral secondary employers from becoming needlessly embroiled in outside disputes. (*Id.* at 576; *NLRB v. Denver Building & Construction Trades Council,* 341 U.S. 675, 679, 71 S. Ct. 943 (1951).)

Certain common situs picketing is prohibited by Section 8(b)(4)(i) when its object is to induce secondary employees not to cross the picket lines and consequently cease working. Section 8(b)(4)(ii) prohibits coercion of employer or employees to cease doing business with the primary employer. The Board and courts attempt, on a case by case application of the four-pronged *Moore* test, to balance the competing interests and fulfill legislative intent. In the influential *Moore* decision, the Board attempted to accommodate lawful primary picketing while shielding neutral secondary employers from involvement in disputes not their own. The relationship in the *Moore* case between the primary and secondary employers was that of supplier to consumer of services. Each employer was neutral regarding the labor disputes of the other. The Board held that when the situs, in this case a ship, of the primary employer was ambulatory, a balance must be struck between the union's right to picket and the secondary employer's freedom from being picketed. The Board outlined circumstances under which picketing at a common situs would be primary and lawful. The *Moore* test established the following four-pronged test:

A. The picketing is strictly limited to times when the situs of the dispute is located on the secondary employer's premises;

B. At the time of the picketing, the primary employer is engaged in its normal business at the situs;

C. The picketing is limited to places reasonably close to the location of the situs; and

D. The picketing discloses clearly that the dispute is with the primary employer. (*Sailors' Union of the Pacific (Moore Drydock)*, 92 N.L.R.B. 547, 549 (1950).)

If all four standards were met, a presumption of valid, primary, and lawful picketing was created. In *Moore,* the Board found that since all of the four conditions were met and there was no persuasive evidence of an illegal objective under the statute, the picketing was presumptively lawful. If the picketing had occurred while the ship was tied at the dock owned by the shipowner, the activity would clearly have been primary, even if secondary employers had incidentally been persuaded not to work on the ship. (*Id.* at 549-50.) The distinction in *Moore* was that the situs of the dispute had shifted to the premises of the secondary employer. If the situs of a dispute shifts, it is called ambulatory. A question arises as to whether the union has a right to follow the situs to the premises of a secondary employer if the only way to picket that situs is in front of the secondary employer's premises. (*Id.*) The Board in such cases balances the rights of a secondary employer to be free from involvement in a dispute not his own with the rights of a union to picket the site of its dispute based upon the four-factor test outlined above.

Moore was originally accepted and applied by the circuit courts. (See *NLRB v. Service Trade Chauffeurs*, 191 F.2d 65 (2d Cir. 1951) and *NLRB v. Chauffeurs, Teamsters, Warehousemen & Helpers, Local Union No. 135*, 212 F.2d 216 (7th Cir. 1954).) Their application was additionally expanded to include disputes at a primary situs where the premises owned by the primary employer was also the work site of a neutral secondary employer. (*Carpenters Local 55*, 108 N.L.R.B. 363 (1954), *enforced*, 218 F.2d 226 (10th Cir. 1954).) The Board held that picketing which did not disclose that the dispute was solely with the primary employer was illegal, and rejected the previously accepted notion that picketing at the site of a primary employer was *per se* lawful. (*Electrical Workers, Local 813*, 85 N.L.R.B. 417 (1949).) The Board also held that picketing that did not attempt to minimize its impact on neutral secondary employees was illegal. (*Retail Fruit & Vegetable Clerks Local 1917*, 116 N.L.R.B. 856 (1956), *enforced*, 249 F.2d 591 (9th Cir. 1957).) The Board received criticism for applying the *Moore* four-pronged test in a *per se* fashion and finding a presumption of illegal activity if any one of the four criterion was not met. (*Local 761, IUE v. NLRB*, 366 U.S. 667, 677, 81 S. Ct. 1285 (1961).) A fifth standard was also imposed and applied which held that if an employer had a permanent place of business to which employees reported, the union was limited to picketing that permanent site and prohibited from following the dispute to other sites. (*Brewery & Beverage Drivers, Local 67*, 107 N.L.R.B. 299 (1953), *enforced*, 220 F.2d 380 (D.C. Cir. 1959).)

Overruling the *per se* application of the *Moore* tests and also the fifth criterion, the Board later declared that no artificial prototype would be applied on a *per se* basis. In announcing a new test, the Board held that the place of picketing was only one factor to be considered in determining whether the activity had the proscribed objectives of the statute. (*Electrical Workers, Local 861*, 135 N.L.R.B. 250, 255 (1962).) Under the new test, the Board looked to evidence of the union's intent and utilized the *Moore* standards to weigh equivocal evidence. In this way, failure to meet one of the *Moore* criteria no longer constituted conclusive *per se* proof of illegal activity. (*Id. See Teamsters, Local 126 (Ready Mixed Concrete)*, 200 N.L.R.B. 253 (1972).) On the other hand, mere compliance with the four *Moore* standards did not automatically assure the union that its picketing had a secondary object, nor did compliance overcome evidence which established an illegal object. (*NLRB v. Local 307, Plumbers*, 469 F.2d 403 (7th Cir. 1972), *IBEW Local 441 (Jones & Jones, Inc.)*, 158 N.L.R.B. 549 (1966). *Compare with IBEW Local 480 v. NLRB*, 413 F.2d 1085 (D.C. Cir. 1969) *and IBEW, Local 441*, 222 N.L.R.B. 99 (1976).)

The Board further upheld as legal a union's picketing at the situs of a primary employer who removed all the employees from a ship in drydock undergoing repairs. The Board's holding was premised upon a showing by the union that its dispute with the employer was primary. The court held that the situs of the dispute was at the ship, the picketing was primary, and that the employer should not be allowed to make the picketing illegal by removing employees from the ship. The fact that the drydocked employees refused to work on the ship due to the picketing was an incidental effect. (*Seafarers International Union v. NLRB*, 265 F.2d 585 (D.C. Cir. 1959).) The Board also held that union picketing "between the headlights" of a struck employer's ready-mix concrete trucks making deliveries at a construction site was legal even though the struck employer had established a reserve gate for the use of employees, and picketing forced neutral employees to walk off the job. The Board reiterated that peaceful primary picketing was explicitly protected under the Act regardless of its effect on the operations of neutral employers. Primary picketing remained a protected union activity even though there were other locations at which it might have been performed without affecting neutral employees. (*Teamsters Local 83*, 231 N.L.R.B. 1097 (1977).) On appeal the Ninth Circuit refused to enforce the Board's ruling. (*Allied Concrete, Inc. v. NLRB*, 607 F.2d 827 (9th Cir. 1979).) The court found that the object of the union's picketing was illegal, and that the union's message was too broad. The court held that the picketing must be conducted so as to minimize its effect on neutral employees without diminishing the effectiveness of the picketing in reaching the primary employees and employer. (*Id.* at 828-33.)

When a union is picketing a fixed common situs, it need not initiate any movement of the picketers closer to the situs of the dispute. Neither must the picketers move closer to the fixed common situs if requested, so long as the picketing is reasonably close to the situs of the primary dispute. (*Wire Service Guild, Local 222, Newspaper Guild, AFL-CIO,* 218 N.L.R.B. 1283 (1975).) The court in *Miami Herald* held that no Section 8(b)(4)(i) or (ii)(B) violation occurred when the union, in furtherance of a primary dispute, picketed entrances to neutral newspaper's office in which the primary had offices and equipment. The primary attempted to confine picketing to the hallway immediately outside the primary's office. The Board found that such restrictions on picketing would seriously impair the union's ability to reach the primary's employees and others who dealt directly with the primary. (*Id.*)

If the common situs of the dispute is ambulatory the union must take the initiative to move as close as possible to the situs. The union must move reasonably closer to the situs if requested by the primary employer. If the union fails to sustain a burden of "reasonably close," the third factor in the *Moore* test is not met and a violation may be found. (*AAA Motor Lines, Inc.,* 211 N.L.R.B. 94 (1974). The shift in initiative arises because in a fixed common situs situation the primary employer is ordinarily located at the situs of the dispute. In an ambulatory situs situation, however, the situs will vary. The union must take the initiative and show that its object is to picket the primary employer and thus is legal, and that it moved as close as reasonably possible to the situs of the primary dispute.

§ 8-5. Consumer Boycotts.

As mentioned above, Section 8(b)(4) of the NLRA was

added in 1959 by the Landrum-Griffin Act. Early Board interpretations of consumer boycotts interpreted Section 8(b)(4) to prohibit all picketing designed to induce customers of one employer not to buy the products of another employer, because the picketing necessarily had the objective of pressuring the selling employer to cease doing business with the supplier, an objective expressly proscribed by Section 8(b)(4)(ii)(B). (*See Minneapolis House Furnishings Co.,* 132 N.L.R.B. 40 (1961), *rev'd,* 331 F.2d 561 (8th Cir. 1964).) In the landmark case of *NLRB v. Fruit & Vegetable Packers & Warehousemen Local 760 (Tree Fruits),* 377 U.S. 58, 84 S. Ct. 1063 (1964), the Supreme Court distinguished between consumer picketing against a struck product and consumer picketing against the seller, reasoning that the former did not pressure the seller but the latter did. The Court recognized the right of the union to "follow the struck product" that is, the union had the right to follow the goods of a struck primary employer so long as to do so did not pressure the seller of the product directly. Accordingly, the Supreme Court held that the consumer picketing of a struck product was a lawful extension of the primary dispute and not a proscribed activity. (*Id.*)

In other words, picketing to persuade customers of secondary employers not to trade at all with secondary employers violates the Act, but picketing to persuade customers of the secondary employer not to buy products of primary employers "followed" to the secondary employer's place of business does not violate the Act. Various factors were presented for consideration. For example, the appeal must be to the public, not to employees of the secondary. The union must take care to narrowly identify the struck product. The picket sign must be drawn carefully. (*Local 24, Meatcutters,* 230 N.L.R.B. 189 (1977). *See also Carpenters, Local 550,* 227 N.L.R.B. 196 (1976).) Picketing must be only at consumer entrances, and picketers must be instructed not to interfere with deliveries. Customers must not be asked not to enter the store. Customers may be asked not to purchase the struck product, but nothing more. The union cannot threaten the primary employer to cease doing business with the secondary employer, but can tell the primary employer that the union will continue its lawful consumer picketing since it is merely a statement of the union's legal rights. (*Tree Fruits,* at 60-61.)

In other words, the union is entitled to follow the primary product to a secondary situs which is ancillary to the primary employer's business as long as a secondary strike is not effectuated. A union may picket to ask the public not to buy goods of the primary sold by the secondary employer. But the union will violate the statute if it asks the public to cease buying altogether from the secondary employer.

Section 8(b)(4) prohibits only picketing which induces the employees of the secondary to cease working. Activities other than picketing are not prohibited. Even conduct within the prohibition, if it is in a form other than picketing, is not proscribed unless it induces a secondary strike. So activities other than picketing which do not induce a secondary strike are protected and legal activities under the publicity proviso to Section 8(b)(4).

In *Servette,* the union had a dispute with Servette. The union went to store managers, asking them to stop selling Servette's goods, and warned that if the managers did not stop the sale of the primary's goods, the union would handbill the public and ask the public not to buy Servette's goods at the secondary's store. The Board found no Section 8(b)(4)(B) violation, but the Court of Appeals found a violation based upon the inducement of "individuals." The Court held that the term "individuals" in this case was precisely used to describe the managers approached by the union. The Court also held that the publicity proviso did not allow the handbilling of distributors, since distributors were not literally producers, as specified in the statute. On appeal, the Supreme Court held that the term "individual" includes managers. The statute prohibits unions from inducing employees to withhold services of neutrals. Here, the union asked the managers to use discretion, not to strike, so no violation of Section 8(b)(4)(B)(i) existed. No secondary strike had been induced by a union request for managerial discretion. Further, the Court held that the Union's threat to handbill under (ii) was not a violation, since informing the public of a dispute with a distributor or producer is legally protected activity. (*NLRB v. Servette, Inc.*, 377 U.S. 46 (1964).)

Cases such as *Tree Fruits* and *Servette* brought into focus whether consumer picketing violates Section 8(b)(4)(ii)(B). Based upon legislative history and the proviso itself, Congress exempted publicity other than picketing, so Congress meant to prohibit picketing. It follows, then, that since a threat to induce a secondary boycott violates Section 8(b)(4)(ii)(B), Congress must have considered picketing to violate Section 8(b)(4)(ii)(B) also. Picketing has both speech and conduct elements, and so pure first amendment protection does not apply to all picketing. The contradiction occurs in that one person can picket a store, but the prohibition is really in the content of the message. Although the picketing is really conduct, the speech element is really being prohibited. Courts strain to interpret the Act, especially Section 8(b)(4)(B), to avoid constitutional problems.

Not all Section 8(b)(4)(B) activities which involve publicity are prohibited. No violation occurs unless a strike ensues, just as not all picketing is violative of the Act. In drawing the line, some types of consumer picketing are legal and other activities are illegal. The union can ask the public, for example, not to buy goods of the primary and seek public support against the primary employer, so long as the appeal is narrow. Narrow means that the appeal is confined to the struck product. A broad appeal, such as asking the public to cease doing business with the secondary employer entirely, is illegal. Although this distinction does not appear to be the original Congressional intent, it is the Court's interpretation.

The dicta in *Tree Fruits* sheds further light on the subject by indicating that if handbilling gives a message which, if written on a picket sign would be illegal, it is pure speech and therefore is protected if it does not create a secondary strike. Such a message may or may not violate the statute, depending on whether or not it induces a secondary strike or boycott, such as the stoppage of work or deliveries. To summarize, Section 8(b)(4)(B) prohibits broad appeal picketing but does not prohibit narrow appeal picketing, and the publicity proviso does not apply in such a case. If secondary picketing induces a strike, then the proviso applies. Handbilling with a narrow appeal is not prohibited by the Section, so the publicity proviso does not apply. Handbilling with a broad appeal which does not induce a strike calls into play the proviso, which was designed to exempt publicity other than picketing that does not induce secondary strikes or boycotts. If picketing with narrow appeal induces a strike, no violation of Section 8(b)(4)(B) occurs. If the union is handbilling with narrow appeal and induces a strike or boycott, a violation of Section 8(b)(4)(B) does occur. The narrow-broad appeal is important in deciding when Section 8(b)(4)(B) is applicable.

An exception to the doctrine purported by *Tree Fruits* is exemplified in the merged product exception. A merged product is one that has lost its identity by incorporation with other products prior to sale to the consumer. For some time the merged product exception has been the most meaningful limitation of the picketing sanctioned by *Tree*

241

Fruits. The Board and appellate courts have interpreted *Tree Fruits* to exclude picketing against a merged product because such picketing involves the other business of the secondary seller and therefore is directed at more than solely the struck employer. (*See American Bread,* 170 N.L.R.B. 91 (1968), *enforced in pertinent part,* 411 F.2d 147 (6th Cir. 1969).) In recent decisions the Board has narrowed the merged product exception by interpreting a picket line against a merged product as a primary area standards line instead of a secondary boycott picket line. The court of appeals reversed the Board for attempting to avoid precedent and prohibiting the picketing of a merged product. (*K & K Construction Co.,* 592 F.2d 1228 (3d Cir. 1979).)

The second limitation upon *Tree Fruits* was imposed in 1976 when it was held that where the struck product constituted substantially all of the seller's business, consumer picketing against the product was coincidental with consumer picketing against the seller. (*NLRB v. Retail Store Employees Union, Local 1001 (Safeco Title Insurance Co.),* 447 U.S. 607 (1980).) One of the emphasis of the Supreme Court in *Tree Fruits* was that the struck product constituted only a small portion of the seller's business. The Board interpreted this emphasis of the Supreme Court to mean that the Court did not intend to allow product picketing which induced consumers to stop doing business with the seller. Such product picketing was the equivalent of consumer picketing against the seller, an activity proscribed by the Supreme Court. The Supreme Court reversed the D.C. Circuit Court and agreed with the Board, but took the entire proposition one step farther. The Court held that the union violated Section 8(b)(4)(ii)(B) when it picketed five neutral title insurance companies which derived more than ninety percent of their gross income from sales of the primary's insurance. The Court found that the union's secondary pressure was "reasonably calculated to induce customers not to patronize the neutrals at all." (Cited in *Dow Chemical,* 226 N.L.R.B. at 757.) The court distinguished these facts from those in *Tree Fruits,* where the primary product being picketed was only one among many in which the secondary retailer dealt. In *Safeco,* the secondary pressure forced the secondary employer to choose between economic survival or allegiance to the primary employer; thus the Court found that the picketing violated the statute. (*Safeco,* 226 N.L.R.B. 754, 756-58 (1976).)

The Court held that *Tree Fruits* and *Safeco* represent the opposite ends of a continuum of lawful and unlawful consumer picketing against a product. The dividing line between the two extremes is whether the secondary appeal is reasonably likely to threaten the neutral secondary party with substantial loss. The issue is particularly clear when the secondary picketing is directed against a product which prepresents a major portion, but not a single dominant product, of the secondary's business. The test is an objective one which scrutinizes *results threatened* and not *intent* of the picketing. It is the scope of the threat presented at the start of the picketing and not the loss incurred, in fact, at the conclusion of the picketing that is controlling. Therefore, the courts are not to wait until actual damage or demise of the neutral seller occurs before enjoining the picketing.

It must be remembered that in consumer picketing, as in other types of picketing, the picket signs must clearly identify the primary employer and the neutral so that no confusion exists between the parties and non-parties to the dispute. If the picket signs may lead the public to confuse the neutral with the primary, then the picketing is a violation of Section 8(b)(4). Additionally, where the picketing is against a product, the product must be identified with enough exactness on the picket signs that it cannot be confused by the public with any other product. Failure of the union to avoid consumer confusion results in a violation of Section 8(b)(4). Handbilling cannot be used to correct vagueness or failure of identification on picket signs. (*Service Food Stores*, 230 N.L.R.B. 189 (1977).)

In summary, handbilling is protected by the publicity proviso to Section 8(b)(4) provided the contents of the handbills are truthful for purposes of advising the public, including consumers and members of a labor organization, and do not have the effect of inducing secondary employees to strike or cut off deliveries to the secondary employer. (*See Operating Engineers, Local 139*, 226 N.L.R.B. 759 (1976); *Pet, Inc.*, 244 N.L.R.B. 1046 (1979).)

CHAPTER 9

REGULATION IN THE CONSTRUCTION INDUSTRY

§ 9-1. Generally.

Labor relations in the construction industry have long been recognized as unique. Unlike other enterprises which are operated on regular schedules at fixed plants, the building trades are characterized by intermittent work scattered at various sites throughout a company's geographic business area. (*See generally* Comment, *Impact of the Taft-Hartley Act on the Building and Construction Industry,* 60 Yale L.J. 673, 677 (1951).) Most construction companies are prevented from maintaining a full compliment of employees year round and are, therefore, forced to select the majority of workers for each project virtually on the spot. (*Id.*) Moreover, in contrast to other businesses, the presence of numerous specialty contractors on projects has often created tension due to placing union and non-union laborers side-by-side. (*See, e.g.,* H. Rep. No. 741, 86th Cong., 1st Sess. 22 (1959).) The unusual problems presented by these and other facets of the construction industry prompted Congress to make special exceptions for the building trades within the National Labor Relations Act. (29 U.S.C. § 151 et seq. (1970).)

The Landrum-Griffin Amendments, 73 Stat. 519 (1959), added Sections 8(e) and 8(f) to the NLRA. (*Id.* at §§ 704-705, codified as amended 29 U.S.C. §§ 158(e) and 158(f).) Section 8(e) prohibited the execution of "hot cargo" agreements whereby an employer voluntarily agreed not to do business with another employer because of the latter's employment policies. (*See Final Report of the Senate Select Committee on Improper Activities in the Labor or Management Fields,* S. Rep. No. 1139, 86th Cong., 2d Sess. 3 (1960).) Congress, however, was concerned with the threat that technological displacement could have on the integrity of jobs in the construction trades and, therefore, included an express exception for agreements in that industry regarding jobsite work (hereinafter referred to as the construction industry proviso). (*Id.* 29 U.S.C. § 158(e).)

In Section 8(f), Congress expressly recognized that hiring and employment practices in the construction trades were necessarily different from other industries. (*See generally* S. Rep. No. 187, 86th Cong., 1st Sess. 28 (1959).) This provision reversed the then existing law on employer recognition of minority-supported unions in the construction industry by allowing agreements in these trades without regard to majority status (hereinafter referred to as prehire agreements). (29 U.S.C. § 158(f).)

These "special concessions" to the building and construction trades have, themselves, presented a variety of interesting but complex legal issues. (*See generally* Comment, *The NLRA's Forbidden Fruit: Valid But Unenforceable Concessions to the Construction Industry,* 47 U. Cinn. L. Rev. 288 (1978).) Sections 8(e) and 8(f), however, were not the beginning of specialized treatment for the industry. Prior to passage of the Taft-Hartley Act, 61 Stat. 136 (1947), the National Labor Relations Board declined to assert jurisdiction over both unfair labor practice and representation cases invloving the building and construction trades. (*See, e.g., Johns-Mansville Corp.,* 61 N.L.R.B. 1 (1945).) The Board utilized its discretionary power to abstain from regulating an industry which it considered as having only a remote impact on the operations of interstate

246

commerce. Even after the passage of Taft-Hartley, the Board's time and budgetary limitations caused special problems in deciding when jurisdiction over the industry should be asserted.

Sections 8(e) and 8(f) likewise appear not to be the last form of specialized approach to construction industry labor matters. Competition from smaller, non-union construction companies is causing some larger concerns to establish non-union affiliates in order to keep their bids on smaller projects competitive. (*See generally* King & LaVaute, *Current Trends in the Construction Industry Labor Relations — The Double-Breasted Contractor and the Prehire Contract,* 29 Syracuse L. Rev. 901 (1978).) These so-called "double-breasted" contractors are raising a new level of consciousness among union officials because of their refusal to apply existing collective bargaining agreements to the new affiliate. *(Id.)* More importantly, in cases challenging these dual operations, the Board is apparently taking an approach at variance with similar situations in other industries.

§ 9-2. Board Jurisdiction Over the Construction Industry.

As originally enacted the NLRA empowered the Board to exercise jurisdiction over labor matters which affected interstate commerce. (29 U.S.C. §§ 159(a) and 160(a).) This jurisdictional mandate was always recognized as co-extensive with the power given Congress under the Commerce Clause. (*See, e.g., NLRB v. Reliance Fuel Oil Corp.,* 371 U.S. 224, 226 (1963) (and cases cited therein).) The Board, however, has traditionally had the discretion to abstain from exercising jurisdiction where the policies of the Act would not be effectuated. (*NLRB v. Denver Building & Construction Trades Council,* 341 U.S. 675, 684 (1951).)

Under the Wagner Act, the Board had repeatedly refrained from asserting jurisdiction over both unfair labor practice and representation cases involving the construction industry. (*See Johns-Mansville Corp.*, 61 N.L.R.B. 1 (1945) (representation case); *Brown & Root Co.*, 51 N.L.R.B. 820 (1943) (unfair labor practice). *Cf. Brown Shipbuilding Co.*, 57 N.L.R.B. 326 (1944) (distinguishing building construction from the shipbuilding trades).) There had never been any doubt but that the operation of a construction project affected interstate commerce. (*Johns-Mansville Corp.*, 61 N.L.R.B. at 2.) For example, the interstate operations of Johns-Mansville Sales Corporation were clearly within the Board's then current standards for asserting jurisdiction. The Sales Corporation, however, was engaged in home insulation, and the Board considered all aspects of residential construction essentially local in nature with only a remote impact on interstate commerce. (*Cf. Ozark Dam Constructors*, 77 N.L.R.B. 1136 (1948).)

Although the Taft-Hartley Act (61 Stat. 136 (1947)) made no change in the Board's jurisdiction in this area, the NLRB reversed its policy after passage of that Act. Noting a clear Congressional desire for greater regulation of the construction industry, particularly certain union activities, the Board began to assert jurisdiction without regard to the small volume of interstate business involved. *See Local 74, United Brotherhood of Carpenters & Joiners (Ira A. Watson Co.,)* 80 N.L.R.B. 533 (1948); *cf. Walter J. Mentzer*, 82 N.L.R.B. 389 (1949) (one of the first cases to exercise restraint in asserting jurisdiction). *But see Plumbing Contractors Ass'n of Baltimore*, 93 N.L.R.B. 1081 (1951) (discussing the appropriate balance between Board jurisdiction over representation cases and that of the National Joint Board for Settlement of Jurisdictional Disputes in the Building and Construction Trades).) The Board found that, in many cases, while the volume of business directly involved in interstate commerce was small, jurisdiction was not determined solely "by the quantitative effect of the activities ... before the Board." (*Ira A. Watson Co.*, 80 N.L.R.B. at 535 (quoting *Polish National Alliance v. NLRB*, 322 U.S. 643, 648 (1944).) The NLRB's new policy was extended to materials suppliers who serviced the construction industry and were, therefore, "closely related" to it. (*Akron Brick & Block Co.*, 79 N.L.R.B. 1253 (1948); *J. H. Patterson Co.*, 79 N.L.R.B. 355 (1948).)

The Board's new philosophy, however, was neither consistent nor unanimous. (*See, e.g., Walter J. Mentzer*, 82 N.L.R.B. 389 (1949).) Frequently, cases appeared in direct conflict. (*Compare Ira A. Watson Co.*, 80 N.L.R.B. 533 (1948) *with Denver Bldg. & Constr. Trades Council (William G. Churches)*, 90 N.L.R.B. 378 (1950)), and jurisdiction sometimes seemed dependent on the claim alleged. (*See William G. Churches*, 90 N.L.R.B. 378 (1950).) But the Board's jurisdictional policy received court approval. (*See, e.g., NLRB v. Denver Bldg. & Constr. Trades Council (Gould & Pressner)*, 341 U.S. 675, 683-84 (1951); *IBEW v. NLRB*, 341 U.S. 694, 699 (1951).)

By October 1950, the Board indicated that an inordinate amount of its time and budgetary funds were being expended merely deciding whether a case should be heard. (*William G. Churches*, 90 N.L.R.B. at 380 n. 5 (1950).) This was particularly true since trial examiners (now Administrative Law Judges) were placed in the position of exercising the Board's discretion in the first instance without clearly defined standards on how that discretion should be exercised. (*See Hollow Tree Lumber Co.*, 91 N.L.R.B. 635 (1950).) For these reasons, the Board abandoned its case-by-case approach based upon all the circumstances (*Ira A. Watson Co.*, 80 N.L.R.B. 533 (1948)) in favor of "jurisdictional yardsticks." (*See* Memeographic Release, NLRB Clarifies and Defines Areas In Which It Will and Will Not Exercise Jurisdiction (October 6, 1950).)

Immediately following its release, the Board issued a series of decisions sometimes referred to as the "yardstick decisions of October, 1950." (*See, e.g., Hollow Tree Lumber Co.,* 91 N.L.R.B. 635 (1950) (summarizing the decisions immediately following their issuance). Comment, *Impact of the Taft-Hartley Act, supra* at 680).) Under the standards promulgated in these decisions, the Board claimed jurisdiction over any construction firm that: (1) performed $50,000 worth of business annually in services for instrumentalities of or firms engaged in interstate commerce; (2) handled an inflow of $500,000 in materials directly from out-of-state or $1,000,000 indirectly purchased from out-of-state; or (3) performed work affecting the national defense. (*But see* NLRB Press Release No. 576 (October 2, 1958) (modifying these standards).) While asserting that these standards reflected the results reached in its recent decisions (*Hollow Tree Lumber Co.,* 91 N.L.R.B. at 636), the Board was abandoning its position in those cases for a more manageable standard.

It was unmistakable that the Board was confining its jurisdiction to relatively large construction firms. (*See* Comment, *Impact of the Taft-Hartley Act, supra* at 681.) Eight years later, the Board expanded its jurisdiction over the construction industry. (*See* NLRB Press Release No. 576 (October 2, 1958).) Nonetheless, the proliferation of small construction firms in the industry, the purchasing practices of general and subcontractors, and the general nature of the business forced the Board to adopt special rules for the construction industry in order to assert jurisdiction in important cases.

This line of special rulings began with the *International Brotherhood of Teamsters, Local 649 (Jamestown Builders Exchange),* 93 N.L.R.B. 386 (1951). In *Jamestown,* the Board was faced with a Section 8(b)(4) secondary boycott case in which neither the general contractor nor the subcontractors individually met the annual services test. For this reason, the trial examiner recommended dismissal. The Board, however, disagreed, and held that in secondary boycott cases, the annual business of both the general contractor and any "affected subcontractors" should be combined to establish the jurisdictional amount. (*Jamestown Builders Exchange,* 93 N.L.R.B. at 387. *Accord International Brotherhood of Teamsters, Local 554 (McAllister Transfer, Inc.),* 110 N.L.R.B. 1769 (1954).) This ruling caused some difficulty for trial examiners who believed that *Jamestown* required establishing a violation vis-a-vis each subcontractor to include that subcontractor's annual business. (*See, e.g., Madison Bldg. & Constr. Trades Council,* 134 N.L.R.B. 517 (1961) (trial examiner's decision).) In *Madison Building,* the Board clarified the meaning of "affected subcontractors." Rather than finding a violation in order to establish jurisdiction, the Board held that the "affected subcontractor" requirement was satisfied if "conduct occurred that involved the secondary employer, . . . [and such] conduct must be considered and ruled upon . . . ." (*Id.* at 518.)

The Board, however, limited its *Jamestown* holding to secondary boycott cases. (*United Assoc. of Journeymen (Frick Co.),* 116 N.L.R.B. 119 (1956).) In *Frick Company,* the Board found that absent any evidence that the subcontract reserved to the general contractor any control over the terms and conditions of employment of the subcontractor's employees, the Board would look only to the subcontractor's business in establishing jurisdiction over a Section 8(b)(2) charge. (*Id.* at 120. *But see IBEW, Local 379 (Fassbach Electric Co.),* 230 N.L.R.B. 626 (1977) (where the trial examiner stated that even absent the presence of a multi-employer association, he would have asserted jurisdiction over an 8(b)(2) charge under the rationale in *Madison Building*). Contra, Local 447, Plumbers & Pipefitters, 172 N.L.R.B. 128 (1968).)

But the *Frick Company* case did not mean that the general contractor could avoid the jurisdictional limits in Section 8(b)(2) or 8(b)(7) cases by delegating purchasing responsibilities to his subcontractors. In *United Brotherhood of Carpenters, Local 1028 (Dennehy Construction Co.,* 111 N.L.R.B. 1125 (1955), the Board held that jurisdiction over a general contractor would be asserted "on the basis of [*either*] the total volume of his business, *or* of the general construction which he [has] undertake[n] to discharge." (*Id.* at 1026 (emphasis added). *See also Operative Plasterers' & Cement Masons' Local 2 (Arnold M. Hansen),* 149 N.L.R.B. 1264 (1964); *Plasterers' Local 739 (Arnold M. Hansen, Inc.),* 157 N.L.R.B. 823 (1966).)

Perhaps the most expansive rule which the Board has developed for asserting jurisdiction in Sections 8(b)(2) and 8(b)(7) cases involving small construction firms is stated in *Reilly Cartage Co.,* 110 N.L.R.B. 1742 (1954). In *Reilly,* the Board asserted jurisdiction over a Section 8(a)(1) charge where the employer did not meet the jurisdictional yardstick but where the employer was involved in the secondary boycott charge within the same case. In doing so, the Board stated that "the desirability for a full and complete record upon the issues as between the parties require that we should consider the merits of the issues in both of these consolidated cases." (*Id.* at 1744.)

The Board's rationale had sometimes been referred to as the "fragmentation of the dispute" theory. (*See, e.g., New Furniture & Appliance Drivers Local 196 (Biltmore Furniture Mfg. Co.),* 120 N.L.R.B. 1728 (1958) (trial examiner's decision).) But later opinions clearly established that the Board was adopting an "ancillary jurisdiction" standard. Thus in *New Furniture,* the Board held that "when respondents are guilty of a 'pattern of conduct affecting enterprises both within and without the jurisdictional standards,' [it] will assert jurisdiction over both . . . in order to make the remedy coextensive with the reach of the unfair labor practices." (*Id.* at 1729. *See also Local 400, Commission House Drivers, (Euclid Foods, Inc.)*, 118 N.L.R.B. 130 (1957).)

Two recent cases have dealt with the question of whether the Board should retain jurisdiction over Section 8(b)(2) or 8(b)(7) charge where Section 8(b)(4) violation is either settled or found not to exist. (*See Carpet, Linoleum & Soft Tile Layers Local 1238 (Robert A. Arnold d/b/a Arnold's Carpet)*, 175 N.L.R.B. 332 (1969); *Plumbers & Steamfitters U.A. Local 460 (L.J. Construction)*, 236 N.L.R.B. 1435 (1978).) In *Arnold's Carpet,* a Section 8(b)(4) was filed against the Carpet Layers Union alleging that the union picketed Vaughn's Home Decorating Center (Vaughn) for the purpose of forcing Vaughn to cease doing business with Arnold's. Because of the inter-relationship between Arnold's and Vaughn, the trial examiner found that Arnold was an employee, not an independent contractor. Despite his finding that the picketing was violative of Section 8(b)(2), the trial examiner recommended dismissal because Vaughn did not fall within the Board's jurisdictional standards. (*Id.* at 335.) The Board adopted his recommendations and dismissed the complaint. (*Id.* at 332.)

The second case, *Plumbers & Steamfitters U.A. Local 460,* 236 N.L.R.B. 1435, involved alleged violations of Sections 8(b)(4) and 8(b)(7). The Section 8(b)(4) charge was settled by informal agreement approved by the Board. The Board retained jurisdiction over the Section 8(b)(7) charge because the "union engaged in conduct arguably in violation of both 8(b)(4)(B) and 8(b)(7)(C) . . ." (*Id.* at 1436.) *Arnold's Carpet* was distinguished on the grounds that there the initial exercise of jurisdiction was improperly predicated on secondary boycott criteria. (*Id.* n. 3.)

It, therefore, appears that the Board will retain jurisdiction over the "ancillary" claim *only* when the conduct could constitute both an 8(b)(4) violation and another unfair labor practice. Since the jurisdictional yardsticks are discretionary and self-imposed, however, there is no real reason why the "ancillary" claim could not be adjudicated. This is particularly true where, as in *Arnold's Carpet,* the issue is fully litigated. *(Cf. United Mine Workers v. Gibbs,* 383 U.S. 715 (1966) (discussing the same problem under the theory of pendent jurisdiction in federal district courts).) At the very least, administrative law judges should have the discretion, in the first instance, to decide whether the policies of the NLRA would be effectuated by retaining jurisdiction. *(Id.* at 726-27. *Cf. Zahn v. International Paper Co.,* 414 U.S. 291, 294-95 (1973) (dealing with the non-discretionary jurisdictional amount imposed in 28 U.S.C. §§ 1331(a) and 1332(a).)

§ 9-3. Section 8(e), Hot Cargo Clauses, and Work Preservation.

In the 1959 Landrum-Griffin Amendments, Congress added Section 8(e) to the Act and made it an unfair labor practice for a union and an employer to enter into an agreement whereby the employer ceased doing business with or refused to handle the products of any other employer. (29 U.S.C. § 158(e).) One purpose of this clause was to close the loophole created by dictum in *Local 1976, United Brotherhood of Carpenters & Joiners v. NLRB (Sand Door & Plywood Co.),* 357 U.S. 93 (1958). In *Sand Door,* the Supreme Court held that an agreement between the employer and union by which the employer agreed not to handle non-union goods was not a defense to what was then a Section 8(b)(4)(A) charge against the union for job action to enforce the agreement. The Court, however, emphasized that the execution of the agreement and its voluntary observance was not violative of Section

8(b)(4)(A). Section 8(e) rendered the mere execution of such an agreement an unfair labor practice. (*See National Woodwork Manufacturers Ass'n v. NLRB,* 386 U.S. 612, 634 (1967).) But Congress provided that the prohibitions of Section 8(e) should not be applied "to an agreement between a labor organization and an employer in the construction industry relating to the contracting or subcontracting of work . . . at the [construction] site . . . ." (29 U.S.C. § 158(e).)

Thus, with slight modification, the construction industry proviso preserved the "status quo" vis-a-vis "hot cargo" agreements between employers and unions in the construction industry. Indeed, as Senator Goldwater, a leading proponent of the section, indicated:

> [t]here is a further exemption from the prohibitions against "hot cargo" agreements . . . with respect to a segment of the building construction industry and the labor unions . . . in that segment of the industry. This exemption applies only where the employer . . . engages only in construction work at the site. . . . Where an employer falls within this limited category, it is not an unfair labor practice for such employer and a labor union to enter into [a hot cargo] agreement. . . .

(II Leg. Hist. of the Labor-Management Reporting and Disclosure Act of 1959, at 1858 (hereinafter 1959 Leg. Hist.).) The Supreme Court first interpreted the scope of Section 8(e) and its qualifying provisos in *National Woodwork Manufacturers Ass'n v. NLRB,* 386 U.S. 612 (1967), and found that Section 8(e) aimed solely at agreements which were secondary in nature. (*Id.* at 638-39.) At the same time, however, the Court appeared to narrow the scope of the construction industry proviso, stating that the proviso was intended only to "allow agreements pertaining to certain secondary activities on the construction site because of the close community of interests there, but to ban secondary objective agreements concerning nonjobsite work. . . ." (*Id.* at 638-39.)

The Supreme Court found a number of factors supported its conclusion that Section 8(e) was never intended to prohibit primary agreements "addressed to the labor relations of the contracting employer vis-a-vis his own employees." (*Id.* at 645 (footnote omitted).) First, the Court noted that Section 8(e) must be read in connection with Section 8(b)(4)(B) since it was designed to fill a gap in secondary boycott analysis. (*Id.* at 649 (Harlan, J., concurring memorandum) ("It is recognized by Court and counsel on both sides that the legislative history of § 8(b)(4)(B) . . . [and] § 8(e) . . . is to be taken *pari passu* . . .").) *See also* 29 U.S.C. § 158(b)(4)(B) ("nothing contained in this clause (B) shall be construed to make unlawful . . . any primary strike or primary picketing"). In addition, earlier cases had declared that certain "will not handle" clauses, aimed at protecting the terms and conditions of employment, were mandatory subjects of bargaining. (*See, e.g., Firebrand Paper Products Corp. v. NLRB,* 379 U.S. 203 (1964).) Finally, the Court believed that the provisos lent support to its interpretation, for otherwise "the construction industry proviso . . . would have the curious and unsupported result of allowing the construction worker to make agreements preserving his traditional work against jobsite prefabrication and subcontracting, but not against nonjobsite prefabrication and subcontracting." (*National Woodwork Manufacturers Ass'n v. NLRB,* 386 U.S. at 638.)

In this last regard, the Court's opinion was probably incorrect. (*Cf.* II 1959 Leg. Hist. 1858 (Comments of Senator Goldwater).) The construction industry proviso would permit the agreement in *National Woodwork* because (1) it relates to the subcontracting of work to be done at the construction site since the work will either be done at the site or subcontracted out, and (2) the signatory employer is one performing work at the construction site. *See, e.g., United Ass'n of Pipefitters Local 455 (American Boiler Manufac-*

256

turers), 154 N.L.R.B. 285 (1965). The Court, however, implied that the proviso only exempts union efforts to secure agreements with a general contractor not to utilize non-union subcontractors. (*See* R. Gorman, Labor Law 271 (1976). *See generally* Comment, *The NLRA's Forbidden Fruit: Valid But Unenforceable Concessions to the Construction Industry,* 47 U. Cinn. L. Rev. 288, 290 & n. 18 (1978).) Moreover, the Court's language leads to the curious result of inducing unions in the construction industry to organize non-union subcontractors if they wish to receive work from the signatory general contractor. (*But see Connell Construction Co. v. Plumbers Local 100,* 421 U.S. 616 (1975) (curtailing the union's power to secure these agreements).)

Despite the Court's narrow language, there are very few situations in which a labor union and an employer in the industry can violate Section 8(e) by executing an agreement outside the scope of the proviso. One situation would be the *Sand Door* "will not handle non-union materials" clause simply because there is no effect on jobsite work involved. (*See* Comment, *NLRA's Forbidden Fruit, supra,* at 290, n. 19.) Such a contract would also violate the Section if the signatory employer were a building materials supplier who performed no work at the construction site. (*See American Boiler Manufacturers Ass'n v. NLRB,* 404 F.2d 547, 556 (8th Cir. 1969), *cert. denied,* 398 U.S. 960 (1970).) Litigation over the proviso, therefore, centers on the union's right to compel agreement to and enforce the observance thereof through job action.

In a series of cases following the 1959 Amendments, the Board held that job action which sought to secure employer agreement to a clause within the proviso was nonetheless violative of Section 8(b)(4)(i)(A). (*See Construction, Production & Maintenance Laborers Local 383 (Colson & Stevens Construction Co.,* 137 N.L.R.B. 1650 (1962); *Orange Belt*

257

District Council of Painters #48 (Calhoun Drywall Co.), 139
N.L.R.B. 383 (1962); *Los Angeles Building & Constructors
Trades Council (Stockton Plumbing Co.)*, 144 N.L.R.B. 49
(1963).) The Board found that the proviso was not
applicable to the proscriptions of Section 8(b)(4), reasoning
that it would be anomalous to allow unions to coerce "voluntary" agreements. (*Colson & Stevens Construction Co.*, 137
N.L.R.B. at 1652.) Federal courts of appeal found the
Board's contention untenable, (*e.g., Construction, Produc-
tion & Maintenance Laborers Local 383 v. NLRB*, 323 F.2d
422 (9th Cir. 1963)), as did some trial examiners. (*Operative
Plasterers' & Cement Masons, Local 2 (Arnold M. Hansen)*,
149 N.L.R.B. 1264, 1280 (1964) (trial examiner's decision).)
After several courts rejected the Board's decisions, the
Board overruled the *Colson & Stevens* doctrine, and found
picketing to secure the agreement to be protected activity.
(*Northeastern Indiana Building & Construction Trades
Council (Centlivre Village Apts.)*, 148 N.L.R.B. 854 (1964).)

In *National Woodstock* the Supreme Court indicated that
the construction industry proviso exempted from the
proscription of Section 8(e) agreements between general
contractors and unions preventing the general contractor
from doing business with non-union subcontractors. The
union, however, may be subjected to liability under the
Sherman Act. (*Connell Construction Co. v. Plumbers, Local
100*, 421 U.S. 616 (1975).) In *Connell*, Plumbers Local 100
picketed a general contractor and thereby forced its
agreement to a clause limiting the subcontracting of work
within the union's trade jurisdiction to subcontractors
having a bargaining relationship with the union. After
signing the agreement and while the union was engaged in
similar practices with other general contractors, Connell
challenged the agreement on anti-trust grounds. Justice
Powell, writing for the majority, stated first that labor's
immunity from the anti-trust laws under the

258

Norris-LaGuardia Act did not protect union-employer combination, despite the use of economic pressure by the union. (*Id.* at 622-23 (*citing Allen Bradley Co. v. Local 3, IBEW,* 325 U.S. 797 (1945).) *But see* Meltzer, *Labor Unions, Collective Bargaining and the Anti-Trust Laws,* 32 U. Chi. L. Rev. 659, 676 (1965) ("[T]he Sherman Act applies to union-employer combinations that institute market restrictions essentially similar to those devised by businessmen *even when they are free from union pressure.*" (emphasis added).)

The Court, however, also recognized that certain labor activities are exempted from anti-trust liability as "an accommodation" between the policies of the National Labor Relations Act and those of the Sherman Act. *Connell* demonstrated that this immunity existed only to the extent that labor policies demanded. Justice Powell found that the agreement went beyond the jobsite and, therefore, exceeded the limits of the judicial exemption. (421 U.S. at 625.)

Most importantly, the Court refused to find that Section 8(e) provided the exclusive remedy for the union's lawful secondary activity. Justice Powell noted the failure of Congress to provide a civil damages remedy as support for imposing anti-trust liability. The purpose of the NLRA, however, is to protect *employees* not *employers.* It makes no sense to reward an employer under the anti-trust law. (*Id.* at 639 (Steward, J., dissenting opinion). *See also,* Note, *The Supreme Court, 1974 Term,* 89 Harv. L. Rev. 47, 239 & n. 38.) This is essentially true when the evils complained of, top-down organization techniques, are not a restraint on competition but rather an infringement upon the employee's rights. (*See,* Comment, *The NLRA's Forbidden Fruit, supra,* at 290 n. 20.) The employer's remedy in this situation should only be an unfair labor charge under Section 8(e).

Job action to enforce a collective bargaining clause within the proviso has always been recognized as unlawful secondary activity. (*See Local 1976 Carpenters & Joiners v. NLRB*, 357 U.S. 93, 106 (1958). *See also* II 1959 Leg. Hist. 1858 (comments of Senator Goldwater).) This finding was reinforced in *National Woodwork* where the Court recognized that primary agreements were outside the scope of Section 8(e). *National Woodwork* and its progeny, however, have created a gray area in which strikes to enforce primary agreement become unlawful secondary activity, an area commonly referred to as "work preservation." (*See generally* Comment, *Secondary Boycotts and Work Preservation*, 77 Yale L.J. 1401 (1968).)

Work preservation clauses generally appear in three forms. (*Id.* at 1405-09.) The first is the subcontracting clause defining the conditions in which the employer can subcontract bargaining unit work. (*See Orange Belt District Council of Painters #48 v. NLRB*, 328 F.2d 534 (D.C. Cir. 1964).) In this regard, a distinction is drawn between (1) union standards clauses which protect the bargaining unit from employer efforts to indirectly receive cheaper labor; (*See Truck Drivers Local 413 v. NLRB*, 334 F.2d 539 (D.C. Cir. 1964), *cert. denied*, 379 U.S. 916; *Lewis v. NLRB*, 350 F.2d 801 (D.C. Cir. 1965)), and (2) union signatory clauses aimed at promoting the status of unions generally. (*Orange Belt District Council of Painters #48 v. NLRB*, 328 F.2d at 538-39.) The second form of work preservation clause refers to job allocation and to whom the employer can subcontract the work. In the construction industry, these situations normally involve union jurisdictional disputes which are primary in nature. (*See* Comment, *Secondary Boycotts and Work Preservation, supra*, at 1409, n. 46.) On the other hand, clauses which permit subcontracting only to sister locals are generally secondary. (*But see Houston Insulation Contractors Ass'n v. NLRB*, 386 U.S. 664 (1967) (where the Court found decisive the involvement of only one employer).) The third form of work preservation clause is the product boycott which is generally considered primary so long as it does not address the union status of the subcontractor. (*See National Woodwork Manufacturers Ass'n v. NLRB,* 386 U.S. 612 (1967).)

In *National Woodwork,* the Court held that job action to enforce a "will not handle" clause was not violative of Section 8(b)(4)(B), provided that, "*under all the surrounding circumstances,* the Union's objective was preservation of work for [its members and not] tactically calculated to satisfy union objectives elsewhere." (*Id.* at 644 (footnotes omitted) (emphasis added).) The crucial factor was "whether the agreement or its maintenance [was] addressed to the labor relations of the contracting employer *vis-a-vis* his own employees." (*Id.* at 645 (footnote omitted).) Perhaps the most important aspect of the *National Woodwork* case was its decided support of union activities to preserve bargaining unit work from technological displacement. (*Id.* at 650 (Harlan, J., concurring memorandum.) *See generally* Comment, *Secondary Boycotts and Work Preservation, supra,* at 1409 ("[*Woodwork*] . . . [is] a signal . . . that the Justices will no longer tolerate hostility toward the work-preservation form of union activity in the guise of secondary reasoning").)

National Woodwork left several unanswered questions in its wake. The first area of confusion concerned the employee group protected and can best be explained by analyzing *Houston Insulation Contractors Ass'n v. NLRB,* 386 U.S. 664 (1967). In *Houston Contractors,* the employer was engaged in a bargaining relationship with both Local 22 and Local 113 of the Insulators Union, both agreements having work preservation clauses. Local 22 made prefabricated steel bands for insulation in the employer's shop for use at a construction site. The jobsite employers, represented by Local 113, refused to handle any prefabricated insulation not made by Local 22. Applying the *National Woodwork* test, the Court found that since both bargaining units were employed by the same contractor, "the agreement [and the work stoppage were] addressed to the labor relations of the contracting employer *vis-a-vis* his own employees" (*National Woodwork*, 386 U.S. at 645 (emphasis added)), and the traditional right of mutual aid and protection enabled the jobsite workers to assist their fellow employees though their own jobs were not in jeopardy. (*Houston Contractors*, 386 U.S. at 668.) Thus, *Houston Contractors* extended the protected group to the employer's employees.

A related problem is created by supposing that Locals 22 and 113 are one local, and that the employer is two employers, one at the jobsite, the other at a home shop. Both employers hire on a part-time basis with the exception of a skeleton staff, and both hire from the same bargaining unit. Can the jobsite workers refuse to handle prefabricated insulation not made by the bargaining unit? No case found is directly on point. The Board, however, appears to consider this primary activity. (*See Ohio Valley Carpenters District Council (Cardinal Industries) v. NLRB*, 136 N.L.R.B. 977, 986-87 (1962), and *Houston Contractors* seems to compel that result.) (*See generally* Comment, *Secondary Boycotts and Work Preservation, supra,* at 1412.)

The second, and perhaps the most controversial, area left unresolved by *National Woodwork* involved the Board's use of the right-to-control test as the determining factor in assessing whether job action aimed at securing compliance with an otherwise primary work preservation clause violated Section 8(b)(4)(B). (*See National Woodwork Manufacturers Ass'n v. NLRB*, 386 U.S. at 616-17, n. 3 (1967).) Although the right to control issue was not presented in *National Woodwork*, Justice Brennan's majority opinion specified that, in determining whether the union's objectives were primary or secondary, all the surrounding circumstances should be considered. (*Id.* at 644.) A virtual war developed between the Board and the Court of Appeals for the District of Columbia. (*Compare Local 438, United Pipe Fitters (George Koch Sons, Inc.),* 201 N.L.R.B. 59, 61 (1973) ("We deem [Phillips' lack of control] crucial in determining the legality of the Respondents' attempts here to enforce the admittedly valid work preservation clauses . . .") *with Local 742, United Brotherhood of Carpenters & Joiners v. NLRB (J.L. Simmons Co.),* 444 F.2d 895, 903 (D.C. Cir. 1971) ("We emphasize once more, however, that as a *per se* rule the "right to control" test must be finally abandoned").) The Board reasoned that the signatory employer's inability to provide the work which the union sought rendered him the neutral in a dispute that was really between the union and the general contractor/owner who specified prefabricated/prefinished materials. (*See Enterprises Ass'n of Steam Pipefitters,* 204 N.L.R.B. 760 (1973).) The District of Columbia Court of Appeals, on the other hand, believed that "an employer who is struck by his own employees for the purpose of requiring him to do what he was lawfully contracted to do to benefit those employees can [n]ever be considered a neutral bystander in a dispute not his own." (*Enterprises Ass'n of Steam Pipefitters v. NLRB,* 521 F.2d 885, 903 (D.C. Cir. 1975).)

The Supreme Court finally resolved the conflict in *NLRB v. Enterprise Ass'n of Steam Pipefitters,* 429 U.S. 507 (1977). In *Enterprise Association,* the Court was faced with the issue not presented in *National Woodwork:* whether the contracting employer's inability to control the assignment of work desired by the union converts an otherwise primary strike into an illegal secondary boycott. Justice White, writing for the majority, initially noted that the validity of a contract under Section 8(e) does not necessarily establish that economic pressure to enforce the agreement is always primary. (*Id.* at 519.) The opinion added that the existence and validity of the provision were, in effect, irrelevant under its holding in *Local 1976, United Brotherhood of Carpenters & Joiners v. NLRB (Sand Door)*, 357 U.S. 93 (1958). However, unlike that "secondary" contract clause in *Sand Door,* the operative provision in *Enterprise Association* was undisputedly primary. (*NLRB v. Enterprise Ass'n of Steam Pipefitters,* 429 U.S. at 521, n. 8.) Thus, in the absence of evidence which demonstrated that the union's insistence upon compliance with the legitimate work preservation agreement was a pretext "for some secondary objective," it was equally primary to enforce it through economic pressure. (*Id.* at 541-42, nn. 8-9 (Brennan, J., dissenting opinion); *see also* Lesnick, *Job Security and Secondary Boycotts: The Reach of NLRA §§ 8(b)(4) and 8(e),* 113 U. Pa. L. Rev. 1000, 1040 (1965).)

The Court sustained the Board's inference of an unlawful secondary objective from the contracting employer's inability to control the assignment of work. (*NLRB v. Enterprise Ass'n of Steam Pipefitters,* 429 U.S. at 521-22.) The court of appeals, however, found this inference to be unsupported by substantial evidence. (521 F.2d at 904.) Justice White stated that there was ample support for the Board's conclusion (429 U.S. at 529), but focused on only one fact; right-to-control. Thus, *Enterprise Association* implicitly established the right-to-control as an element of law in primary/secondary analysis. (*Id.* at 540 (Brennan, J., dissenting opinion); *Cf. George Koch Sons, Inc.,* 201 N.L.R.B. at 64 ("the Board has always proceeded with an analysis of (1) whether under all the surrounding circumstances the union's objectives were work preservation *and then (2) whether the pressures exerted were directed at the right person* . . .") (emphasis added).)

One factor which could place the right-to-control element into proper perspective is the concept of the "non-unoffending employer." (*See Painters District Council #20 (Uni-Coat Spray Painting, Inc.)*, 185 N.L.R.B. 930 (1970).) In *Uni-Coat*, the Board held that the employer's lack of control was not determinative where it actually and knowingly contracted away its control and, in fact, initiated the very problem. (*Id.* at 932.) The employer's action prevented it from being "unoffending" and caused it to lose neutral status. (*Id.*) In cases before and after *Enterprise Association*, the Board clearly stated that it would evaluate the way in which the employer came to be in the pressured situation, and would not protect employers who created their own problem. (*E.g., George Koch Sons, Inc.*, 201 N.L.R.B. at 63.) This analysis evidenced a fear that collusive action between the contractors would completely foreclose any union efforts to preserve unit work by ensuring that subcontractors never had the right-to-control. (*See generally* Yates & Kaplan, *Prefabricated Work in Construction: New Technology Versus Work Preservation — Who Controls the Job Site?*, 23 St. Louis L.J. 270, 275 (1979).)

Three Board decisions demonstrated, however, that establishing an employer's non-unoffending status is not an easy task. The first case was *George Koch Sons, Inc.*, 201 N.L.R.B. 59 (1973). In *George Koch*, the pressured employer had no bargaining power with respect to the desired work because the prime contractor was under specifications from the owner to prefabricate the piping prior to delivery. Therefore, the contracting employer never surrendered the right-to-control, nor did it, precipitate the problem. (*Id.*) The second case, *Local 742, United Brotherhood of Carpenters & Joiners (J.L. Simmons Co.)*, 201 N.L.R.B. 70 (1973) (supplemental decision and order — see 178 N.L.R.B. 351 (1969)), was consolidated with *George Koch* for the purposes of oral argument. (201 N.L.R.B. at 70, n. 5.) Interestingly, the Board failed to examine how the pressured employer, Simmons, came to be in that situation. (*But see Local 742, United Brotherhood of Carpenters & Joiners (J.L. Simmons Co.)*, 237 N.L.R.B. 564, 565 n. 7 (1978).)

The specifications in *Simmons* provided for the use of either "plastics faced" (herein prefabricated doors) doors, or wood doors (unfinished doors), depending on owner's choice which in turn was based upon its financing arrangements. At the time that Simmons signed the subcontract, unfinished doors were to be installed. One month later, a change order was approved by Simmons and the owner under which the prefabricated doors were ordered in lieu of the unfinished doors. The record indicated that: (1) the owner's only reason for choosing plastic faced doors was their lower maintenance cost; (2) the plastic faced doors have been finished at the jobsite; (3) Simmons never made any effort to honor the collective bargaining clause; and (4) that in the end, Simmons netted a $14,000 additional profit from the change order, 86% of which was at the expense of the union employees. (178 N.L.R.B. at 354-58 (trial examiner's findings).) Moreover, Simmons refused to negotiate a "premium pay" settlement with the union officials.

Simmons Company appears to present the situation in which the pressured employer helped precipitate the problem. There is very little indication that the owner would have objected to unfinished plastic clad doors. In the words of the Court of Appeals for the Fourth Circuit, "[c]ertainly where the employer was initially in a position to accede to potential union demands through the negotiating stages of the contract, then he should later not be deemed a neutral if he intentionally forfeited his potential for control." (*George Koch Sons, Inc. v. NLRB*, 490 F.2d 323 (4th Cir. 1973).)

Two years later, the Board explained why the situation in *J.L. Simmons Company* would not make the contractor an "offending employer." (*IBEW, Local 501 (Atlas Construction Co.)*, 216 N.L.R.B. 417 (1975).) In *Atlas,* like *Simmons,* the pressured employers had some bargaining power over the desired work, but never actually sought that work. (*Id.* at 417.) The Administrative Law Judge found that the employers had voluntarily forfeited their potential for control, and could not, therefore, be deemed "unoffending." The Board, however, disagreed. The three-member panel found that any "attempt to define the parameters of "unoffending employer" based solely on an expenditure of effort [or more accurately, the lack thereof] on the part of the employer . . . [was] futile . . . [and] administratively unmanageable." (*Id.* at 418.) In the absence of some affirmative conduct, actively and knowingly undertaken, in conflict with the collective bargaining obligation and not demanded by an independent third party, the employer must be considered "unoffending." (*Id.* at 417.)

On petition of the union for review of the Board's order, the District of Columbia Court of Appeals, affirmed the Board's conclusions and granted enforcement. (*IBEW, Local 501 v. NLRB,* 566 F.2d 348 (D.C. Cir. 1977).) In sustaining the Board, the court found two factors persuasive. First, the court agreed that scrutiny of the negotiation process for employer good faith would be administratively unmanageable. (*Id.* at 353.) Second, the Board's analysis was supported by *Enterprise Ass'n of Steamfitters v. NLRB,* 429 U.S. 507 (1977), which, according to the appellate court, foreclosed scrutiny of the employer's good faith in contract negotiations. (*IBEW, Local 501,* 566 F.2d at 353.) Although the court was apprehensive of the Board's definition of an "unoffending employer," it deferred to the Board's expertise. (*See NLRB v. United Steelworkers,* 357 U.S. 357, 362 (1958).)

The third area of confusion which resulted from *National Woodwork* concerned its reference to work preservation/work acquisition analysis as a sword/shield situation. (*National Woodwork Manufacturers Ass'n v. NLRB*, 386 U.S. at 630.) The Court's analogy intimated that work *acquisition* was always secondary. (*See* Comment, *Secondary Boycotts and Work Preservation, supra*, at 1410.) Thus, after *National Woodwork*, employers argued that work preservation could only encompass work which was currently, continually, and exclusively performed by unit employers. Both the Board and the Courts have rejected this strict standard. (*See, e.g., United Association of Pipefitters Local 539 (American Boiler Manufacturers Ass'n)*, 167 N.L.R.B. 606 (1967), *enforced sum nom. American Boiler Manufacturers Ass'n v. NLRB*, 404 F.2d 547, 551 (8th Cir. 1968), *cert. denied*, 398 U.S. 960 (1970) (work "reacquisition" fell within the permissible primary scope of *National Woodwork*).) Later cases extended this concept to jobs that were "fairly claimable" by the unit because the jobs required the same skills and abilities although never actually performed by unit employees. (*See, e.g., Retail Store Employees, Local 876 (Canada Dry Corp.)*, 174 N.L.R.B. 424 (1969), *enforced sub nom. Canada Dry Corp. v. NLRB*, 421 F.2d 907 (6th Cir. 1970).)

In *International Ass'n of Heat & Frost Insulators, Local 12*, 193 N.L.R.B. 40 (1971), the Board began to retract from this position. *Insulators* involved a union which had traditionally performed the insulation work for steam turbines and claimed that its object was the preservation of the same work for the newly introduced gas turbines. (*Id.* at 40, n. 5.) The Board, however, rejected this contention without examining whether the work was fairly claimable, relying instead on the fact that other workers had traditionally done the work involved. (*Id.* at 40. *See International Longshoremen's Ass'n (Dolphin Forwarding, Inc.)*,

236 N.L.R.B. 525 (1978); *International Longshoremen's Ass'n (Consolidated Express, Inc.)*, 221 N.L.R.B. 956 (1975), *enforced*, 537 F.2d 706 (2d Cir. 1976), *cert. denied*, 429 U.S. 1041 (1977).)

The Supreme Court recognized the fairly claimable test in *NLRB v. Longshoremen's Ass'n*, 447 U.S. 490 (1980), to the extent that the union has attempted "to accommodate change while preserving as much of their traditional work . . . as possible." (*Id.* at 506.) The Court also overruled the Board's improper approach of looking to the traditional work of non-unit workers. Justice Marshall, writing for the majority, stated that "the Board must focus on the work of bargaining unit employees, not the work of other employees . . . doing the same or similar work." (*Id.* at 507.) The Supreme Court's opinion also indicated that the "surrounding circumstances" test of *National Woodwork* and the right-to-control element by *Enterprise Association* must be considered in analyzing this form of work preservation. (*Id.* at 511-12.)

International Longshoremen's Association finally establishes what has been lacking since before the passage of the 1959 Amendments. First, its re-emphasis of *National Woodwork* and *Enterprise Association* provides a coherent, complete framework for primary/secondary analysis in the work preservation area. Second, and more importantly, by extending *National Woodwork* to situations in which the union accepts technological advances and seeks to adapt the union's traditional work, rather than perpetuate "the old way of doing things," the Court strikes an appropriate balance between competing concerns. The owner/contractor can bring technological advances to the project, where the union can protect the job security of its members.

The Supreme Court's balance between technology and job security can also be seen as supportive of two alternative methods by which labor unions can seek to enforce valid work preservation clauses, or in the construction industry, secondary "will not handle" clauses which fall within the construction industry proviso. The first alternative involves the traditional remedy for collective bargaining disputes, arbitration. In *Hadley-Dean Glass (Glaziers & Glass Workers Union, Local 513)*, 69 Lab. Arb. 1057 (1977), the union filed a grievance to enforce a work preservation clause. The arbitrator stated that the union's grievance would be sustained if the work preservation clause barred the subcontracting of work involved and the contracting employer's employees had traditionally, and as a past practice, performed that work. The grievance in *Hadley* was denied because of numerous exceptions to the traditional work claimed by the union. (*Id.* at 1065-66. *See IBEW, Local 501 v. NLRB*, 566 F.2d 348, 354 (1977).)

The second alternative was attempted but rebuffed by the Board in *J.L. Simmons*, 237 N.L.R.B. 564 (1978) (second supplemental decision). In *Simmons*, the union offered to install pre-machined doors in exchange for premium pay. The Board, however, deemed the premium pay proposal as a substitution of one form of coercion for another. (*Id.* at 565.) Chairman Fanning seemed willing to allow a premium pay provision within the work preservation clause. (*Id.* at 565, n. 8.) Such a contractual clause might be subjected to the scrutiny of the courts as an unlawful penalty. Moreover, the Board took an all too quick glance at this solution. Provided that negotiations could be exhausted before the encroaching materials arrived, the union could still resort to arbitration, thereby avoiding a strike all together. At that point, however, the union would be required to gamble on the grievance and handle the materials to avoid secondary impact. It would be contrary to the substantial evidence if the Board found secondary objectives under such circumstances.

§ 9-4. Section 8(f) Prehire Contracts.

The building and construction trades differ from other enterprises mostly in the employment and hiring practices used in the industry. Construction contractors need a full complement of employees for each project but are unable to maintain this labor staff throughout the entire year. This situation causes uncertainty in the supply and cost of labor for each project, which, in turn, materially affects the contractor's ability to make complete and accurate bids. (*See* S. Rep. No. 187, 86th Cong., 1st Sess. 28 (1959).)

Under the Board's policy of abstention, the construction industry developed the union hiring hall into customary practice. Although the practice was an unfair labor practice, *Matter of Guy F. Atkinson Co. & J.A. Jones Construction Co. (Atkinson-Jones),* 90 N.L.R.B. 143 (1950) (applying Wagner Act after Taft-Hartley because the agreement pre-dated the new Act and finding a violation of Section 8(3)), it provided contractors with a ready supply of labor at a definite cost. (S. Rep. No. 187, *supra,* at 28.) Taft-Hartley added further limitations to the use of this practice. (*See* 29 U.S.C. §§ 8(a)(3) and 8(b)(2) (1947)), which caused serious problems in the construction industry. (H. Rep. No. 741, 86th Cong., 1st Sess. 19 (1959).)

Recognizing the peculiar needs of the construction trades, Congress included a provision permitting the execution of collective bargaining agreements in the industry regardless of (1) the majority status of the union, (2) the inclusion of a union security clause, or (3) the requirement that the employer notify the union of employment opportunities or give the union an opportunity to refer qualified applicants based upon training, experience or seniority qualifications. (29 U.S.C. § 8(f). *But see* II 1959 Leg. Hist. 1289 (remarks of Senator Goldwater to the House Committee on Education and Labor).) Congress, however, specifically limited the

271

provision to prevent the use of union shop provisions in right-to-work states (Labor-Management Reporting and Disclosure Act of 1959, Public Law 86-357, § 705(b) (September 14, 1959)), and further to preclude any discrimination under Section 8(a)(3). (29 U.S.C. § 8(f) (first proviso).) Moreover, Congress provided that the prehire contract would not constitute a contract bar to a representation petition under Section 9. (29 U.S.C. § 8(f) (second proviso).)

Early Board decisions dealing with the prehire contract established that the provision was addressed to the preliminary stages of union organization vis-a-vis an employer. Thus, *Island Construction Co.,* 135 N.L.R.B. 13 (1962), held that while a Section 8(f) agreement was not a contract bar to a certification proceeding, when the union obtained majority status, the contract was no longer governed by the prehire provision but instead by the general principles of Sections 8(a)(5), 8(b)(3) and 8(d). (*See Mishara Construction Co.,* 171 N.L.R.B. 471 (1968) (applying the contract bar prevented a decertification petition).) Likewise, in *Dallas Building & Construction Trades Council,* 164 N.L.R.B. 938 (1967), the Board held that the union violated Section 8(b)(7)(A) by picketing when a question concerning representation (QCR) could not be raised in light of the employer's pre-existing contracts. Applying its *Island Construction* rationale, the Board found "successive renewals of [8(f)] agreements would [not] be subject to the second proviso of Section 8(f) . . . [because these contracts] . . . were not initial agreements, but the latest fruits of continuing bargaining relationships. . . ." (*Id.* at 943.) Five months earlier, the Board had found that while the duty to bargain in good faith was not applicable to the initial Section 8(f) contract, it would be enforced with respect to renewal negotiations. (*Bricklayers & Masons Local 3 (Eastern Washington Builders),* 162 N.L.R.B. 476 (1966).)

272

The Board also appeared determined to promote continuing relationships between employers and unions initialed under prehire contracts. Pointing to Congressional findings of the need for stable, long-term relationships between employers and unions (*See Daniel Construction Co.,* 133 N.L.R.B. 264 (1961)), the Board indicated that Section 8(f) contracts were only terminable at the expiration of the contract period, subject only to Section 9 proceedings. (*Oilfield Maintenance Co., etc.,* 142 N.L.R.B. 1384 (1963).) *Oilfield Maintenance* also demonstrated the Board's desire to prevent employer domination and assistance of minority unions to insure *bona fide* bargaining. (*Id.* at 1385 and 1387 n. 9.)

In *Oilfield Maintenance* the Board intimated that the execution of a Section 8(f) contract raised, in effect, a presumption of majority status that could only be challenged within the auspices of the Board's Section 9 proceedings. (*See Celanese Corp. of America,* 95 N.L.R.B. 664 (1951); *Barrington Plaza & Tragniew, Inc.,* 185 N.L.R.B. 962 (1970).) While in traditional Section 9 contracts, this presumption would be conclusive, a modified application of *Celanese* and *Barrington* corresponded with the Congressional intent of Section 8(f). (*See Local 150, Operating Engineers v. NLRB,* 480 F.2d 1186 (D.C. Cir. 1973); *R.J. Smith Construction Co.,* 191 N.L.R.B. 693 (1971) (Member Brown, dissenting); *Ruttmann Construction Co.,* 191 N.L.R.B. 701 (1971) (Member Fanning, concurring) (Member Brown, dissenting).) In the companion cases of *R.J. Smith* and *Ruttmann Construction,* the Board retreated from its earlier stance.

In *R.J. Smith,* the union had never obtained majority status, partially because the prehire agreement did not contain a union security clause. The employer repudiated its contract before its expiration date. Ignoring its prior decisions, the Board stated that since the proviso to Section 8(f)

"expressly permit[ted] the testing of the signatory union's
majority status at any time . . . it would be anomalous . . .
to hold that Section 8(f) prohibit[ed] examination of those
questions in the litigation of refusal-to-bargain charges."
(191 N.L.R.B. at 694. *But see Local 150, Operating Engineers v. NLRB*, 480 F.2d 1186 (D.C. Cir. 1973) (denying
enforcement of *R.J. Smith*).) In *Ruttmann Construction*, the
Board extended this concept to permit an employer's
repudiation of a prehire contract prior to expiration date.
(191 N.L.R.B. at 701.) Although peculiar facts in *Ruttmann
Construction* justified the Board's conclusion, (191 N.L.R.B.
at 702-03 (Member Fanning, concurring)), the Board never
limited the scope of its holding.

In *Irvin-McKelvy Co.*, 194 N.L.R.B. 52 (1971), another
case with peculiar facts, the Board restricted the *Smith*
holding to cases where there was no union security clause.
(*Id.* at 53.) Unfortunately, *Irvin-McKelvy* involved a
contract which, by operation of a "most favored nations"
clause, expired upon completion of each project. (*Id.*) Thus,
the Board held that the contract could only be terminated
upon the project's completion and other prehire contracts
could be executed as to all future projects provided that the
union did not represent a majority of the workers employed.
(*Id.* at 52.) But where there was independent proof of the
union's majority status, the contract continued in force
according to its terms. (*See Williams Enterprises, Inc.*, 212
N.L.R.B. 880 (1974) (independent proof established by
enforced union security clause); *Barwise Sheet Metal Co.*,
199 N.L.R.B. 372 (1972) (employer checked off union dues
of all 13 employees pursuant to authorization from
employees); *Ted Hicks & Associates, Inc.*, 232 N.L.R.B. 712
(1977) (membership in a multi-employer bargaining association). *See generally* King & LaVaute, *Current Trends in
Construction Industry Labor Relations — The
Double-Breasted Contractor and the Prehire Contract*, 29
Syracuse L. Rev. 901, 932-34 (1978).)

The Board's position contrasted sharply with that of the Court of Appeals for the District of Columbia. In *Local 150, Operating Engineers v. NLRB, (R.J. Smith Construction Co.)*, 480 F.2d 1186 (D.C. Cir. 1973), the appellate court set aside the Board's order on the ground that it misconstrued Section 8(f). The court specifically noted that this section was passed to help contractors in their bidding practice. (*Id.* at 1189.) Moreover, the Act provided employers with the opportunity to challenge the union's status under Section 9(c) if, after a reasonable period of time, the union seemed unable to achieve majority status. The court pointed out that in light of this remedy, there was no purpose, indeed it was against the purpose of Section 8(f), to permit employers to abrogate a valid agreement or commit unfair labor practices in the face of one. (*Id.* at 1190.) Otherwise, the prehire contract is virtually a nullity at the employer's prerogative.

In *Iron Workers Local 103 (Hidgon Contracting Co.)*, 216 N.L.R.B. 45 (1975), the Board held that a prehire contract was virtually a nullity. After execution of a valid prehire contract, without a union security clause, the employer refused to apply the contract and the union picketed to enforce it. The Board stated that since the union never achieved majority status, the contract was unenforceable and terminable at will. (*Id.* at 46.) The Board declared that there could be no presumption of majority status until the employees for a particular project are hired, and concluded that an employer could terminate the agreement for any project not underway. (*Id.*)

The Supreme Court adpted the Board's position and affirmed its order. *NLRB v. Iron Workers Local 103*, 434 U.S. 335 (1978). Justice White, writing for the majority, noted that Section 8(f) was an exception to the general rule forbidding employer recognition of minority unions, subject to challenges under the proviso eliminating the contract bar. (*Id.* at 345.) The Court found nothing in the statutory

scheme which precluded the Board's approach and rejected
the union's contention that the Board had rendered Section
8(f) meaningless. Stating that the Board's resolution "is
entitled to great deference," (*Id.* at 350), the Court proceeded to accept that resolution without analyzing the
Board's inappropriate and incorrect foundation. (*Id.* at 352,
354 (Stewart, J., dissenting opinion).)

The Court's position on the contract itself is clearly contrary to the intent of Congress in passing Section 8(f). As
the dissent notes, "an employer in the construction industry
. . . is under *no obligation* to bargain with [minority] labor
organization[s]. . . ." (*Id.* at 352.) Congress, however, in
recognition of the employer's particular needs, empowers it
to do so without committing an unfair labor practice. Yet,
that power does not enable the employer to accept the benefits of the prehire contract without undertaking its duties.
Indeed, basic contract principles require that it do so, as do
the policies expressed in the National Labor Relations Act.
(*Id.* at 353.) While it would stretch the purposes of Section
8(f) to imply that a prehire contract should stand on the
same ground as a Section 9 collective bargaining
agreement, there is no reason to permit employers to render
the contract a nullity. Rather, the provision leaves the
employers and unions in the construction industry free from
the entanglements of Section 9. (*See* Aaron, *The
Labor-Management Reporting and Disclosure Act of 1959,*
73 Harv. L. Rev. 1086, 1121-22 (1960).)

In *Hidgon Contracting,* the Supreme Court likewise
declined to examine the Board's legal foundation. The Court
approved the Board's focus on an improper bargaining unit;
the project work force. In the construction industry,
employees are normally represented on an area-wide basis.
(*See* King & LaVaute, *Current Trends in Construction
Industry Labor Relations,* 29 Syracuse L. Rev. at 934.) In
addition, the Board cited *Irvin-McKelvy* despite the fact

that there the contract terminated on *completion* of a project by its terms, and the Board's order required the employer to maintain the agreement *until completion*. In *Hidgon,* the employer terminated the prehire contract before the project started and without giving the union a reasonable chance to achieve majority status. The Board also failed to distinguish or overrule prior cases which directly contradicted its present finding. While the Court correctly noted that "[a]n administrative agency is not disqualified from changing its mind" (434 U.S. at 351), that agency should be required to clearly enunciate its approach. (*Cf. Seafarer's Local 777 v. NLRB,* 603 F.2d 862 (D.C. Cir. 1978).) Finally, the Court found that the Board's policy was rooted in the general principles preventing recognition of unions with only minority support. (434 U.S. at 344.) While recognizing that in Section 8(f) Congress made a specific exemption to that rule, the Board and the Court never gave effect to that effort.

Hidgon Contracting was also the first case explicitly dealing with union picketing to enforce its prehire contract and found such action violative of Section 8(b)(7)(C). In this regard, the Board and the Court, with ample support from the legislative history, were correct. (*See, e.g.,* II 1959 Leg. Hist. 1715 (Senator J. Kennedy). *Id.* at 1289 (Senator Goldwater).) Section 8(b)(7), which was also added in 1959, aimed at preventing unions, without sufficient support from bargaining unit employees, from forcing themselves upon the employer through economic pressure. As noted by the Court, repeated concerns were expressed in the Congressional debates over the use of economic pressure in connection with prehire contracts. (*Id.*) Additionally, the fear that unions might force themselves on employees was considered by both the Board and the Court, and found to be sufficiently real to constitute a threat. (434 U.S. at 346.) Although Section 9 collective bargaining agreements may be enforced through job action, (*Building & Construction Trades Council of Santa Barbara County (Sullivan Electric Co.)*, 146 N.L.R.B. 1086 (1964)), modification of this principle in prehire contract cases was consistent with the intent of Congress in passing Section 8(f).

In *Dee Cee Floor Covering, Inc.*, 232 N.L.R.B. 421 (1977), the Board extended its *Hidgon* rationale and held that the existence of majority support at previous jobsites was irrelevant since the union was required to demonstrate its majority at each new project to invoke the protection of Section 8(a)(5). The appellate courts treated this view as aberrational and refused to give it effect. (*See, e.g., NLRB v. SAC Construction Co.*, 603 F.2d 1155 (5th Cir. 1979).) This Board, itself, repudiated this concept in *G.M. Masonry Co.*, 245 N.L.R.B. 267 (1979). (*See also VM Construction Co.*, 241 N.L.R.B. 584 (1979) ("an employer is [not] free to repudiate an 8(f) agreement where . . . a majority of the *unit* employees supported the union at the time of repudiation." (*Id.* at 584, n. 1) (emphasis added).)

More recent cases have indicated a Board reconsideration of the ramifications of certain language in *Hidgon Contracting,* particularly the misplaced reliance on *Irvin-McKelvy*. The most notable opinion in this regard was *Haberman Construction Co.,* 236 N.L.R.B. 79 (1978), *enforced,* 618 F.2d 288 (5th Cir. 1980), *modified en banc,* 641 F.2d 351 (1981). In *Haberman Construction,* the Board noted that an employer under a prehire contract was not free to repudiate its obligations where the union had attained majority status at the time of repudiation. (*See G.M. Masonry Co.,* 245 N.L.R.B. 267 (1979).) In so stating, the Board initiated the process of clarifying the somewhat inconsistent language found in *NLRB v. Iron Workers, Local 103,* 434 U.S. 335 (1978). Furthermore, the Board limited the impact of *Irvin-McKelvy* by fashioning a remedy which included projects not yet underway and, in effect, created a presumption, *albeit* rebuttable, that the union retains its majority status as a result of normal carryovers. (*Cf. Hageman Underground Construction,* 253 N.L.R.B. 60 (1980) (limiting this presumption to employers having a stable work force).)

The Board's clarification of *Hidgon Contracting* was enforced and expressly approved by a panel court of the Fifth Circuit Court of Appeals. (*NLRB v. Haberman Construction Co.,* 618 F.2d 288 (5th Cir. 1980).) The first *Haberman* opinion held that upon attainment of majority status of the union within the unit, the prehire contract was no longer governed by Section 8(f), but rather was transformed by Section 9(a) into a collective bargaining agreement executed with a representative union. (*Id.* at 303.) Moreover, the court pointed out that the contract matured with respect to the bargaining unit rather than project work force. (*Id.* at 303-04.) The court also found that the Board's presumption of continuing majority status conformed with *Hidgon* and the *NLRA* and should, therefore, be approved. On rehearing *en banc,* the full court endorsed everything ascribed to above, except the broadness of the remedial order. (641 F.2d 351 (5th Cir. 1981).) The court acknowledged that a prehire contract matured into a traditional collective bargaining agreement when the union attained majority status. (*Id.* at 357.) The opinion, however, expressed concern with the Board's inconsistent approach, particularly with respect to *Dee Cee Floor Covering, Inc.,* 232 N.L.R.B. 421 (1977). The court expressly rejected the concept of a presumption of continuing majority status and considered the Board's order to have exceeded the proper realm of establishing the status quo because the union had not shown that the majority status would be retained and the Administrative Law Judge expressly found that the employer intended to go open shop. (641 F.2d at 369.) The court therefore, limited

279

the Board's order to projects which had begun before repudiation. (*Id.* at 370.)

While the court's action in this regard would normally be improper since the employer's unfair labor practice prevented the union's continuing majority (*See* Gorman, *Labor Law* 532-39 (1976)), the Board's inconsistent approaches have created a great deal of confusion in Section 8(f) contracts. (*See Hageman Underground Construction Co.,* 253 N.L.R.B. 60 (1980).) More importantly, the Board had characterized Haberman as a project-by-project employer, and under the standards enunciated in *Dee Cee Floor Covering,* such an employer could repudiate the contract as to projects not yet underway. The court correctly noted that *Dee Cee* was neither distinguished nor overruled in *Haberman* and, therefore, the remedy conflicted with Board precedent. Nevertheless, in its *en banc* opinion, the court did not admonish the Board to clarify its stance. Perhaps this is a result of the Board's recent stable work force/project-by-project hiring practice dichotomy. (*See, e.g., Hageman Underground Construction,* 253 N.L.R.B. 60 (1980).) This distinction, with its apparent administrative convenience, may well establish some consistent enforceability of Section 8(f) contracts which mature into collective bargaining agreements. While this position is, nonetheless, far short of the original Congressional intent of Section 8(f), it is far more desirable than the Board's prior approach and should serve to promote stable relationships between employers and the representative of the majority of their employees.

§ 9-5. The Double-Breasted Contractor.

One of the most disruptive occurrences in a collective bargaining relationship is the refusal of an employer to honor its contractual obligations and bargain with the majority representative of its employees. An equally difficult problem in the business world is the employer's inability to compete with other firms in the market place. The development of the double-breasted contractor presents the clash of these interests in the construction industry. (*See generally* King & LaVaute, *Current Trends in Construction Industry Labor Relations,* 29 Syracuse L. Rev. at 901-28.)

A double-breasted contractor is one which operates both a union subsidiary and a non-union contracting company. Many reasons are given for these dual operations. Employers contend that, often times, they are unable to bid competitively on smaller projects against smaller non-union businesses. (*See* Bornstein, *The Emerging Law of the "Double Breasted" Operation in the Construction Industry,* 28 Lab. L.J. 77 (1977).) Unions, on the other hand, may regard these operations as evasive devices aimed at disintegrating the organization's base and destroying its majority status. (*Id.* at 88.)

The first double-breasted contractor case before the Board was *Gerace Construction Co.,* 193 N.L.R.B. 645 (1971). The principal owner of Gerace formed a subsidiary corporation in order to secure a project which required the employer to guarantee no work interruptions. Gerace could not have made such a guarantee because of the expiration date on its collective bargaining agreement. The new company, Helger, did, in fact, obtain the project. The facts further established that: (1) Gerace was concerned with its inability to bid competitively on smaller projects (under $100,000); (2) after the first six months of operation, Helger was an entirely separate business entity *vis-a-vis* normal business operations; (3) the two firms operated on completely different scales; and (4) the companies never bid against one another and the principal owners never intended that they should. (*Id.* at 646-49.)

The union filed Sections 8(a)(3) and 8(a)(5) charges, alleging that the two companies were a single employer within the meaning of the Act and that its collective bargaining agreement should, therefore, be applied to Helger. The trial examiner agreed and found the Helger employees accreted to the union's bargaining unit. (*Id.* at 651.) The Board, disagreed. The three-member panel found that common ownership was not determinative of a single employer where actual, active common control over labor relations was not shown. (*Id.* at 645.) The Board, however, ignored the trial examiner's findings that "Helger was organized to do work which Gerace was equipped to do, had done and ... wanted to do ... in order that the [e]mployer's obligations under the [collective bargaining] contracts ... could be circumvented." (*Id.* at 651.)

There were several factors upon which the Board could logically have rested its decision. Most important in the context of the double-breasted contractor was the complementary, not substitutionary, nature of the two companies. But the Board chose instead to focus on the lack of common control over labor relations. (*Id.* at 645-46. *See also NLRB v. Condenser Corporation of America*, 128 F.2d 67, 71 (3d Cir. 1942). *But see Canton, Carp's, Inc.*, 125 N.L.R.B. 483 (1959).) This factor was one of the controlling criteria for single employer status approved by the Supreme Court in *Radio & Television Broadcast Technicians Local 1264 v. Broadcast Service of Mobile, Inc. (Radio Union)*, 380 U.S. 255 (1965). The other factors included: common ownership, common management and interrelation of operations. (*Id.* at 256.) Additional indicia are sometimes mentioned. (*See, e.g., Gerace Construction Co.*, 193 N.L.R.B. at 649 (trial examiner's decision) (financial dependence and interchange of employees).) Depending on the case, the importance attached to any one criterion has varied. (*See Great Atlantic & Pacific Tea Co. (Family Savings Center)*, 140

N.L.R.B. 1011 (1963).)

In the context of the double-breasted contractors, over-emphasis of common control of labor relations seems inappropriate. (*See* King & LaVaute, *Current Trends in Construction Industry Labor Relations,* 29 Syracuse L. Rev. at 909.) As noted earlier, the prime motivation for these dual operations is the inability to compete in certain markets. The union's main concern is the disintegrating effect on their organizational base. More appropriate factors are the interchange of employees, and the competition among subsidiaries. First, the interchange of employees is crucial because they form the union's base, especially in the construction industry where most hiring is done on a project by project basis. The second factor is interrelated. If the non-union subsidiary displaces workers by "robbing" the union company of projects, this, likewise, threatens the union's base. On the other hand, non-union affiliates, which complement the union company's business by working projects that the company would otherwise forego, cause no harm to the union.

Frank N. Smith Associates, Inc., 194 N.L.R.B. 212 (1971), demonstrated the difficulty in the Board's approach. In *Smith,* the labor relations of each company were completely separate. The trial examiner's mechanical application of the *Radio Union* factors led him to find separate employers. (*Id.* at 218.) The Board adopted his conclusions specifically noting the similarity with *Gerace Construction,* 193 N.L.R.B. 645 (1971). (*Id.* at 212, n. 1.) The non-union affiliate in *Smith,* however, displaced workers from the union company and utilized carpenters that previously worked under the union contract. (*Id.* at 216-17.) These factors, coupled with the principal's statement that "Keuka was reincorporated . . . to negotiate for or to bid on jobs as an open shop," demonstrated the employer's desire to evade its contractual obligations. (*Id.* at 213.) The trial examiner found that the companies did not compete and that the interchange of employees was at the employer's initiation. (*Id.* at 217-19.) But the emphasis, itself, clearly disclosed that Keuka's non-union work force increased while Smith's (union company) decreased.

Likewise, the Board's decision in *Peter Kiewit Sons Co. (South Prairie Construction Co.)*, 206 N.L.R.B. 562 (1973) is another example of the Board engaging in a mechanical application of the *Radio Union* test, with critical emphasis on the labor control criteria. In contrast to *Smith,* where the union perhaps failed to provide sufficient proof to substantiate its claim, the Administrative Law Judge made extensive findings which detailed an attempt to avoid contractual obligations. (*Id.* at 567 and 571-73.) These findings included: (1) frequent interchange of employees; (2) clear displacement of union work by the non-union affiliate; and (3) admissions and other circumstantial evidence that refuted any contention that Peter Kiewit (union company) was unable to bid competitively on projects that South Prairie (non-union company) could. (*Id.* at 571-73.) The Administrative Law Judge further discounted the labor control criteria, claiming that she found "such evidence insufficient . . . in view of the record as a whole," (*id.* at 575), and distinguished *Gerace* and *Smith* on the facts elicited above. The Board, however, ignored these facts and held the labor control criteria determinative. (*Id.* at 562.)

The Board's mechanical approach was rejected by the District of Columbia Court of Appeals. (*Local 627 IUOE v. NLRB,* 518 F.2d 1040 (D.C. Cir. 1975).) The court first noted the *Radio Union* criteria and stated that all the criteria need not be present. (*Id.* at 1045.) Rather, the question was whether, under all the circumstances with those factors in mind, " 'there [was an] arm's length relationship found among unintegrated companies.' " (*Id.* at 1046.) The court further instructed that in evaluating whether there was a Section 8(a)(5) violation, the interchange of employees and displacement of union work were important factors to be considered. (*Id.* at 1048.) The court found these factors persuasive, holding "that a reasonable likelihood that . . . Kiewit employees would lose work has been established, so that application of the 'single employer' principle would serve to protect the union's agreement." (*Id.* at 1049.)

The Supreme Court affirmed the court's single employer holding, but remanded the cause to the Board for an initial determination regarding the question of appropriate bargaining unit. (*South Prairie Construction Co. v. Local 627, IUOE,* 425 U.S. 800 (1976).) The *per curiam* opinion, however, neither approved nor rejected the appellate court's approach. Instead, the Court sustained the single employer finding, stating "[t]he Board's finding to the contrary was, therefore, . . . not warranted by the record." (*Id.* at 803.) Thus, the Supreme Court interpreted the court of appeals as having overturned an order unsupported by the substantial weight of the evidence.

In light of the Supreme Court's ambiguous ruling, the Board has maintained its "common control over labor relations" approach. Thus, in *United Constructors & Goodwin Construction Co.,* 233 N.L.R.B. 904 (1977), the Board held that the affiliates were separate employers, disregarding evidence of competition between the affiliates, three instances of sub-contracting, family relationships among principals of the affiliates, and interchange of employees. (*Id.* at 912-13. *See also Don Burgess Construction Corp. (d/b/a Burgess Construction),* 227 N.L.R.B. 765 (1977).) Moreover, the Board interestingly made no mention of *Kiewit,* despite *United Constructors* clear inability to satisfy the "arm's length relationship" test. (*See* King & LaVaute, *Current Trends in Construction Industry Labor Relations,* 29 Syracuse L. Rev. at 911.)

In addition to the ambiguous resolution of the single employer problem, the Supreme Court also declined to address the factors which should be considered in deciding whether an employer-wide unit is appropriate. (*South Prairie Construction Co. v. Local 627, IUOE*, 425 U.S. at 805.) The Court cited with approval Board cases which held that "a determination that firms constitute[d] a single employer 'does not necessarily establish that an employer-wide unit is appropriate . . .' ". (*Id. See also Central New Mexico Chapter, National Electrical Contractors Ass'n*, 152 N.L.R.B. 1604 (1965); *B & B Industries, Inc.*, 162 N.L.R.B. 832 (1967)), but found that the Board should be granted, initially, the opportunity to fully address this question. (425 U.S. at 805-06.)

Central New Mexico involved a representation proceeding under Section 9(c) in which the union sought clarification of the multi-employer unit for which it had been recognized as bargaining representative. (152 N.L.R.B. at 1604.) The employer association involved only represented the member employers upon the signing of one of two assent letters. The dual operation was found to be a single employer. (*Id.* at 1608.) The Board found, however, that the separate supervision, location and labor policies of the firms, combined with the different nature of their work, prevented their employees from having the necessary "community of interest." (*Id. See also B & B Industries, Inc.*, 162 N.L.R.B. 832 (1967).)

The D.C. Circuit's first *Kiewit* opinion distinguished this case from the South Prairie situation. (*Local 627, IUOE v. NLRB*, 518 F.2d at 1048-49.) While that portion of the opinion was vacated, (425 U.S. at 806), it was nonetheless instructive. The court found *Central New Mexico* inapplicable because *South Prairie* and *Peter Kiewit* were both involved in the same class of construction at the same location. (518 F.2d at 1048.) *B & B Industries* was recognized to be on all fours with the *Kiewit* case except that South Prairie was brought in after the signing of the contract and without any knowledge on the union's part of its intended entry. (*Id.* at 1049, n. 16. *But see A-1 Fire Protection, Inc.,* 233 N.L.R.B. 38 (1977).)

The Board did not find the court persuasive. (*Peter Kiewit Sons Co.,* 231 N.L.R.B. 76 (1977) (on remand), *enforced,* 595 F.2d 844 (1979).) While the supplemental decision recognized a great deal of common interest between the firms' employees, the Board considered two factors important in reaching a contrary result. (*Id.* at 77.) First, the labor policies of the two firms originated at different sources. Second, there was no common supervision over day-to-day labor conditions. (*Id.*) Therefore, according to the Board, the two groups have a "distinct and separate community of interests." (*Id.* at 78. *But see Don Burgess Construction Corp. (d/b/a Burgess Construction),* 227 N.L.R.B. 765 (1977) (finding that employees of two affiliated firms having the same skills, performing the same functions, sharing the same general working conditions and normally working at the same site have the requisite community of interest).)

The Board's approach to double-breasted contractors has demonstrated a willingness to approve conduct evasive of the employer's contractual responsibilities. (*But see Appalachian Construction, Inc.,* 235 N.L.R.B. 685 (1978) (interpreted by King & LaVaute, *Current Trends in Construction Industry Labor Relations,* 29 Syracuse L. Rev. at 924, as suggesting recognition and adoption of the D.C. Circuit's *Kiewit* opinion).) But unions have apparently not exhausted all avenues of Board proceedings. (*See e.g., Central New Mexico Chapter, National Electrical Contractors Ass'n,* 152 N.L.R.B. 1604 (1965).) In *Central New Mexico,* the union filed a certification petition which, in light of the union's recognized majority status, the Board treated as a petition for clarification under Section 102.60(b) of the Board's Rules and Regulations. While the result is, of course, in the Board's hands, it may be more receptive to union action under this procedure. The petition would also clarify the union's status in regard to a subsequent organizational drive, particularly in light of Section 8(b)(7).

CHAPTER 10

DEFERRAL TO ARBITRATION BY THE LABOR BOARD

Parties to a collective bargaining agreement may include in their contract an arbitration clause which provides for resolution of differences which arise during the term of the agreement. The parties may enter into "voluntary and binding" arbitration for many reasons, including the desire to avoid the disruptions associated with resorts to self-help and the desire to avoid expensive litigation in more formal forums. The statute encourages "the friendly adjustment of industrial disputes (29 U.S.C. § 151 (1970)), and the United States Supreme Court has identified a congressional policy favoring agreements to arbitrate grievances and encouraging parties to settle their differences voluntarily. (*See Textile Workers Union v. Lincoln Mills of Alabama,* 353 U.S. 448 (1957). *See also United Steelworkers of America v. American Mfg. Co.,* 363 U.S. 564 (1960).)

In some cases, a dispute which is channeled through the contractual grievance process, and ultimately submitted to arbitration, may also be the subject of an unfair labor practice charge or charges filed with the National Labor Relations Board. This concurrence of jurisdiction raises questions of the proper relationship between the relatively informal, voluntary process of arbitration and the more formal, involuntary statutory processes administered by the Labor Board. The Board has long grappled with this problem, and has changed its approach from time to time when new Board members have been appointed.

As a matter of law, the Board is not bound by any arbitration award. In *NLRB v. Walt Disney Productions,* 146 F.2d 44 (9th Cir. 1944) the court said:

The Act itself contemplates a continuing jurisdiction by the Board over employer-employee relationships, for Sec. 160(a) includes a provision that the Board's power over unfair labor practices "shall be exclusive, and shall not be affected by any other means of adjustment or prevention that has been or may be established by agreement, code, law or otherwise." Clearly, agreements between private parties cannot restrict the jurisdiction of the Board. ... Therefore, we believe the Board may exercise jurisdiction in any case of an unfair labor practice when in its discretion its interference is necessary to protect the public rights defined in the Act. (*Id.* at 48.)

In *Monsanto Chemical Co.,* 97 N.L.R.B. 517 (1951), the Board recognized the principle of the *Disney* case, declaring there can "be no justification for deeming ourselves bound, as a policy matter, by an arbitration award which is at odds with the statute." (*Id.* at 520.) And in *Wertheimer Stores Corp.,* 107 N.L.R.B. 1434 (1954), the Board restated the principle that as a matter of law, it is not bound by an arbitration award.

Although the Board may ignore arbitration awards, it has shown a willingness to accept the arbitration process as a method of settling labor disputes both in cases where there has been an arbitration award and those where arbitration is available but has not been invoked. In a number of cases, the Board has declined to exercise its jurisdiction where the agreement between the parties provided for the settlement of disputes through arbitration and the parties had not made use of that process prior to the filing of charges with the Board. (*See Collyer Insulated Wire,* 192 N.L.R.B. 837 (1971) and *Jos. Schlitz Brewing Co.,* 175 N.L.R.B. 141 (1969).) The Board has also deferred to arbitration awards issued pursuant to the procedures set out in the collective bargaining agreement between the parties.

(*See Spielberg Manufacturing Co.*, 112 N.L.R.B. 1080 (1955).)

In *Timken Roller Bearing Co.*, 70 N.L.R.B. 500 (1946), the Board declined to exercise jurisdiction, in deference to an arbitrator's decision, despite the fact that the Board would otherwise have found that an unfair labor practice had been committed. In reaching its decision, the Board reasoned:

> It would not comport with the sound exercise of our administrative discretion to permit the Union to seek redress under the Act after having initiated arbitration proceedings which, at the Union's request, resulted in a determination upon the merits. (*Id.* at 501.)

In 1955, the Board definitively set out its policy regarding deferral to an arbitration award in *Spielberg Manufacturing Co.*, 112 N.L.R.B. 1080 (1955). There the Board established the rule that it would defer to an arbitrator's award where the arbitration proceedings appear to have been fair and regular, all the parties agreed to be bound, and the decision of the arbitrator was not clearly repugnant to the purposes and policies of the Act.

The facts of *Spielberg* were as follows: In about April or May of 1953, the Leather and Luggage Workers Union, Local No. 160, began organizing the employees of the Spielberg Manufacturing Company. On August 5, the Union called a strike which lasted until August 24. Approximately 100 of the Company's 220 production employees participated in the strike. On September 22, the Company and the Union executed a contract effective for a period of 5 years. All of the striking employees whose reinstatement was requested by the Union were reinstated with the exception of four persons who were denied reinstatement because of misconduct on the picket line. The Company and the Union also signed a separate agreement in which they agreed to a special arbitration procedure to

291

determine the reinstatement of the four employees, and on October 5, a special board of arbitration met to hear the cases. The arbitration panel, consisting of a Union representative, a Company representative and a third party mutually agreed upon by the parties, decided by a two to one majority that the Company had valid and sufficient reasons for refusing to reinstate the four individuals and that the Company was not obligated to reinstate them.

After the issuance of the arbitration award, the four individuals filed a charge with the National Labor Relations Board alleging that the Company had engaged in unfair labor practices in violation of Section 8(a)(1) and (3) of the Labor Management Relations Act of 1947, and the Board's General Counsel issued a complaint. Finding that the Company's refusal to reinstate the four individuals violated the Act, the Trial Examiner rejected the Company's defense based upon the arbitration award, on the ground that the Board is not bound by such an award.

The National Labor Relations Board, citing *Disney,* *Monsanto* and *Wertheimer,* agreed with the Trial Examiner that the Board was not bound, as a matter of law, by an arbitration award. However, the Board declared:

> In the instant case the factors which impelled the Board to exercise its jurisdiction in *Monsanto* and *Wertheimer* are not present. Thus, the arbitration award is not, as it was in *Monsanto,* at odds with the statute. This does not mean that the Board would necessarily decide the issue of the alleged strike misconduct as the arbitration panel did. We do not pass upon that issue. And unlike *Wertheimer,* all parties had acquiesced in the arbitration proceeding. In summary, the proceedings appear to have been fair and regular, all parties had agreed to be bound, and the decision of the arbitration panel is not clearly repugnant to the purposes and policies of the Act. In these circumstances we believe that the desirable objective of encouraging the voluntary settlement of labor disputes will best be

292

served by our recognition of the arbitrator's award. (*Id.* at 1082.)

Accordingly, the Board held that the Company did not violate the Act when, in accordance with the arbitration award, it refused to reinstate the four individuals, and the complaint was dismissed in its entirety.

In 1963, the Board added another requirement to the "Spielberg Doctrine." In *Raytheon Co.,* 140 N.L.R.B. 883 (1963), *enforcement denied,* 326 F.2d 471 (1st Cir. 1946), the Board held that the arbitrator must have considered the unfair labor practice issue and have ruled on it. This additional requirement, however, has not been followed consistently in Board decisions.

In *Kansas City Star Co.,* 236 N.L.R.B. 866 (1978), the Board deferred to an arbitration award even though the arbitrator made no specific finding that the company's action was legally permissible, since the factual findings made by the arbitrator precluded any other finding. However, Chairman Fanning and Member Jenkins dissented in part, and according to concurring Member Truesdale, showed their "willingness to engage in a *de novo* review of the evidence." Member Truesdale warned: "This willingness to review the evidence exhaustively and then substitute their judgment for that of the arbitrator can only serve to undermine the integrity of the arbitral process." (*Id.* at 868.)

Again, in *Atlantic Steel Co.,* 245 N.L.R.B. 814 (1979), the Board stated the requirement added to *Spielberg* that, in order for the Board to defer to an arbitration award, the arbitrator must have considered the unfair labor practice in his decision. The Board conceded:

> there has been little discussion by the Board as to what this requirement means. Must the arbitrator actually discuss the unfair labor practice, or is it sufficient that he or she considered all of the evidence relevant to

293

the unfair labor practice in determining whether the discharge was lawful under the contract? A review of the decisions shows that, while it may be preferable for the arbitrator to pass on the unfair labor practice directly, the Board generally has not required that he or she do so. Rather, it is necessary only that the arbitrator has considered all of the evidence relevant to the unfair labor practice in reaching his or her decision. (*Id.* at 815.)

This interpretation of the added requirement was short lived. In *Suburban Motor Freight, Inc.,* 247 N.L.R.B. 146 (1980), the Board declared that it would refuse to honor the results of an arbitration unless the arbitrator actually ruled on the unfair labor practice issue. The Board stated that it would "no longer honor the results of an arbitration proceeding under *Spielberg* unless the unfair labor practice issue before the Board was both presented to and decided by the arbitrator." (*Id.* at 146-47.) A number of subsequent Board decisions have upheld this interpretation and ignored arbitration awards because the statutory issues were not specifically decided. (*Triple A Machine Shop, Inc.,* 245 N.L.R.B. 136 (1979); *Van Haaren Specialized Carriers, Inc.,* 247 N.L.R.B. 1185 (1980); and *Sachs Electric Co.,* 248 N.L.R.B. 669 (1980).)

Recently, the Board seems to have abandoned the interpretation of *Spielberg* espoused in *Suburban Motor Freight* and returned to the interpretation in *Kansas City Star* and *Atlantic Steel.* In *Bay Shipbuilding Corp.,* 251 N.L.R.B. 809 (1980), the Board deferred to an arbitration award, finding that it fully met the *Spielberg* standards for deferral, even though the arbitrators specifically refused to pass upon the statutory issue since "the arbitrator's factual determination of the meaning of the contract has resolved the unfair labor practice issues herein." (*Id.* at 811.)

It remains to be seen, however, whether *Bay Shipbuilding's* return to *Kansas City Star* and *Atlantic*

Steel will be permanent, whether the Board will return to *Suburban Motor Freight* or continue to vascillate between the two. Since such changes depend on Board appointments, it is difficult to determine which of these alternatives will be the law or if the Board will take an entirely different course. For example, the newly appointed Board majority recently overruled *Suburban Motor Freight* and adopted standards under which it will conclude that an arbitrator has adequately considered an unfair labor practice issue if it was factually parallel to the contractual issue, the arbitrator was presented with facts relevant to the unfair labor practice issue, and the arbitrator was not palpably wrong. (*Olin Corp.,* 268 N.L.R.B. No. 86 (1984).)

Another of the *Spielberg* deferral standards that has recently been subject to some modification is the "not clearly repugnant" standard. In *Babcock & Wilcox Co.,* 249 N.L.R.B. 739 (1980), the Board, citing *Atlantic Steel,* refused to defer to an arbitration award holding that the absence of "substantial evidence to support the arbitrator's finding" made the arbitrator's decision "repugnant to the purposes and policies of the Act." (*Id.* at 740.)

The Board decisions reviewed above seem to indicate that the preferred status afforded to the arbitration process in *Spielberg* has been somewhat lessened. This diminished deference is exemplified to some extent in *Roadway Express, Inc.,* 246 N.L.R.B. 174 (1979); *Roadway Express —* Supplemental Decision & Order, 250 N.L.R.B. 393 (1980), in which the Board declined to extend the principals of deferral espoused in *Spielberg* to the settlement of a grievance without resort to an arbitration proceeding.

As a practical matter this trend away from deference seems to encourage two Board activities which *Spielberg* attempted to discourage, *i.e., de novo* review of arbitration decisions, and deferral to only those arbitration awards with which the Board agrees. At a time when the Board's docket is extremely crowded, and Federal budget cuts threaten to affect every Federal Agency, this trend does not appear to be in the best interest of the Board or the persons and entities it regulates.

In recent years the Board has redefined its policy concerning deferral to arbitration. In *Collyer Insulated Wire,* 192 N.L.R.B. 837 (1971), the Board concluded that the purposes of the National Labor Relations Act could best be served by deferring to the arbitration process those complaints which the parties agreed to resolve through arbitration.

In *Collyer* the employer was charged with unfair labor practices by allegedly making certain unilateral changes in wages and working conditions. The Board declined to exercise its jurisdiction, agreeing with the employer that the arbitration provision of the bargaining agreement intended that the arbitration process be the sole forum for resolving contract disputes. The majority held that the Board should dismiss a complaint alleging breach of the bargaining agreement when the arbitration provision provides for its resolution, even though an alleged violation of the Act may also be involved.

While the majority recognized that Congress had granted the Board exclusive jurisdiction over complaints of unfair labor practices it stated that the circumstances of *Collyer* "weigh[ed] heavily in favor of deferral." (192 N.L.R.B. at 842.) The circumstances considered determinative by the Board were that the parties had a long and productive bargaining relationship, there was no claim of hostility by the employer toward employees' exercise of protected rights, the employer indicated its willingness to arbitrate a broad range of disputes under the arbitration clause, and the dispute was "eminently well suited to resolution by arbitration." (*Id.*)

Members Fanning and Jenkins disagreed in a strongly worded dissent. Member Fanning stated that the majority's decision not only reversed *Spielberg* but stripped employees of statutory rights. Member Jenkins added that "this practice of refusing to decide is directly contrary to the decision[s] of the Supreme Court." (192 N.L.R.B. at 850.) At the center of the dissenting opinions is a concern over the protection of statutory rights and the fear of compulsory arbitration. The majority dismissed member Fanning's fear over loss of protection of statutory rights as unfounded, stating that "by our reservation of jurisdiction . . . we guarantee that there will be no sacrifice of statutory rights if the parties' own processes fail to function in a manner consistent with the dictates of our law." (192 N.L.R.B. at 843.)

The majority also refused to acknowledge the validity of the argument concerning compulsory arbitration. Member Jenkins stated that "to compel parties to return to the arbitration route when they have chosen another seems to reduce the 'voluntary' quality of the arbitration to zero." (192 N.L.R.B. at 855.) The majority disagreed, holding that since the bargaining agreement contained a standard arbitration provision, a directive to utilize it was not compulsory but "merely giving full effect to the parties' voluntary agreements . . . rather than permitting such agreements to be side-stepped and permitting the substitution of our processes, a forum not contemplated by their own agreement." (*Id.* at 842.)

The Board reaffirmed the *Collyer* doctrine in *Roy Robinson, Inc.,* 228 N.L.R.B. 828 (1977) where the disputed conduct involved a contract violation as well as an unfair labor practice charge. The complaint alleged that Section 8(a)(5) of the Act had been violated by the employer's unilateral decision to eliminate its body shop operation without notifying or bargaining with the union.

The arbitration provision of the bargaining agreement was a standard one, covering " 'any complaint arising . . . over the interpretation of the agreement.' " (228 N.L.R.B. at 828.) The Board held that arbitration of the contract dispute would also resolve the unfair labor practice charge, thus making dismissal of the complaint appropriate since it fit the deferral procedure outlined in *Collyer*.

The majority spent a substantial amount of time defending the *Collyer* doctrine, relying upon the "massive judicial approval of *Collyer* by the courts" to buttress the decision of applying the doctrine to *Robinson*. (228 N.L.R.B. at 829.) The majority cited a Supreme Court case in which the *Collyer* doctrine was referred to as "Board policy" and the Court stated that " 'the fundamental objectives of Federal law [are] to require the parties . . . to honor their contractual obligations rather than, by casting [their] dispute in statutory terms, to ignore their agreed-upon procedures.' " (228 N.L.R.B. at 829, citing 417 U.S. 12, 18 (1974).)

Dissenting members Fanning and Jenkins rejected this rationale claiming that the majority incorrectly cast the statutory violation dispute in contract terms. The dissenting members felt there was no contract provision which covered the disputed conduct, thus making arbitration an ineffectual alternative. Lacking a contract provision to interpret, an arbitrator's determination would indeed be ineffectual since it "has no precedential value, . . . may not decide or touch upon the statutory violation, . . . may not remedy present statutory violations and cannot control future conduct, however unlawful the present conduct." (*Collyer*, 192 N.L.R.B. at 851.) Thus, members Fanning and Jenkins concluded that without a contract provision in dispute, deferral to arbitration would be an empty gesture.

In *General American Transportation Corp.*, 228 N.L.R.B. 808 (1977), the dissenters of *Collyer* and *Robinson* become the majority. The majority position upheld the Board's "statutory duty to hear and to dispose of unfair labor practices" and refused to "abdicate or avoid its duty by seeking to cede its jurisdiction to private tribunals." (228 N.L.R.B. at 808.) More importantly, the majority announced that "the *Collyer* doctrine of deferral has failed." (*Id.*) Other than abandoning *Collyer,* the majority advances no new theories concerning Board deferral to arbitration. A substantial part of the majority opinion is devoted to expanding the rationale of the *Collyer* and *Robinson* dissents and denouncing the claims of *Collyer* adherents as having a "decidedly hollow ring." (*Id.* at 809.)

The complaint in *General American* alleged that the employer laid off an employee because of his union activities. Such a discharge would constitute a violation of Section 8(a)(3) of the Act. The bargaining agreement contained a provision which authorized the employer to lay off employees because of "lack of work or for other legitimate reasons" so long as the employer did not use the authorization to discriminate against employees. (228 N.L.R.B. at 813.) The employer argued that the employee had not been laid off because of union activities and requested that the issue be submitted to the sort of arbitration provided for in the bargaining agreement.

The majority considered deferral inappropriate. By the majority's own admission the decision was based on their "longstanding opposition to the policy established by *Collyer* and its progeny, and is not based merely on the particular circumstances of the instant case." (228 N.L.R.B. at 808.)

Hence, the majority opinion in *General American* deals with the two main concerns discussed in the dissenting opinions of *Collyer* and *Robinson,* compulsory arbitration and protection of statutory rights. Since the employee sought to go before the Board rather than an arbitrator, a decision to defer would amount to compulsory arbitration. It is situations such as this which the majority felt the *Collyer* adherents had "repeatedly ignored" in the past when deferring to arbitration. (228 N.L.R.B. at 809.)

In the past the majority members opposed the decisions of the *Collyer* adherents because "they would defer in any case where the contract incorporates sections of the Act, thus stripping employees of the protection afforded by the Act." (*Id.*) In *General American* the majority was not satisfied that the portion of the contract covering no discrimination against employees would make the case an appropriate one for deferral. In fact, the majority went on to say that the contention by the dissenters that it would, was an "example of the way the *Collyer* adherents foster the destruction of statutory protection." (*Id.*)

Again, evincing the importance of new appointments to the NLRB, the Board majority has recently overruled *General American Transportation* and returned to a policy of deferral to arbitration in cases alleging violations of Sections 8(a)(3), 8(a)(1), 8(b)(1)(A), and 8(b)(2) of the Act. (*United Technologies Corp.*, 268 NLRB No. 83 (1984).)

TABLE OF CASES

303

Roadway Express, Inc., 246 N.L.R.B. 174 (1979) — ch. 10.

Robesky v. Qantas Empire Airways, Ltd., 573 F.2d 1082 (9th Cir. 1978) — § 7-7.

Rock Island Franciscan Hosp., 226 N.L.R.B. 291 (1976) — § 3-2(A)(2).

Rossmore House, 269 N.L.R.B. No. 198 (1984) — § 3-2(C).

Rowan v. Howard Sober, Inc., 384 F. Supp. 1121 (E.D. Mich. 1974) — § 7-11.

Royal Typewriter Co. v. NLRB, 533 F.2d 1030 (8th Cir. 1976) — § 3-2(A)(2).

Royal Typewriter, NLRB v. Business Machines Local 459, IUE, 228 F.2d 553 (2d Cir. 1955) — § 8-2.

Roy Robinson, Inc., 228 N.L.R.B. 828 (1977) — ch. 10.

Ruan Transport Corp., 234 N.L.R.B. 241 (1978) — § 2-2(A).

Ruffalo's Trucking Serv., Inc., 114 N.L.R.B. 1549 (1955) — §§ 1-2(A)(3)(k), 3-1.

Russell Stover Candies, Inc., 221 N.L.R.B. 441 (1975) — § 3-2(D)(1), ch. 4.

Ruttmann Constr. Co., 191 N.L.R.B. 701 (1971) — § 9-4.

Ruzicka v. General Motors Corp., 523 F.2d 306 (6th Cir. 1975) — § 7-1.

Ryan v. N.Y. Newspaper Printing Pressman's Union No. 2, 590 F.2d 451 (2d Cir. 1979) — § 7-7.

S

Sachs Elec. Co., 248 N.L.R.B. 669 (1980) — ch. 10.

Safeco, 226 N.L.R.B. 754 (1976) — § 8-5.

Sailor's Union of the Pacific (Moore Drydock), 92 N.L.R.B. 547 (1950) — § 8-4.

Sanabria v. International Longshoremen's Ass'n, Local 1575, 597 F.2d 312 (1st Cir. 1979) — § 7-11(B).

S & H Grossinger's, Inc., 156 N.L.R.B. 233 (1965) — § 3-2(B).

San Diego Bldg. Trades Council v. Garman, 359 U.S. 236 (1959) — § 7-10(B).

Sangamo Constr. Co., 188 N.L.R.B. 159 (1971) — § 2-2(B).

Sav-On Drugs, Inc., 138 N.L.R.B. 1032 (1962) — §§ 2-1(A)(1), 2-1(A)(4).

Scott v. Teamsters, Local 377, 548 F.2d 1244 (6th Cir. 1977) — § 7-11(B).

Seafarers Int'l Union v. NLRB, 265 F.2d 585 (D.C. Cir. 1959) — § 8-4.

Seafarers Local 777 v. NLRB, 603 F.2d 862 (D.C. Cir. 1978) — § 9-4.

Seeler v. Trading Port, Inc., 517 F.2d 33 (2d Cir. 1975) — ch. 4.

Seeler v. Teamsters, Local 375 (W.D.N.Y. 1972) — § 8-2.

Self Cycle & Marine Distributors, 237 N.L.R.B. 75 (1978) — § 5-2.

Seminole Asphalt Refining, Inc. v. NLRB, 497 F.2d 247 (5th Cir. 1974) — § 3-3(B)(5).

United Dairy Farmers Coop. Ass'n, 107 L.R.R.M. 1577 (1981) — ch. 4.

United Mine Workers v. Gibbs, 383 U.S. 715 (1966) — § 9-2.

United Parcel Serv., Inc. v. Mitchell, 451 U.S. 56 (1981) — § 7-11.

United Screw & Bolt Corp., 91 N.L.R.B. 916 (1950) — § 3-2(D)(2).

United States Lingerie Corp., 170 N.L.R.B. 750 (1968) — § 2-2(B).

United States Plywood-Champion Papers, Inc., 174 N.L.R.B. 292 (1969) — § 2-1(B).

United States Postal Serv., 232 N.L.R.B. 556 (1978) — § 1-1(B)(2)(a).

U.S. Postal Serv., 252 N.L.R.B. 61 (1980) — ch. 6.

U.S. Postal Serv., 254 N.L.R.B. 703 (1981) — ch. 6.

U.S. Postal Serv., 256 N.L.R.B. 78 (1981) — ch. 6.

United Steelworkers v. NLRB, 496 F.2d 1342 (5th Cir. 1974) — § 3-2(A)(2).

United Steelworkers of America v. American Mfg. Co., 363 U.S. 564 (1960) — ch. 10.

United Steelworkers of America, AFL-CIO v. NLRB, 405 F.2d 1373 (D.C. Cir. 1968) — § 3-3(B).

United Supermarkets, Inc., 110 L.R.R.M. 1173 (1982) — ch. 4.

United Technologies Corp., 268 NLRB No. 83 (1984) — ch. 10.

United Tel. Co. of Florida, 251 N.L.R.B. 510 (1980) — ch. 6.

Universal Camera Corp. v. NLRB, 340 U.S. 474 (1951) — §§ 1-2(B)(6), 3-3(B)(4).

Universal Insulation Corp., 149 N.L.R.B. 1397 (1954) — § 2-2(B).

V

Vaca v. Sipes, 386 U.S. 171 (1967) — §§ 1-2(B)(4), 7-1, 7-2, 7-5, 7-6, 7-10(B), 7-11, 7-11(A).

Van Haaren Specialized Carriers, Inc., 247 N.L.R.B. 1185 (1980) — ch. 10.

Vickers, Inc., 124 N.L.R.B. 1051 (1959) — § 1-2(A)(3)(j).

Vicksburg Hosp., Inc. v. NLRB, 633 F.2d 1070 (5th Cir. 1981) — § 2-1.

Victoria Station, Inc. v. NLRB, 586 F.2d 672 (9th Cir. 1978) — § 2-1(A)(1).

VM Constr. Co., 241 N.L.R.B. 584 (1979) — § 9-4.

W

W.A. Jones Foundry & Mach. Co., 30 N.L.R.B. 809 (1941) — § 3-2(A)(1).

Wallace Corp. v. NLRB, 323 U.S. 248 (1944) — § 7-4.

Walter J. Mentzer, 82 N.L.R.B. 389 (1949) — § 9-2.

Warehousemen & Mail Order Employees, Local No. 743 v. NLRB, 302 F.2d 865 (D.C. Cir. 1962) — § 3-3(B).

W.A. Sheaffer Pen Co. v. NLRB, 486 F.2d 180 (8th Cir. 1973) — § 3-2(C).

Index

A

ARBITRATION.
National labor relations board.
Deferral to arbitration by board, ch. 10.
ATTORNEYS AT LAW.
National labor relations board.
Staff for members of board, §1-2(A).
ATTORNEYS' FEES.
Fair representation.
Award by court, §7-11(B).

B

BARGAINING UNITS.
Appropriateness, §1-2(A).
Principles governing unit appropriateness decisions, §2-1.
Community of interest factors.
Centralized administration, §2-1(A).
Generally, §2-1(A).
Geographic proximity, §2-1(A).
Interchange of employees, §2-1(A).
Previous bargaining history, §2-1(A).
Single-plant v. multi-plant units, §2-1(A).
Craft unit certification and severance, §2-1(B).
Concerted activity in absence of labor organization.
See CONCERTED ACTIVITY IN ABSENCE OF LABOR
ORGANIZATION.
Fair representation, §§7-1 to 7-13.
See FAIR REPRESENTATION.
Multi-employer bargaining units, §2-2.
Formation, §2-2(A).
Withdrawal from unit, §2-2(B).
Selection.
Bargaining orders in lieu of selection by election, ch. 4.

D

DAMAGES.
Fair representation.
Remedies in courts, §7-11(A).
DISCHARGES.
Unfair labor practices.
Pretext and dual motive cases, §3-3(A).
See UNFAIR LABOR PRACTICES.
DISCIPLINARY ACTION.
Predisciplinary interview.
Employee's right to representation, ch. 6.
DISCRIMINATION.
Fair representation.
Personal discrimination or animosity, §7-5.
Specific applications of duty.
Race, sex and national origin, §7-3.

F

FAIR REPRESENTATION.
Arbitrary representation, §7-6.
Attorneys' fees.
Award by court, §7-11(B).
Contracts.
Exhaustion and finality of contractual remedies, §7-10(C).
Damages.
Remedies in courts, §7-11(A).
Discrimination.
Personal discrimination or animosity, §7-5.
Specific applications of duty.
Race, sex and national origin, §7-3.
Duty.
Generally, §7-2.
Specific applications, §7-3.
Exhaustion and finality of contractual remedies,
§7-10(C).
Historical development of doctrine, §7-1.
Injunctions.
Remedies in court, §7-11(A).

J

JURISDICTION.
  Construction industry.
    National labor relations board, §9-2.
  Fair representation, §7-10.
    Preemption doctrine, §7-10(B).
    Statutory jurisdiction, §7-10(A).
  National labor relations board.
    See NATIONAL LABOR RELATIONS BOARD.

L

LIMITATION OF ACTIONS.
  National labor relations board.
    Unfair labor practice case procedures.
      Six months statute of limitations, §1-2(B).
  Unfair labor practices.
    National labor relations board.
      Unfair labor practice case procedures.
        Six months statute of limitations, §1-2(B).

N

NATIONAL LABOR RELATIONS ACT, §1-1.
  Generally, §1-1(A).
  National labor relations board.
    See NATIONAL LABOR RELATIONS BOARD.

NATIONAL LABOR RELATIONS BOARD.
  Administrative law judges.
    Unfair labor practice case procedures.
      Decisions, §1-2(B).
        Exceptions.
          Filing with labor board, §1-2(B).
      Hearings, §1-2(B).
  Appointment of board, §1-2(A).
  Arbitration.
    Deferral to arbitration by board, ch. 10.
  Attorneys at law.
    Staff for members of board, §1-2(A).

U

UNFAIR LABOR PRACTICES.
Discharges.
Pretext and dual motive cases.
Distinction between pretext and dual motive cases, §3-3(A).
"Dominant motive" test, §3-3(A).
"In part" test, §3-3(A).
Mt. Healthy test, §3-3(A).
Wright line test, §3-3(A).
Limitation of actions.
National labor relations board.
Unfair labor practice case procedures.
Six months statute of limitations, §1-2(B).
National labor relations board.
Unfair labor practice procedures, §1-2(B).
See NATIONAL LABOR RELATIONS BOARD.
Premature recognition, §3-1.
Selection of bargaining unit.
Benefits.
Employer promises of benefits and conduct relating to benefits.
Grants of benefit, §3-2(D).
Threats to reduce or withhold benefits, §3-2(D).
Wage increases, §3-2(D).
Withholding of promised benefit, §3-2(D).
Employer conduct during selection process, §3-2.
Employer statements during campaign, §3-2(A).
Critical period, §3-2(A).
Laboratory conditions standard, §3-2(A).
Lawful predictions distinguished from unlawful threats, §3-2(A).
Polling employees, §3-2(C).
Promises of benefits and conduct relating to benefits, §3-2(D).
Rules restricting to outsiders, §3-2(B).
Statements during campaign, §3-2(A).
Premature recognition, §3-1.
Strikes.
Rights of strikers, §3-3(B).